International Series on Computer Entertainment and Media Technology

Series Editor

Newton Lee

The International Series on Computer Entertainment and Media Technology presents forward-looking ideas, cutting-edge research, and in-depth case studies across a wide spectrum of entertainment and media technology. The series covers a range of content from professional to academic. Entertainment Technology includes computer games, electronic toys, scenery fabrication, theatrical property, costume, lighting, sound, video, music, show control, animation, animatronics, interactive environments, computer simulation, visual effects, augmented reality, and virtual reality. Media Technology includes art media, print media, digital media, electronic media, big data, asset management, signal processing, data recording, data storage, data transmission, media psychology, wearable devices, robotics, and physical computing.

More information about this series at http://www.springer.com/series/13820

Patrick C. K. Hung

Editor

Big Data Applications and Use Cases

 Springer

Editor
Patrick C. K. Hung
Faculty of Business and Information Technology
University of Ontario Institute of Technology
Oshawa, ON, Canada

Department of Electronic Engineering
National Taipei University of Technology
Taiwan

ISSN 2364-947X   ISSN 2364-9488   (electronic)
International Series on Computer Entertainment and Media Technology
ISBN 978-3-319-30144-0   ISBN 978-3-319-30146-4   (eBook)
DOI 10.1007/978-3-319-30146-4

Library of Congress Control Number: 2016931871

This Springer imprint is published by Springer Nature
The registered company is Springer International Publishing AG Switzerland

Contents

Introduction to Big Data

William Rafferty, Laura Rafferty, and Patrick C. K. Hung

Abstract Big data is a term that has been gaining considerable attention in recent years. Big data is essentially a massive amount of data that can be analyzed and used to make decisions. There are three main characteristics associated with big data: volume, variety and velocity. There are many motivations for the adoption of big data; this data has remarkable potential to drive innovation, the economy, productivity and future growth. Big data analytics has become very popular in the area of marketing, driving up value by understanding and engaging customers more effectively. There are many industries that have adopted the use of big data analytics and are experiencing fantastic results; the healthcare, retail, insurance and telecommunications industries have all displayed the endless possibilities of implemented big data into their operations. However, as more information is collected through big data, there becomes more concern for individuals' privacy. To mitigate these potential risks, policies have been put into place such as the Personal Information Protection and Electronic Documents Act (PIPEDA). Furthermore, due to the nature of the technologies within the Internet of Things (IoT), there are security concerns. These systems are very resource-constrained which results in a large amount of attention in cryptography and security engineering. This paper provides an introduction to the concepts of big data, motivations, some case studies, and a brief discussion on privacy.

Keywords Big data • Privacy • Pervasive computing • Internet of things

W. Rafferty (✉) • L. Rafferty
Faculty of Business and IT, University of Ontario Institute of Technology,
Oshawa, ON, Canada
e-mail: William.Rafferty@uoit.net; Laura.Rafferty@uoit.net

P.C.K. Hung
Faculty of Business and IT, University of Ontario Institute of Technology,
Oshawa, ON, Canada

Department of Electronic Engineering, National Taipei University of Technology, Taiwan
e-mail: Patrick.Hung@uoit.ca

© Springer International Publishing Switzerland 2016
P.C.K. Hung (ed.), *Big Data Applications and Use Cases*, International Series
on Computer Entertainment and Media Technology, DOI 10.1007/978-3-319-30146-4_1

1   Introduction to Big Data

1.1   What is Big Data?

Big data is a buzzword that has soared in popularity in recent years. Big data is the description of large amount of either organized or unorganized data that is analyzed to make an informed decision or evaluation. The data can be taken from a large variety of sources including browsing history, geolocation, social media, purchase history and medical records. Big data consists of complex data that would overwhelm the processing power of traditional simple database systems. There are three main characteristics associated with big data: volume, variety and velocity [1]. An ideal big data analytics system would be able to demonstrate each of these three characteristics of big data to the greatest extent, which would allow it to perform at its optimum level [2] discussed as follows.

- *Volume* is a characteristic used to describe the vast amounts of data that is utilized by big data. The amounts of data usually range from gigabytes to yottabytes. The big data should be able to handle any amount of data even as it expectedly grows exponentially [2].
- *Variety* is a characteristic used to describe the many different types of data sources that are used as part of a big data analytics system. There are multiple data storage formats that are utilized by computer devices throughout the world. There are structured data such as databases, .csv, video, SMS and excel sheets. The unstructured data could be in the form such as handwritten notes. All the data from these sources would ideally be useful to a big data analytics system [2].
- *Velocity* is a characteristic used to describe the speed at which data is generated. It is also used to describe the speed at which the generated data is processed. With a click of a button, an online retailer is able to quickly view large data about a certain customer. Velocity is also important to ensure that data is current and updated in real-time, thus allowing the system to perform the best it can. This speed is essential as real-time data generation helps organizations speed up operations processes; which can save organizations a large amount of money [2].

Digitalization of information is the foundation of big data, and the amount of available data is increasing at a rapid pace. In the 1950s, John Hancock's insurance company was thought to have more data than any other organization, with 600 megabytes of data. Throughout history, this number has continued to increase incrementally. The Federal Express had the greatest reported amount of data by the 1970s with 80 gigabytes. By the 1990s, Walmart took the lead with the largest amount of data with 180 terabytes of data, 2250 times the reported amount in the 1970s. To this day, Facebook is reported to have the largest amount of data; approximately 100 petabytes worth [3].

In our modern age, the amount of data being generated is tremendous. In 2010, the International Data Corporation reported that the amount of data stored was approximately 1 zetabyte. By 2011, the International Data Corporation reported the amount of data has increased to almost 2 zetabytes [3].

The amount of data being stored is so much more in our modern age because we are following a trend of digitalizing everything. There are vast amounts of emails, social media updates, and geolocation tags; everything is made available online in the form of data. This type of information is what is being mined to process and make use for big data analytics. Being able to understand just how great the amount of data available this date is challenging, but it is reported that there are "nearly as many bits of information in the digital universe as stars in our physical universe" [3].

1.2   Uses for Big Data

There are many motivations for the adoption of big data. Data has a tremendous potential to drive innovation, the economy, productivity and future growth. An outstanding example of the benefits of big data is Google Flu Trend; a service that predicts and locates flu outbreaks. This service uses aggregate search queries for processing. This service has the potential to reduce the impact of influenza [4].

Many corporations are taking advantage of big data to boost their Return on Investment (ROI). As IBM stated, "Plenty of customers are seeing tangible ROI using IBM's big data and analytics platform" [5]. Within the healthcare industry there has been a 20 % decrease in patient mortality by analyzing streaming patient data. The telecommunications experienced a 92 % decrease in processing time by analyzing networking and call data. Further, the utilities industry witnessed a 99 % improvement in accuracy 99 % in placing power generation resources by analyzing 2.8 petabytes of untapped data. These are just some of the industries making use of big data analytics. When organizations can make use of the full potential of big data analytics rather than just a segment, they gain a truly powerful tool to boost their Return on Investment [5].

1.2.1   Marketing

Big data analytics has become very popular in the area of marketing. Big data marketing is about driving up value by engaging customers more effectively. This can be done in many forms. For example, a coffee shop could be making great use of big data marketing by combining a potential customer's geolocation and search history. This way they could engage customers who they know both like coffee and are in the area. This is called target marketing and is a very effective way of segmenting the market into a subset of who is most likely to respond to the advertisement [6].

This form of marketing sounds simple at first, but big data marketing is rather complex. Technological advancements are making this form of marketing easier, allowing modern organizations to fully take advantage of the digital information made available. The old ways of non-segmented marketing focused at consumers are over. In our modern age, organizations must engage consumers, act on customer feedback and deliver services that are truly personalized towards the consumer in a timely manner. In order to meet these demands, marketing teams need to promote their services online through websites, mobile apps, and social media pages. This allows organizations to allocate their spending from less productive marketing strategies to much more productive elements of their marketing mix [6]. The modernization of marketing is full of potential. Marketing teams must take advantage of new technology, and revaluate current processes to fully leverage their full grasp of the marketing industry. This is essential as, "Companies that integrate people, processes, and technology will deliver a ROMI that is 50 % higher than those that don't" [6].

Behavioral profiling is one of the ways marketing teams can segment their marketing toward a target market. With the latest technology, a combination of complex algorithms and large amounts of data enables the creation of customer profiles. Organizations in a vast array of industries are taking advantage of behavioral profiles, to completely understand and connect with potential customers. Combining data from social media, blogs, surveys, search history, sales data, geolocation and many other sources can create detailed profiles on customers and allow marketing teams to segment their advertisements to those who are most likely to respond positively. This allows organizations to more fully understand the customer; their interests, what they are doing and even as far as what they are thinking, from mining texts or social media updates. This is a new age of marketing [7].

These marketing teams that can identify their customer's behavioral profile in such complexity, they can send very personal and truly targeted messages to the customer, creating a personal relationship, even if they have millions of other customers. For example, a user who has been searching the internet for toddler toys, who also has provided details of his location, can be effectively delivered advertisements for toy stores near his current location [7].

With behavioral profiling, there are certain aspects that need to be addressed. There must be an understanding of the users' online and offline behavior: How do they interact online and/or in person? What does this person purchase? What is the quantity in which the customer purchases and how often? These are all important topics which help marketing teams understand what exactly their customers want and allow them to reach out on a personal level and create a relationship [7].

1.2.2 Pervasive Computing

Pervasive computing is becoming a key form of gathering data for big data analytics. Pervasive computing, also known as ubiquitous computing, is a growing trend associated with inserting technology into everyday life. Pervasive means that it is everywhere, hence the implementation into our everyday life. These gadgets are completely connected and always available in real-time [8]. This form of computing is vast; it is a modernized version of the traditional desktop environment. This includes smart watches, smart phones, and even smart homes that communicate with appliances within the residency. Day-to-day equipment is being equipped with microprocessors which truly connect our devices and lives.

Pervasive computing makes daily activities easier through a wide range of technologies including Wi-Fi compatibility, voice recognition, Bluetooth, networking, etc. These technologies simplify our lives, which is why they are becoming a growing trend. With the addition of such pervasive technologies collecting mass amounts of data on our daily lives, there are security and privacy risks. To defeat this issue, trust models should be put in place to make these devices more secure. There are also other drawbacks to this form of computing; slow communication, expensive and limited bandwidth. These all cause a security risk to pervasive computing due to the system vulnerabilities they can create [8].

1.2.3 Internet of Things (IoT)

The Internet of Things (IoT) is becoming the primary grounds for data mining for big data analytics. The concept of IoT involves embedding sensory and network capable devices into our everyday lives. IoT has been growing in popularity with the adoption of wearable devices such as smart watches that track heartbeats, smart home technology, and users publishing their lives on social media via Smartphones. These devices are all communicating together and storing information in the cloud. The immense amount of data being collected and processed by big data analytics from the IoT introduces privacy as a major concern [9].

Furthermore, due to the nature of such technology, there are also security concerns. These systems are very resource-constrained, resulting in a large amount of attention in cryptography and security engineering. These technologies usually work in uncontrolled environments where they are vulnerable to malicious misuse. In order to alleviate these issues special attention needs to be focused on the following areas as stated by Antonio Skarmeta and M. Victoria Moreno [10]:

1. Design of lightweight security protocols and cryptographic algorithms.
2. Lightweight and efficient implementations of security protocols and cryptographic algorithms.
3. Secure implementations in hardware and/or software.

1.2.4 Smart Cities

Smart Cities are cities that use technology to improve processes, reduce environmental footprint and improve citizen's lives through the use of technology. Technological advances in information and communication technologies are enticing the movement into smart cities. For example, a city could analyze the traffic during peak hours with big data analytics and design traffic lights and new road ways to take these elements into consideration.

Advances in information and communication technologies are creating a movement in the environment in which we live; it is creating intelligent systems known as Smart Cities. These intelligent environments capture data using sensors in the boundaries of the city. From processing the data captured by these sensors, the city is able to adapt their behavior to better fit the citizens in the community [11].

2   Big Data Analytics

The benefits of using big data analytics are significant. Many organizations are adopting the use of this new technology and are experiencing substantial results. As reported by IBM [12]:

- Sixty-three percent of respondents reported that the use of information—including big data and analytics—is creating a competitive advantage for their organizations
- When compared to companies that rely on traditional analytics alone, organizations that implemented big data and analytics pilot projects or deployments are 15 % more likely to report a significant advantage from their information assets and analytics

Companies that use big data analytics outperform in their industry. This data allows companies to identify their most profitable customers and enables them to reach out to them on a personal level, enabling a better customer experience. This technology also allows organizations to improve the speed of processes, better understand customer needs, and improve innovation. By properly understanding customer needs, companies know exactly what type of innovations will be successful; where they should invest in with their R&D department [12].

The implementation of big data analytics also helps manage risk. Without the speed of big data analytics, companies often cannot find the proper information quick enough, which can often lead to unnecessary risk from poor decisions. Companies need a proactive way of finding valuable information when they need it; making the use of data analytics a valuable tool. Big data analytics can help companies acquire and retain customers. With the use of this technology, organizations are able to create customer profiles. They understand how their customers interact, they purchasing history, their interests, quantity of purchases and much more. With this information they are able to attract the right customers through target marketing and then attain their business by providing the proper experience that the customer requires.

Companies can improve operations and lower their costs with data analytics. They can do this by drastically improving process efficiency and through the ability to make quality decisions faster. Through improving operations, organizations are better prepared to identify and pinpoint fraudulent activity. This can be accomplished through processing data and identifying trends [12].

> Using a powerful analytics-based software platform, MoneyGram International can now better understand their users. These insights helped them prevent more than 37.7 million US dollars in fraudulent transactions, reduce customer fraud complaints by 72 percent, and promptly address stringent regulatory requirements. [12]

With big data analytics, it makes revamping products much more efficient. This analysis helps organizations understand how customers perceive their products. Simply mining text on social media about the related product provides endless customer opinions. With big data, you can test thousands of new variations of the product based on customer needs for costs, lead times, and performance [12].

Big data can also keep organization's sensitive data safe. Companies can now map their data landscape allowing them to analyze threats before they occur and then mitigate them. This allows them to detect sensitive information that is not properly protected. This could potentially save companies millions through preventing sensitive data leaks. This can also save companies their integrity to the public.

The use of big data is also making our cities smarter. This technology mitigates the risks of fast expansion. For example, Oslo, a city in Norway, managed to reduce the street light energy consumption by approximately 62 % [13]. Police in Memphis began to implement the use of big data predictive technology; resulting in 30 % reduction in serious crime. "The city of Portland, Oregon, used technology to optimize the timing of its traffic signals and was able to eliminate more than 157,000 metric tonnes of CO_2 emissions in just 6 years—the equivalent of taking 30,000 passenger vehicles off the roads for an entire year" [13]. These are just some of the many examples of cities that are making improvements for both the environment and their citizens with the use of big data technology.

3 Case Studies

3.1 Healthcare

Within the Canadian healthcare industry, the adoption of streamline big data analytics has started.

The industry began to be able to properly control the huge amount of data and process it into truly helpful data. Some of the benefits the healthcare industry noticed that IBM has reported include [5]:

- Reduce the din of monitors emitting patient health data to a manageable set of signals that can be acted by interjecting algorithms into the streaming data path coming from patient monitoring equipment.
- Improve healthcare outcomes by providing timely and meaningful insights to nurses, physicians and other care providers, who can then proactively administer the most effective treatments.
- Lower anxiety and stress levels among healthcare professionals by arming them with the most relevant patient information, enhancing their ability to provide effective care.

Surgeons in the UCLA Medical Center are adopting the use of big data streaming analytics and have had amazing results. As reported they were able to "cull real-time insights from more than 80,000 data points generated each minute in the critical care unit, so as to proactively identify patients whose conditions show subtle signs of worsening" [5]

3.2 Retail

Within the Canadian retail industry, there has also been a widespread adoption of predictive big data analytics.

Using this new technology, retailers are able to accurately estimate inventory demands by making customer buying patterns more transparent. Some of the benefits the retail industry noticed that IBM has reported include [5]:

- Plan and execute assortment at the local level by analysing specific product attributes—size, color, style and more—and accurately predicting which products are most in demand.
- Avoid stock-outs and overstocks by analysing all types of data from merchandise management and warehouse management systems to better optimise inventory levels.
- Predict uptrends in demand for certain products by applying real-time analytics to streaming social media feeds to see what customers want and need.

From the use of predictive big data analytics, it became possible to accurately estimate daily demand at singular bakeries from data obtained by the weather forecast [5].

3.3 Insurance

Within the Canadian insurance industry, the limitless capabilities of big data analytics were displayed.

From the use of this technology, they were able both speed up their processes and reduce the number of fraud through the identification of patterns in the data. Some of the benefits the insurance industry noticed that IBM has reported include [5]:

- Make better decisions about claims assignment, Special Investigation Unit (SIU) referrals, recoveries and reserves by analysing massive amounts of claims and claimant claims data faster.
- Identify low-risk claims and high-value clients by analysing all types of data—transactions, demographics, geolocation and more—and fast-track these claims to improve efficiencies and customer satisfaction.
- Detect fraud before a claim is paid by using predictive analytics to detect patterns, and analysing all data pertinent to the claim—in real time.

By using big data analytics to identify patterns in the data, the Insurance Bureau of Canada was able to identify two criminal fraud rings. They were able to identify them in as little as 2 weeks, in the past this would have taken up to 2 years [5].

3.4   Google Flu Trends

Another example of the excellent use of big data analytics is Google Flu Trends (GFT). GFT was created to deliver the number and location of flu cases around the world in real-time. As Google has explained:

> We have found a close relationship between how many people search for flu-related topics and how many people actually have flu symptoms. Of course, not every person who searches for "flu" is actually sick, but a pattern emerges when all the flu-related search queries are added together. We compared our query counts with traditional flu surveillance systems and found that many search queries tend to be popular exactly when flu season is happening. By counting how often we see these search queries, we can estimate how much flu is circulating in different countries and regions around the world [14].

Google has been able to make these predictions based on flu-related search results around the world. Although, this method is not 100%, as people can be searching for flu-related pages while they are not immediately sick with this virus. This complication has been displayed as Google has overestimated the number of humans with the flu from 2011 to 2013 by more than 50%. Google Flu Trends has over-predicted this number in 100 out of 108 weeks. This truly shows that big data analytics still can be improved, as it is still an emerging technology [15]. Although, regardless of Google's overestimation, this service has the potential to reduce the impact of influenza [4].

3.5   Telecommunications

With over 33 million customers, T-Mobile, a USA-based telecommunications company, used big data analytics to reduce their number of lost customers by over 50%. T-Mobile did this in just one quarter. To properly visualize their customer's data, they used different data zones [16]:

- Customer data zone: a 360° view of each customer used to attack customer dissatisfaction;
- Product and Services zone: which products and services are used by whom and when in order to drive innovation;
- Customer experience zone: what are the channels that interact with the customer and when? Used to regain and optimize service levels;
- Business Operations zone: containing all billing and accounting information as well as the finance and risk management. Used to define the best areas for optimization and performance;
- Supply Chain zone: How do the purchase-order, shipment and logistics operate? Used to drive innovation within the supply chain and to cut costs;
- Network zone: All (raw) data that is stored to support management. Used to drive innovation and grow quality customers.

T-Mobile used these data zones to create a customer model. The essence of this model assumes that there are people with very large social groups, if they switch to a different telecommunications provider, it will create a domino effect. T-Mobile created a 'Customer Lifetime Value' which is calculated on how influential their customers are on others. From T-Mobiles experience with Big Data analytics, they managed to reduce the amount of customers leaving from 100,000 in the first quarter, to 50,000 lost customers in the second quarter; a 50 % decrease [16].

4 Security and Privacy Concerns

One of the main concerns users have related to big data is the concept of privacy. As big data's popularity increases, there becomes more of a concern for the privacy of the mass amounts of data that is being collected and used. The mass amounts of data that is collected can sometimes be personal or sensitive data that could otherwise be used to identify the owner; leading to embarrassment or malicious acts. In the healthcare industry, information about an illness that another patient may prove to be crucial in aiding another. However that illness may be an embarrassing medical illness that they would not want to be disclosed with someone else. For example with the use of big data analytics, Target had identified a teenager whom was pregnant, before the teen wanted the information shared with her father [17].

Information that is obtained from a third party such as a data broker should be anonymized to protect the identity of the individual unless given consent. Data brokers in particular have a habit of selling information that can come from social media websites where some users post personal text or images [17]. Occasionally when individuals surrender such information to data brokers they do not realize that the information could be shared with others and possibly be linked to their identity.

A large concern with collecting information of the public (data mining) is the invasion of privacy. There is a security threat related to geolocation tracking. By law one cannot track an individual without a warrant; although if the information being used for tracking is considered to be public data or the user has given "consent", then there are no legal complications. Consent could be as simple as having your location services turned on your mobile device, or through accepting an app's terms of use.

HAPPYFOOT is a program that is used exploit mobile apps. Many apps place a cookie on a cellular device, this is what the program exploits by piggybacking on the cookie and tracking the user. The use of cookies is what this program functions on; tracking the cellular device without the user's awareness [18].

Another tracking exploit involves the use of a smartphone's accelerometer. Due to imperfections in these devices, it is possible to track the device with 96 % accuracy [18]. The accelerometer data signal can be used to uniquely identify a smartphone and track them without any knowledge of the phone's number, or even the IMEI of the device. With this type of tracking it is possible to know the exact direction the device is moving based on the cellular device's swinging during movement [18]. This creates not only a powerful tracking tool, but also a tool which can also be used to invade privacy creating a security threat.

The data that is mined for big data analytics is stored in databases; without proper security precautions of these databases, the information could be leaked. Researchers in Switzerland have recently conducted a study in which they found 1 petabyte of data exposed by misconfigured databases. The majority of these databases had no authentication configured. The first solution they analyzed was Redis, the most popular key-value database. They concluded that there was 35,330 Redis instances with no authentication; exposing 13 terabytes of data from this database software alone [19]. They also analyzed MongoDB, the most popular noSQL database system. The researchers found 39,000 instances that had no authentication configured. There were 620 terabytes of data exposed on this software [19].

Without proper configuration of databases the risk of data being exposed is a real threat. If this data has personal identifying elements, it could be a large scale threat to the security and privacy of the user. Database admins should follow standard security procedures and allows configure authentication within their database.

To help address the problem of big data privacy, certain countries have created legislations to help ensure organizations such as data brokers provide the best with privacy of the public in mind. In Canada, legislations have been introduced to help address some of the privacy concerns; such as the Personal Information Protection and Electronic Documents Act (PIPEDA) and the Personal Health Information Protection Act (PHIPA). The legislations seek to provide users with more control over their information and how a business can use it. They also allow users to ensure that any information used by organizations is kept up to date by providing them opportunities to change the stored information [20].

4.1   Personal Information Protection and Electronic Documents Act (PIPEDA)

PIPEDA, the Personal Information Protection and Electronic Documents Act, is a privacy legislation within Canada. The objective of this legislation is to control how organizations may collect, use and or disclose personal information. This legislation legally allows Canadians to both access and makes corrections to their personal information that companies have composed [21]. We are now living in a period of technological excellence, and the confidentiality and handling procedures of personal data must be secured now more than ever before. PIPEDA's purpose is exactly that; to standardize how organizations may collect, use and or disclose personal information. This legislation accepts that we all have the right of privacy in relation to our personal information. PIPEDA also understands the risks of improper handling practices of personal information [22].

PIPEDA affects every Canadian. It also affects any company that collects personal information as the way that they collect, use and or reveal personal information is now being governed. This also affects any employee that collect, uses or discloses personal information [22].

This privacy legislation applies to all organizations and federal organizations that operate within the boundaries of Canada. Although, if the company is located within a province or territory that has its own privacy legislation, Alberta for example, then that company must adhere to the specific privacy legislation which is standardized within their location [23]. Furthermore, organizations that are not involved in commercial activities are not affected by the privacy legislation [24].

Compliance with the metrics of PIPEDA is mandatory; with the exception of the previously discussed groups which are any organization that is not involved in commercial activities, and if your company is located in another Province or Territory that follows their own privacy legislation. It is up to all Canadian companies who are affected by PIPEDA to be aware of their responsibilities regarding the legislation's respected processes concerning the collection, use and disclosure of personal information. Organizations that do not adhere to the standards will be sanctioned; both financial and ethical consequences. There is a process which is followed if there is a PIPEDA related complaint. First, the whistleblower will report their allegations to the Privacy Commissioner of Canada. Although the Commissioner is not allowed to sanction fines, except in the situation where an organization fails to record and report data breaches they can receive a maximum fine of $100,000. In either case, the Privacy Commissioner of Canada can investigate and attempt to diffuse the situation [25]. If the allegations were not solved by the Commissioner, the next step is to take your allegations to the Federal Court of Canada. Unlike the Privacy Commissioner of Canada, these courts are allowed to sanction fines [25]. If PIPEDA related allegations are made against a company are made public, then the organization could be labeled unethical and lose potential future business [26].

4.2   Personal Health Information Protection Act (PHIPA)

PHIPA, the Personal Health Information Protection Act, is a privacy legislation residing within Ontario. This legislation has many intentions, but the main focus is to control rules for the collection, use and disclosure of personal health information. Furthermore, this legislation attempts to protect both the confidentiality and privacy of the personal health information. PHIPA, similar to PIPEDA, also gives individuals the right to both access and request changes to their health information [27].

This legislation affects any company that works with personal health information residing within Ontario. Similarly to PIPEDA, there are special situations regarding this legislation that could still apply when access is granted to access to personal health information [27].

PHIPA is an Ontario specific legislation; PHIPA applies to all organizations and individuals within Ontario that collect personal health information. This legislation will apply to any organization that collects personal health information. This legislation would also apply to any Ontario bound company which collects health information from their employees [28].

Compliance with the metrics of PHIPA is mandatory for organizations that reside within Ontario and collect personal health information. It is up to all Ontario companies who are affected by PHIPA to be aware of their responsibilities regarding the legislation's respected processes concerning the collection, proper use and disclosure of personal health information. Organizations that do not adhere to the standards will be sanctioned; financial and ethical consequences. Similar to PIPEDA, if a company's noncompliance of the legislation they could be labeled unethical and lose future business. Unlike in PIPEDA where the Privacy Commissioner of Canada is in charge of investigating allegations, The Attorney General of Canada is accountable for the initiation of sanctions regarding PHIPA. If the Attorney General deems the allegations are deserved, the individual responsible can receive a fine of up to $50,000 and an organization up to $250,000 [29].

5 Conclusions

Big data is a wildly growing topic which has been proven to be a beneficial tool. The implications of being able to collect and analyse such vast amounts of information are phenomenal in a range of applications including marketing, healthcare, telecommunications, and more. Businesses and governments are beginning to adopt big data solutions to address a wide range of issues.

This chapter has provided an introduction to big data for the rest of the book. We provided an overview of big data concepts, motivations for using big data, as well as some case studies where big data solutions have been applied to solve important problems. Finally, we discussed some privacy concerns as well as a discussion on Canadian privacy legislations (PIPEDA) and (PHIPA).

References

1. MongoDB. Big data explained. (2015). Retrieved from Mongodb.com: http://www.mongodb. com/big-data-explained
2. P. Dave, What is big data - 3 Vs of big data. (2013, 10 2). Retrieved from SQL Authority Blog: http://blog.sqlauthority.com/2013/10/02/big-data-what-is-big-data-3-vs-of-big-data-volume-velocity-and-variety-day-2-of-21/
3. K. Bottles, E. Begoli, B. Worley. Understanding the pros and cons of big data analytics. (2014). Retrieved from http://go.galegroup.com.uproxy.library.dc-uoit.ca/ps/i.do?p=AONE&u=ko_ acd_uoo&id=GALE|A377410232&v=2.1&it=r&userGroup=ko_acd_uoo&authCount=1

4. O. Tene, J. Polenetsky. Data, privacy in the age of big data. (2012, February 2). Retrieved from Stanford Law Review: https://www.stanfordlawreview.org/online/privacy-paradox/big-data
5. IBM. Big data and analytics. (2015, June). Retrieved from IBM: http://www.ibm.com/big-data/ca/en/big-data-and-analytics/operations-management/industries/index.html
6. L. Arthur, in *Big Data Marketing*, ed. by L. Arthur (John Wiley & Sons, 2013). Retrieved Aug 2015, from http://library.books24x7.com.uproxy.library.dc-uoit.ca/assetviewer.aspx?bookid=58128&chunkid=174813851&rowid=235
7. M. V. Rijmenam, Why 360-degrees customer profiles created with big data are nothing new. (2015). Retrieved from DATAFLOQ: https://datafloq.com/read/360-degrees-customer-pro files-created-big-data-not/109
8. Techopedia. (n.d.). Pervasive computing. Retrieved from Techopedia: http://www.techopedia.com/definition/667/pervasive-computing
9. Datamation. Why big data and the internet of things are a perfect match. (2015). Retrieved from Datamation: http://www.datamation.com/applications/why-big-data-and-the-internet-of-things-are-a-perfect-match.html
10. A. S. Moreno. Internet of Things Security, Privacy and Trust Considerations. (2014)
11. K. B. Ahmed, M. Bouhorma, M. Ahmed, Age of big data and smart cities: privacy trade-off. (2014, October). Retrieved from arXiv: http://arxiv.org/ftp/arxiv/papers/1411/1411.0087.pdf
12. IBM. Better business outcomes with IBM Big Data & Analytics. (2014, January). Retrieved from IBM: http://www.ibmbigdatahub.com/sites/default/files/whitepapers_reports_file/59898_Better%20Business%20Outcomes_White%20Paper_Final_NIW03048-USEN-00_Final_Jan21_14.pdf
13. Data Science Series. (n.d.). Examples of what you can accomplish with big data. Retrieved from Data Science Series: http://datascienceseries.com/stories/ten-practical-big-data-benefits
14. Google. Google Flu Trends. (2014). Retrieved from Google.org: https://www.google.org/flutrends/about/how.html
15. B. Walsh, Google's flu project shows failings of big data (2014). Retrieved from Time: http://time.com/23782/google-flu-trends-big-data-problems/
16. M. V. Rijmenam, T-Mobile USA cuts down churn rates by 50% with big data. Retrieved from DATAFLOQ: https://datafloq.com/read/t-mobile-usa-cuts-downs-churn-rate-with-big-data/512
17. M. Goldberg. Cloud computing experts detail big data security and privacy risks. (2013). Retrieved from Data Informed: http://datainformed.com/cloud-computing-experts-detailbig-data-security-and-privacy-risks
18. J. Crampton, Collect it all: National Security, Big Data and Governance (2014). Retrieved from SSRN: http://poseidon01.ssrn.com/delivery.php?ID=482106013031117031067120096090003111052032042016084026027093126022114105102031026109096023059100025126046118024078119029025068024015069044007119073083087122127114100052018084084121071090025016025013076098015110022119065027005015007076104030109093069025&EXT=pdf
19. E. Kovacs, Researchers Find 1PB of Data Exposed by Misconfigured Databases (2015, August). Retrieved from SecurityWeek: http://www.securityweek.com/researchers-find-1pb-data-exposed-misconfigured-databases
20. Ontario's Privacy Legislation. (2015). Retrieved from http://www.privacysense.net/privacylegislation/canadian/ontario/
21. Office of The Privacy Commissioner of Canada. The Personal Information Protection and Electric Documents Act (PIPEDA). (2013). Retrieved from Office of The Privacy Commissioner of Canada: https://www.priv.gc.ca/leg_c/leg_c_p_e.asp
22. Government of Canada. Personal Information Protection and Electric Documents Act. (2015). Retrieved from Justice Laws Website: http://laws-lois.justice.gc.ca/eng/acts/P-8.6/FullText.html
23. Office of The Privacy Commissioner of Ontario. Privacy Legislation in Canada. (2014). Retrieved from Office of The Privacy Commissioner of Ontario: https://www.priv.gc.ca/resource/fs-fi/02_05_d_15_e.asp

24. Privacy Protection in Canada. (2015). Retrieved from Office of the Privacy Commissioner of Canada: https://www.priv.gc.ca/resource/tooloutil/infographic/leg_info_201405_e.pdf
25. Mondaq. (2014). Canada's digital privacy rethink: fines, enforceable compliance agreements. Retrieved from Mondaq: http://www.mondaq.com/canada/x/305856/data+protection/Canadas+Digital+Privacy+Reth
    ink+Fines+Enforceable+Compliance+Agreement s+And+More
26. Incident Summary #4. (2014). Retrieved from Priv.gc.ca: https://www.priv.gc.ca/cfdc/inci dents/2014/004_140919_e.asp
27. A. Cavoukian. A Guide to the Personal Health Information Protection Act. (2004, December). Retrieved from Information and Privacy Commissioner: https://www.ipc.on.ca/images/resources/hguide-e.pdf
28. Ontario.ca. Personal Health Information Protection Act, 2004. (2010). Retrieved from Ontario.ca: http://www.ontario.ca/laws/statute/04p03
29. A. Cavoukian. Frequently Asked Questions: Personal Health Information Protection Act. (2005, Febuary). Retrieved from Information and Privacy Commissioner: https://www.ipc.on.ca/images/Resources/hfaq-e.pdf

A Bloom Filter-Based Approach for Supporting the Representation and Membership Query of Multidimensional Dataset

Zhu Wang and Tiejian Luo

Abstract Bloom filter has been utilized in set representation and membership query. However, the algorithm is not quite suitable for representing multidimensional dataset. The paper presents a novel data structure based on Bloom filter for the multidimensional data representation. We further give the theoretical analysis and experimental evaluations of the algorithm. Results show that the algorithm can achieve the same false positive rate when dealing with exact membership queries. It can provide extra support of by-attribute membership query.

1 Introduction

Bloom filter [2] is widely used in Internet applications [3]. It has also been adopted in multidimensional indexing because of its space-efficient and time-efficient characteristics in supporting approximate membership queries. Standard Bloom filter takes the entire multidimensional data as a whole and generates the indices. Therefore, it cannot support by-attribute queries, in which only a subset of attributes in the queried item are provided. Multidimensional dynamic Bloom filter [4] and parallel Bloom filter [5, 6] store each dimensional data in a separate Bloom filter to answer by-attribute queries. However, when adopted with high-correlated queries, the performance of the algorithm degrades a lot. In this paper, we try to maintain the advantages mentioned in the algorithms above and avoid their shortages by using a Cartesian matrix of Bloom filters to store the dataset.

An index for a dataset is a data structure that is used to record the items of the set. In a multidimensional data search, the membership query is a request with several

---

This work gives real world based experiments of our paper [1] published previously.

Z. Wang (✉)
Data Communication Technology Research Institute (DCTRI), Beijing, China
e-mail: wangzhu09@mails.ucas.ac.cn

T. Luo
University of Chinese Academy of Sciences, Beijing, China
e-mail: tjluo@ucas.ac.cn

© Springer International Publishing Switzerland 2016   17
P.C.K. Hung (ed.), *Big Data Applications and Use Cases*, International Series
on Computer Entertainment and Media Technology, DOI 10.1007/978-3-319-30146-4_2

attributes keyed into the database system. It asks for the response of whether there is an item (data object) in the set that has all the wanted attributes. Exact membership query refers to a request which can provide all wanted attributes simultaneously, whereas by-attribute memberships query requests for the search result in response to queries containing a subset of all attributes that compose a data object. Let us look at an example to see the scenario of these queries. There are two items in a set, S = {(a, b),(x,y)}, each item has two dimensions. An exact membership query is a question like "Is there an item in S whose two attributes are (a,b)?" In contrast, a by-attribute query only contains partial dimension information, such as "Is there an item in S whose first attribute is x?" In addition, a correlative query contains the shared attributes with the set. For example, "Is (a,m) in the set?" is a correlative query because it shares "a" with the set. The more likely the query shares attributes with the set, the higher correlative it is. To fulfill these queries, various indexing structures are designed in applications. For example, one indexing technique [4] is to store each dimension in one container separately. For the set S, we maintain the first dimensional container $D_1 = \{a,x\}$ and the second $D_2 = \{b,y\}$. When a query arrives, the system just examines the containers dimension by dimension to locate the requested result and merges the result. However, this processing will cause a false positive mistake. E. g., query (a,y) will be judged as inside S because $a \in D_1$ and $y \in D_2$, but actually it is not. Thus in this technique like [4], any mix-up of existing items' attributes will cause such mistakes. Obviously, the high-correlative queries will boost this error.

Bloom filter is a data structure that can give fast response to queries but have a low false positive rate. In typical applications like [7], the false positive occurrence may lead to a waste of time. However, the short response delay characteristic overweighs the previous cost and the overall system performance can be improved by using Bloom filter as an index.

The key for multidimensional data management is to establish a reliable data structure for data indexing, which is capable of supporting exact and by-attribute membership queries. The time and space overhead should be very low and the mix-up false rate caused by correlative queries must be reduced.

The remainder of the paper is organized as follows. In Sect. 2 we survey the existing Bloom filter based algorithms for multidimensional data indexing. Section 3 gives the theoretical analysis of false rate and optimal hash number of the Cartesian-join of Bloom Filters. The time and space complexity is also demonstrated. Experimental evaluation is shown is Sect. 4. Finally, Sect. 5 concludes the research and suggests future directions.

2   Related Work

There have been quite a few previous attempts to apply Bloom filters in multidimensional data indexing. Standard Bloom Filter (SBF) [2] offers an efficient way to represent multidimensional data. It uses a bit vector as an index of items of a set S. When an item is inserted, the algorithm uses a group of hash functions to map the item onto several locations in the bit vector and sets the corresponding bits to one. When a membership query is submitted, the algorithm uses the same hash functions to calculate the hash positions of the queried item and checks if all the corresponding bits are one. If the answer is yes, the Bloom filter concludes that the queried item belongs to the set. Otherwise it reports that the query does not belong to the set. It needs to be mentioned that for each item belonging to S, since all the bits of the hash locations are already set to 1, the lookup procedure for the very item will definitely have the positive answer. So there will be no false negatives. However, there is a probability that items do not belong to the set be judged as inside S by the Bloom filter because its hash locations might have been set to 1 by some other items' hashing. That is to say, Bloom filter has a false positive rate. Research [8] shows that the false positive rate can be represented as follows:

$$f_{SBF} = \left(1 - e^{-\frac{kn}{m}}\right)^k \tag{1}$$

Here m is the bit vector length. n is the item number. k is the hash number and f_{SBF} is false positive rate of SBF. Study [8] also shows that f_{SBF} reaches the minimal value when k values

$$k_{opt\_SBF} = \frac{m}{n} ln2$$

k_{opt_SBF} is the optimal hash number. The time complexity is O(k).

In multidimensional indexing, the standard Bloom filter first joins the attributes of an item and then operates with the joint result. In that way, SBF can easily avoid the false rate caused by the cross-dimensional mix-up. However, the method requires the entire attributes of a query and therefore is not capable of handling by-attribute search.

Guo et al. propose an algorithm called multidimensional dynamic Bloom filter (MDDBF) to support data indexing [4]. The algorithm builds one attribute Bloom filter as the index for each dimension of the multidimensional set. In item insertion it simply inserts each of dimensional attribute into the corresponding Bloom filter. When a query is submitted, the algorithm checks whether all of its attributes exist in the corresponding Bloom filter. If all the answers are yes, then it reports a positive response. It can be seen that while the method is capable of handling exact and by-attribute queries, it introduces a new type of false positive occurrence: the mix-up of attributes in different dimensions. For example, if (a,b) and (x,y) are in the set S, then the query (a,y) will be judged as inside S because both attributes of the query exists in each dimensional Bloom filter. The reason for that is the idea of storing the item's attributes of different dimensions separately splits the entire item and the relationship between the attributes of one item is lost. In the example, one cannot tell that attribute a and b belong to one item due to the separate storage.

Parallel Bloom filter (PBF) [5, 6] tries to solve the problem by adding a verification value of each attribute insertion for the item. Then it stores the verification value in a summary Bloom filter. The new Bloom filter's hash functions are actually a composite function of attribute hashes, verification function and summary hash functions. So the approach is equivalent to adding a SBF for the integrated item besides the attribute Bloom filters for the separate dimensions. Therefore, PBF cannot support by-attribute query because it requires all attribution information, just like SBF.

3   CBF Design and Analysis

Table-based index can support flexible queries but takes too much time and space. SBF is an efficient indexing structure but do not allow by-attribute query. MDDBF provides that functionality but performs poorly with correlative queries. Designing a fast, accurate and space-efficient indexing mechanism for multidimensional dataset to support both exact and by-attribute membership queries which can achieve a high performance even with correlative queries is indeed a challenging task in multidimensional data management. Our proposal, the CBF Bloom filter is capable of satisfying those requirements. In this section we present the design of the CBF. We then analyze the false positive rate and the optimal hash function number of the algorithm. The time and space complexity is also given.

3.1   CBF Algorithm and Structure

The CBF is designed to support both exact and by-attribute membership queries. In order to avoid the mix-up mistake with the correlative queries (which is the main source of the false positive rate in MDDBF), we try to maintain the inner relationship between different attributes of a same item.

3.1.1   CBF Structure

We use one Bloom filter to represent one dimension's attributes of the d-dimensional dataset. The Bloom filter is called an attribute Bloom filter. All attribute Bloom filters have the same hash number k (yet the hash functions are independent). To avoid the loss of relationship between one item's attributes, we establish a d-dimensional CBF matrix which is the Cartesian product of empty attribute Bloom filters. That matrix is used to store the membership information of the dataset. To answer membership queries, the items should be inserted into the matrix: we store the hash result in the matrix by combining the corresponding results into a d-dimensional point in the CBF matrix.

CBF indexing works in the following procedure: in order to establish the index of the multidimensional database, we insert all the items into the CBF matrix using item insertion algorithm. When a membership query of a certain item is submitted to the system, we look up the query in the CBF matrix using the same hash functions in the insertion period. Then we give the yes/no answer of the query.

Now we illustrate the insertion method of a d-dimensional item $A = (a_1, a_2, \ldots, a_d)$. The ith attribute Bloom filter is ABF_i. The hash function group for the ith attribute Bloom filter is $H_i = \{h_{i1}, h_{i2}, \ldots, h_{ik}\}$. The length of the ith ABF is m_i. For the first dimension a_1, we use the hash functions group H_1 of the ABF_1 to calculate the first hash results group $H_1(a_1) = \{h_{11}(a_1), h_{12}(a_1), \ldots, h_{1k}(a_1)\}$, which contains k hash results. We do the same with the second dimension using second hash function group until the last dimension. Now we obtain the hash result groups $\{H_1(a_1), H_2(a_2), \ldots, H_d(a_d)\}$, each contains k hash results. In each group, we select the first hash results in each hash result groups and join the selections to form a d-dimensional data point $(h_{11}(a_1), h_{21}(a_2), \ldots, h_{d1}(a_d))$. We set the corresponding point in CBF matrix to one. We do the same for the rest of hash result groups until all k hash result points are set to one. Figure 1 shows the data structure of CBF matrix. We take $d = 2$ as an example.

Here the CBF matrix is the Cartesian product of empty ABFs.

$$CBF = ABF_1 \times ABF_2 \times \ldots \times ABF_d$$
$$= \left\{X \mid X = (x_1, x_2, \ldots, x_d), x_i \in [0, m_i)\right\}$$

Unlike the MDDBF and the PBF algorithm which put the multidimensional items in several parallel Bloom filters, CBF makes Cartesian-join of Bloom filters to form a matrix. That indicates the major difference of our algorithm. Recall the example in the related work, the query (a,y) has a large possibility to be judged as outside S by CBF because the hash points of items (a,b), (x,y), and (a,y) in CBF can be different.

3.1.2 Item Insertion

The item insertion procedure has already been described in the section above. Now we give the detailed algorithm in Fig. 2.

The major advantage of the indexing algorithm is that unlike MDDBF, the CBF manages to preserve the inner relationship between attributes of the same item. That goal is achieved by combining the same-order hash results of each dimension belonging to one item into one data point. Each dimension value of the data point comes from one attribution Bloom filter's hash results. When the corresponding position is set to 1 in the CBF matrix, the inner relationship of the item's different attributes is maintained.

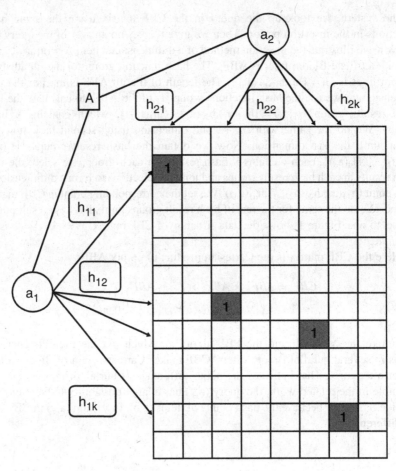

Fig. 1 CBF structure: inserting item A

3.1.3 Exact Membership Query

In an exact membership query, all attributes of queried item are provided. The processing of such query follows the similar way as the item insertion procedure. Let a query $Q = (q_1, q_2, \ldots, q_d)$ where no attribute q_i is empty. The algorithm first uses the same attribute Bloom filters' hash function groups to find the hash results of the item's attributes $H_i(q_i) = \{h_{i1}(q_i), h_{i2}(q_i), \ldots, h_{ik}(q_i)\}$. Then it combines the same-order hash results into query points and checks if all the query points in the CBF matrix are one. If the answer is yes, it concludes that the queried item exists in the set. Otherwise it returns a negative answer. The algorithm is given in Fig. 3.

The algorithm handles the exact membership query by using the same hash function groups to calculate the hash results. If the queried item does exist in the set, then it must have been inserted into the CBF matrix through the item insertion method. So the corresponding data points in CBF must have been set to 1. The look

```
Input
    A=(a_t,a_2,....,a_d): the d-dimensional item needs to be
inserted
Output
    Updated CBF matrix
Method
    (1) Calculate hash results for each dimension using
hashes.
        H_j(a_j)={h_{i1}(a_j),h_{i2}(a_j),...,h_{jk}(a_1)}, i=1,2,...,d
    (2) Join the hash results to form k data points.
        X_j=(h_{1j}(a_1),h_{2j}(a_2),...,h_{dj}(a_d)), j=1,2,...,k
    (3) Set the corresponding positions in CBF to 1.
        CBF(X_j)=1, j=1,2,...,k
```

Fig. 2 The item insertion algorithm

```
Input
    Q=(q_t,q_2,...,q_d): the submitted d-dimensional query
Output
    E: whether the queried item exists, 1 if exist, 0
otherwise
Method
    (1) Calculate hash results for each dimension using
hashes.
        H_j(q_j)={h_{i1}(q_j),h_{i2}(q_j),...,h_{jk}(q_1)}, i=1,2,...,d
    (2) Combine the hash results to form k query points.
        X_j=(h_{1j}(q_1),h_{2j}(q_2),...,h_{dj}(q_d)), j=1,2,...,k
    (3) Check if all corresponding query points are 1.
        E=0 if at least one of the query points is 0 in the
CBF.
        E=1 otherwise.
```

Fig. 3 The exact membership query algorithm

up procedure will surely get a positive response. That is to say, the algorithm will have no false negative mistakes. Yet for a queried item that does not belong to the set, it is possible that it be judged as inside the set because its corresponding data points in the CBF have been set to 1 by some other items, so the algorithm has a false positive rate. We will analyze that in Sect. 3.2.

It needs to mention that since the inner relationship between one item's attributes is preserved, the algorithm prevents the occurrence of mix-up mistake between attributes. For instance, the set $S = \{(a,b),(x,y)\}$. Hash number $k=1$. $h_{11}(a)=1$, $h_{11}(x)=2$, $h_{21}(b)=3$, $h_{21}(y)=4$. In the insertion of (a,b) and (x,y), we set the corresponding data points in the CBF to 1. CBF(1,3) = 1,CBF(2,4) = 1. Now let's see whether the mix-up (a,y) will be judged as inside S. Using the hash results, the query point will be $X_1 = (1,4)$. The corresponding position CBF(1,4) is 0. So the mix-up query (a,y) does not belong to S. In the example, provided that there are no hash collisions, the hash points of different items will never coincide. More broadly, when storing a multidimensional item, the CBF algorithm maintains the inner relationship between its attributes by combining the hash results of each attributes Bloom filter. In that way, the algorithm avoids the mix-up false positive mistake. Later we will see in experiment Sect. 4.2 that false rate is a major part of false positive mistakes with correlative queries.

3.1.4 By-Attribute Membership Query

In by-attribute query, only some of the attributes in the queried item is provided. Some attributes are empty. When the query is submitted, the user intends to ask whether there is an item in the set which has the same attributes as the non-empty attribute of the query. For example, the dataset is composed of students of a class, with two dimensional attributes: age and gender. An exact membership query is "Is there a 12-years-old boy in the class?" A by-attribute membership query is "Is there a girl in the class?" Without loss of generality, we assume that the last p attributes are not provided in the query.

The query $Q = (q_1, q_2, \ldots, q_d)$, $q_{d-p+1} = q_{d-p+2} = \ldots = q_d = \text{NULL}$. Now we want to find whether there is an item in the set whose first d-p attributes are $q_1, q_2, \ldots, q_{d-p}$ respectively. Assume that there is an item A that satisfies the query,

$$A = (a_1, a_2, \ldots, a_d) = (q_1, q_2, \ldots, q_{d-p}, a_{d-p+1}, \ldots, a_d),$$
$a_{d-p+1}, \ldots, a_d$ can be any value,

Since all the items have been inserted into the CBF, using the insertion algorithm, the corresponding hash data points of item A must have been set to 1. That is,

$$CBF\big(h_{1j}(q_1), \ldots, h_{(d-p),j}(q_{d-p}), h_{(d-p+1),j}(a_{d-p+1}), \ldots, h_{dj}(a_d)\big)$$
$$= 1, j = 1, 2, \ldots, k$$

As well as there exist $a_{d-p+1}, \ldots, a_d$ that satisfy the conditions' above, we conclude the queried item exists in set S.

In the look up procedure of query Q, (j values from 1 to k,) for each j, we first calculate $h_{1j}(q_1), h_{2j}(q_2), \ldots, h_{(d-p),j}(q_{d-p})$ and search all points whose first d-p dimensions values $h_{1j}(q_1), h_{2j}(q_2), \ldots, h_{(d-p),j}(q_{d-p})$, correspondingly. We call these points a query bunch. If all these point in the bunch are zero in CBF, it means that no such points exist, and therefore the query doesn't exist in the set. Otherwise it means it is possible that the query exists, so we continue the j + 1 hashes and repeat the same procedure. If all k procedures receives the positive answer (Fig. 4).

```
Input
    Q=(q_t,q_2,...,q_{d-p},NULL,....,NULL): the submitted d-
dimensional query
Output
    E: whether the queried item exists, 1 if exist, 0
otherwise
Method
    (1) Calculate hash results for each dimension using
hashes.
        H_j(q_j)={h_{i1}(q_j),h_{i2}(q_j),...,h_{ik}(q_j)}, i=1,2,...,d-p
    (2) Combine the hash results to form k query bunches.
        X_j=(h_{1j}(q_1),h_{2j}(q_2),...,h_{dj}(q_d),*), j=1,2,...,k
    (3) Check if all query bunches have a 1 in CBF
        E=1 if exists X_1,....,X_k s,t.
    CBF(X_1)=1,....,CBF(X_k)=1
        E=0 otherwise.
```

Fig. 4 The by-attribute membership query algorithm

3.2 False Rate and Optimal Hash Number

As stated above, the CBF algorithm has zero false negative rate because all queries for an existing item will receive a positive response. However, it is possible that a query outside the set S is judged as inside S because its corresponding data points in the CBF have been set to 1 by some other items. Now we analyze the false positive rate. Since in the latter experiments, we will compare the false positive rate between different Bloom filter-based algorithms, we don't use other algorithms as a comparison in this experiment.

Given the attribute Bloom filters ABF_i with size m_i and hash number k, the size of CBF is $m_1 m_2 ... m_d$. For one item, the possibility that the first hash functions of each dimension hit a certain position in CBF is $p_{hit} = 1/(m_1 m_2 ... m_d)$ because each hash has a uniform distribution in the ABF and the hash functions are independent from each other. After inserting n items, each using k hash function groups, the probability that a certain place in CBF is still zero is

$$p = (1 - p_{hit})^{kn}$$

Here $1-p_{hit}$ is the probability that the position is not hit by one hash. After inserting n items, each with k hash groups, the probability that the position remain zero is p, as conducted.

The case in which a non-existent item is judged as inside S happens when all k hashed data points are set to 1 by other items. So the false positive rate of CBF is

$$f_{CBF} = (1-p)^k = \left(1 - \left(1 - \frac{1}{m_1 m_2 \ldots m_d}\right)^{kn}\right)^k$$
$$\approx \left(1 - e^{-\frac{kn}{m_1 m_2 \ldots m_d}}\right)^k \qquad (2)$$

The corresponding optimal hash number can be conducted using similar method as that in [8].

$$k_{opt-CBF} = \frac{m_1 m_2 \ldots m_d}{n} ln2$$

When the length of ABFs and the item number is fixed, the CBF can reach its lowest false positive rate when k reaches that optimal number. That is similar to the optimal hash number of SBF.

It needs to mention that Bloom filter does not contain the actual data. It can just support membership queries of certain sets and give a yes/no response. The applications have to access the data eventually and eliminate the false rate.

3.3 Space Efficiency and Time Complexity

We further look into the false positive rate of CBF, which is the main description of the algorithm's performance. Comparing Eqs. (2) and (1), we find that the only difference between the false rate of CBF and SBF is the product $m_1 m_2 \ldots m_d$, which happens to be the total size of CBF. Replace $m_1 m_2 \ldots m_d$ with data structure size M, the two expressions are the same. So we have

$$f_{CBF} = F_{SBF} = \left(1 - e^{-\frac{kn}{M}}\right)^k \qquad (3)$$

It means that if the total sizes of the two data structures are the same, they will have the same false positive rate. That is to say, the space efficiency of CBF and SBF are the same. As we all know from [3, 9] that, standard Bloom filter has a very high space efficiency, so does CBF.

For every d-dimensional query, the algorithm will have to calculate k hash functions to find the result. So the time complexity for a query is O(dk), higher than that of SBF (O(k)). However, in actual use case, d and k are fixed. So the time complexity of CBF is O(C), which is independent of n (number of items in the set). That is lower than the O(logn) of B-trees.

3.4 Growth of Dimensions

Now we analyze what will happen when the dimension number grows. From Eq. (3) we can see that if we want to maintain the false rate, we need to only keep the total size of CBF unchanged. When the dimension grows, we can keep the false rate without enlarging the CBF size. Actually, we can reduce the average ABF length to achieve that. The only limitation is that the length of each Bloom filter should be no less than 2. So long as the dimension number is less than $\log_2 M$, it has no impact on the false rate of CBF.

The time complexity is O(dk), which has a linear relationship with dimension. However, most applications' dimension size is not very large, say $2 \sim 100$. In that case, the time complexity can be constant, as stated in Sect. 3.3.

4 Experimental Evaluation

In this section we use three experiments to validate our design objectives. We first show the correctness of the false rate and hash number derivation. In the second and third experiments, we present the CBF performance in exact query and by-attribute search respectively, in comparison with baselines.

4.1 False Positive Rate and Optimal Hash Number

In this experiment we want to find the relationship between the false positive rate and the hash number. Then we can identify the optimal hash number from the experiment and compare it with that derived from theoretical analysis.

The role of CBF is to find if a certain query exist in a dataset. It verifies if there is a same item in the dataset, but pays no attention on what the attributes of the query is. That reminds us to use datasets and queries with different items, but to ignore what the attributes of the queries really are. To verify our assumption, we use real world dataset in this experiment.

We use real-world dataset—the Truck dataset from the ChoroChronos Website [10]. The dataset is composed of 112,203 rows. We use the fourth, fifth, sixth and seventh column of the dataset and get rid of the rows that shares the same coordinates to have 29,018 different four dimensional items. The size of CBF is $2^{18} = 262144$. The hash number k ranges from 1 to 16. The result is given in Fig. 5.

The experimental false rate is in accordance with the theoretical one. Here we can see that our analysis of false rate and optimal number is correct and the conclusions drawn from that have a convincible base.

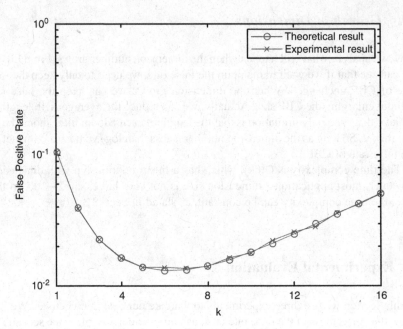

Fig. 5 Effect of hash number

4.2 *Exact Membership Search*

In this experiment we compare the performance of CBF with other indexing algorithms. The baseline approaches are SBF, PBF and MDDBF. We further want to see the effect of relationship between the query and the dataset. Let α be the possibility that one attribute of the query can find a match in the set. So $\alpha = 0$ means all attributes of the query are new. For the set $S = \{(a,b),(x,y)\}$, the query may be (c,d). $\alpha = 1$ means all attributes of the query can find a copy in the corresponding dimensions of the dataset, the query is just a mix-up of the existing items of the dataset, but it is different from any of the existing items in the dataset. For the set $S = \{(a,b),(x,y)\}$, the query may be (a,y).

In the experiment, the dataset has 29,018 four dimensional items. The size of data structures is all the same, $2^{18} = 262144$ bits. The hash number reaches the optimal value for all algorithms. The query number is 29,018. We choose α from 0 to 1 and calculate the false positive rate. The result is shown in Fig. 6.

When $\alpha = 0$, the algorithms have the similar performance. However, the false rates of MDDBF and PBF grow linearly with α, MDDBF even reaches 100 %. That is because of the mix-up mistake. The more similar the query is with the dataset, the more likely its attributes find a match in the set, i.e., the higher false rate.

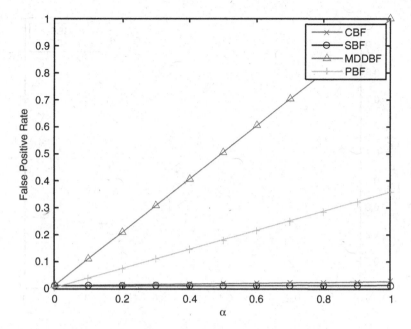

Fig. 6 Effect of query similarity

The false rate of SBF remains stable as α increases, while that of CBF increases very slowly with α. The two algorithms' performance is both acceptable but CBF can support the by-attribute search, while SBF cannot.

It needs to mention that the average space per query is about 10 bits and it remains stable when dimension increases, while in a table only one attribute can use up more than ten bytes of storage. The false positive rate is about 3 % for CBF.

4.3 By-Attribute Membership Search

Now let's look at the by-attribute search performance of CBF. Since only MDDBF can support by-attribute search besides CBF, we use MDDBF as a comparison.

The experimental settings are the same as that in Sect. 4.2. All queries have one missing attribute. The result is given below in Fig. 7.

We see that the false rate of CBF grow very slowly with the increase of α. In comparison, the performance of MDDBF is unacceptably high when α is large.

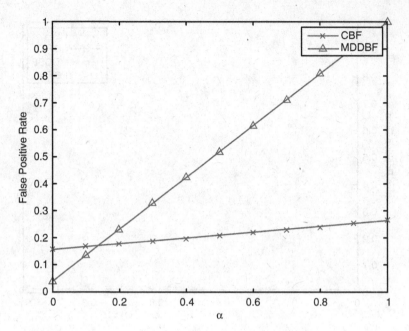

Fig. 7 By-attribute search

5 Conclusion and Future Work

In this paper, we have proposed the Cartesian-join of Bloom Filters to represent multidimensional dataset. The method has low time and space complexity. Our algorithm can support both exact membership query and by-attribute membership query of multidimensional data. In the paper we use theoretical method to analyze the false positive rate, space complexity, time complexity and dimensional scalability of CBF. We use real-world multidimensional dataset to test the performance of our algorithm. The experiments prove the correctness of our theoretical deduction.

The CBF algorithm uses many hash functions to calculate hash results. That causes the time complexity of CBF to be $O(dk)$, which grows linearly with dimension number. In future research, we plan to reduce the time complexity of CBF to achieve better performance. The analysis of the Bloom filter size's impact on system performance will also continue.

References

1. Z. Wang, T. Luo, G. Xu, X. Wang, The application of cartesian-join of bloom filters to supporting membership query of multidimensional data, in *2014 I.E. International Congress on Big Data (BigData Congress)*. IEEE, 2014, pp. 288–295

2. B.H. Bloom, Space/time trade-offs in hash coding with allowable errors. Commun. ACM **13**, 422–426 (1970)
3. S. Tarkoma, C.E. Rothenberg, E. Lagerspetz, Theory and practice of bloom filters for distributed systems. Commun. Surv. Tut. IEEE **14**(1), 131–155 (2012)
4. D. Guo, J. Wu, H. Chen, X. Luo et al., Theory and network applications of dynamic bloom filters, in *INFOCOM*, 2006, pp. 1–12
5. B. Xiao, Y. Hua, Using parallel bloom filters for multiattribute representation on network services. IEEE Trans. Parallel Distrib. Syst. **21**(1), 20–32 (2010)
6. Y. Hua, B. Xiao, A multi-attribute data structure with parallel bloom filters for network services, in *High Performance Computing-HiPC 2006*. Springer, 2006, pp. 277–288
7. Z. Wang, T. Luo, Optimizing hash function number for bf-based object locating algorithm, in *Advances in Swarm Intelligence*. Springer, 2012, pp. 543–552
8. J.K. Mullin, A second look at bloom filters. Commun. ACM **26**(8), 570–571 (1983)
9. A. Broder, M. Mitzenmacher, Network applications of bloom filters: a survey. Internet Math. **1** (4), 485–509 (2004)
10. Trucks—chorochronos.org, http://www.chorochronos.org/?q=node/5

Automatic Speech and Singing Discrimination for Audio Data Indexing

Wei-Ho Tsai and Cin-Hao Ma

Abstract In this study, we propose a technique of automatically discriminating speech from singing voices, which can be of great use for handling big audio data. The proposed discrimination approach is based on both timbre and pitch feature analyses. In using timbre features, voice recordings are converted into Mel-Frequency Cepstral Coefficients and their first derivatives and then analyzed using Gaussian mixture models. In using pitch feature, we convert voice recordings into MIDI note sequences and then use bigram models to analyze the dynamic change information of the notes. Our experiments, conducted using a database including 600 test recordings from 20 subjects, show that the proposed system can achieve 94.3 % accuracy.

Keywords Discrimination • Pitch • Singing • Speech • Timbre • Voice

1 Introduction

The rapid advances in Internet connectivity and signal processing technologies have led to a dramatic increase in the availability of audio material. Ironically, the dramatic increase of audio material also makes it increasingly difficult to locate desired items from the innumerable options. Thus, techniques that could help users acquire the item they want quickly are highly desired. In this work, we attempt to develop an automatic technique for discriminating singing from speech voices.

In addition to serving as a front-end process of an audio retrieval system, the automatic discrimination between singing and speech voices can also be helpful for speech recognition of broadcast news, when there is a need to disable the speech recognizer during the non-speech portion of the audio stream. Another application of distinguishing speech from singing is to assist low bit-rate speech/audio coding. As speech coders generally perform better on speech than on music, and audio coders perform better on music than on speech, it would be necessary to distinguish

W.-H. Tsai (✉) • C.-H. Ma
Department of Electronic Engineering, National Taipei University of Technology,
Taipei, Taiwan
e-mail: whtsai@ntut.edu.tw; t101419012@ntut.edu.tw

© Springer International Publishing Switzerland 2016   33
P.C.K. Hung (ed.), *Big Data Applications and Use Cases*, International Series
on Computer Entertainment and Media Technology, DOI 10.1007/978-3-319-30146-4_3

between speech and singing before a coding scheme is used, i.e., using either speech coding scheme or audio coding scheme.

So far, there is very limited prior literature devoted to this problem. Most related works investigate the differences between singing and speech. In [1, 2], a number of comparisons between singing and speech are discussed. Another related topic in the research field of audio classification is concerned with discriminating between speech signals and music signals [3–11] or locating singing voice segments within music signals [12]. As an initial study of the problem of discriminating between speech and singing voices, we focus only on solo voice without accompanied by music or other sounds. In addition, this study does not attempt to investigate the speech/singing discrimination for multi-language vocals, but only deals with single-language vocals.

The reminder of this paper is organized as follows. Sect. 2 introduces an intuitive speech/singing discrimination approach based on speech recognition. Sect. 3 introduces the proposed speech/singing discrimination approach based on timbre and pitch analyses. Sect. 4 discusses the experiments for examining the two systems. In Sect. 5, we present the conclusions and direction of our future works.

2   An Intuitive Approach Based on Speech Recognition

State-of-the-art speech recognition systems use stochastic pattern modeling and matching techniques to evaluate the likelihood of a given test recording for each defined class. As singing could be viewed as a twisted version of speech, it is natural that a speech recognition system performs poorly for singing voices than speech voices. Because of this, we can assume that if the likelihood of a test recording resulted from a speech recognizer is lower than a certain threshold, the recording is likely to be a singing voice.

Our speech recognition system is based on context dependent state tied Hidden Markov Model (HMM) [13] sets with Gaussian mixture output distributions. It is built using the HMM Toolkit (HTK) [14]. The acoustic data is represented by a stream of 39 dimensional feature vectors with a frame spacing of 10 ms, based on MFCC_E_D_A_Z defined in HTK. Briefly, MFCC_E_D_A_Z, which consists of zero-meaned Mel-Frequency Cepstral Coefficients (MFCCs) [15] appended with delta coefficients, acceleration coefficients, and log energy, is computed as shown in Fig. 1. At this stage, we only consider Mandarin speech and singing data, but the system could be extended to handle other languages. The training data used for our speech recognition system stem from TCC-300 [16], which is composed of Mandarin speech utterances recorded in quiet environments.

There are 151 context-dependent phones used in this study. Each individual phone is represented by an HMM. In addition to models for speech, the acoustic model set contains two silence models, one for silence, and one for short inter-word pauses with the latter preserving context across words. The HMM can be regarded as a random generator of acoustic vectors. An HMM consists of a sequence of states

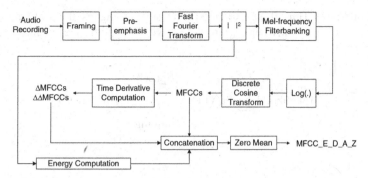

Fig. 1 Computation of acoustic feature MFCC_E_D_A_Z

connected by probabilistic transitions. The entry and exit states are provided to join different phone models together. Specifically, the exit state of one phone model can be connected with the entry state of another phone model in order to cover complete utterances. The transition probabilities model the durational variability in speech and the output probabilities model the spectral variability. In summary, an HMM consisting of N states is completely characterized by the parameters, $\Theta = \{ \mathbf{A}, \mathbf{B}, \mathbf{\Pi} \}$

- $\mathbf{A} = [a_{ij}]_{N \times N}$: the probability transition matrix, representing the probability of occurring a transition from state i to state j.
- $\mathbf{B} = [b_j(O_t)]_{N \times 1}$: the output probability matrix, representing the probability of observing O_t given that the model is in state j.
- $\mathbf{\Pi} = [\pi_i]_{N \times 1}$: the initial state probability vector, representing the probability that state i is the initial state.

In addition, recognizing the fact that contextual effects cause large variations in the way that different sounds are produced, we use different HMMs for each phone with different context. Intuitively, the simplest approach is to use context-phones, where every phone has a distinct HMM for every unique pair of left or right neighbors. However, when context-phones are used, they may result in a system that has too many parameters to train. The problem of too many parameters can be detrimental when the amount of training data is not sufficient. To solve this problem, a number of approaches, such as state-tying [17, 18] and phone-based component tying [19] have been studied. It is found that using these tying techniques with continuous-density HMMs has led to substantial improvements in modeling accuracy.

During the recognition phase, probabilities $\Pr(O|\Theta_i)$ are evaluated for all the models $\Theta_1, \Theta_2, \ldots, \Theta_i, \ldots$ under consideration. Then, the observation sequence $\mathbf{O}$ is determined as one of the potential phones via the maximum-likelihood decision rule. For computational efficiency, probabilities $\Pr(O|\Theta_i)$ are often computed using the Viterbi algorithm, which only considers the most possible state sequence instead of all the possible state sequences. In this study, we use module "HVite" in HTK to decode audio recordings to 1-best phone sequences. It is assumed that the result of decoding singing voice should be much poorer than that of decoding speech utterance. Thus, if the likelihood of a test recording resulted from the speech recognizer is lower than a certain threshold δ, we can hypothesize that the recording is a singing voice, i.e.,

$$\text{Likelihood} \sum_i \Pr(\mathbf{O}|\Theta_i) \overset{\text{Speech}}{\underset{\text{Singing}}{\overset{>}{\underset{\leq}{}}}} \text{Threshold } \delta \qquad (1)$$

3 Proposed Approach

Figure 2 shows the proposed speech/singing discrimination system. In the training phase, the system extracts the timbre and pitch features of all available speech and singing samples and represents them separately as four parametric models. In the testing phase, the system evaluates the timbre and pitch features of an unknown sound recording by matching them with the parametric models generated in the training phase. The resulting likelihoods are then combined to form a basis for decision. Specifically, the unknown sound recording is decided as either speech or singing according to Eq. (2)

$$\alpha \log \frac{\Pr(\mathbf{X}|\Lambda^{\text{Speech}})}{\Pr(\mathbf{X}|\Lambda^{\text{Singing}})} + (1-\alpha)\log \frac{\Pr(\mathbf{Y}|\lambda^{\text{Speech}})}{\Pr(\mathbf{Y}|\lambda^{\text{Singing}})} \overset{\text{Speech}}{\underset{\text{Singing}}{\overset{>}{\underset{\leq}{}}}} 0, \qquad (2)$$

where $\Pr(\mathbf{X}|\Lambda^{\text{Speech}})$ and $\Pr(\mathbf{X}|\Lambda^{\text{Singing}})$ are the likelihoods of the extracted timbre-based feature $\mathbf{X}$ matching speech and singing models Λ^{Speech} and Λ^{Singing}; $\Pr(\mathbf{Y}|\lambda^{\text{Speech}})$ and $\Pr(\mathbf{Y}|\lambda^{\text{Singing}})$ are the likelihoods of the extracted pitch-based feature $\mathbf{Y}$ matching speech and singing models λ^{Speech} and λ^{Singing}; and α is a tunable weight.

3.1 Timbre-Based Feature Extraction and Modeling

Although the organs of a human body for speech and singing are the same, the vocal configurations resulted from the ways people use to speak and sing are different. Figure 3 shows the spectrograms of an example speech utterance and singing recording produced by the same person and based on the same lyrics. We can see from Fig. 3 that the harmonic structures of speech and singing voices are significantly different. Specifically, there are salient regular harmonics like parallel curves in the spectrogram of the singing signal, while this is not the case in the spectrogram

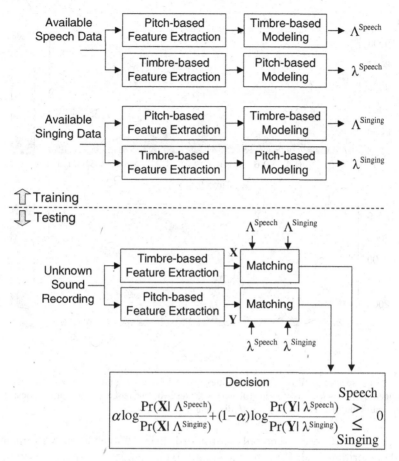

Fig. 2 The proposed speech/singing discrimination system

of the speech signal. It can also be seen that the energy of the speech signal is decayed largely in the frequency higher than 5000 Hz, while there is still strong energy in the high frequency region of the singing signal. Such timbre differences would also make their Mel-Frequency Cepstral Coefficients (MFCCs) rather different.

To characterize the timbre differences between speech and singing voices, we propose building a Gaussian mixture classifier by its success in many pattern recognition problems. The classifier operates in two phases: training and testing. During the training phase, two Gaussian mixture models (GMMs), Λ^{Speech} and $\Lambda^{Singing}$, are created using the available speech data and singing data, respectively. It is known that GMMs provide good approximations of arbitrarily shaped densities of a spectrum over a long span of time [20], and hence can reflect the collective vocal tract configurations in speech or singing voices. The parameters of each GMM consist of means, covariances, and mixture

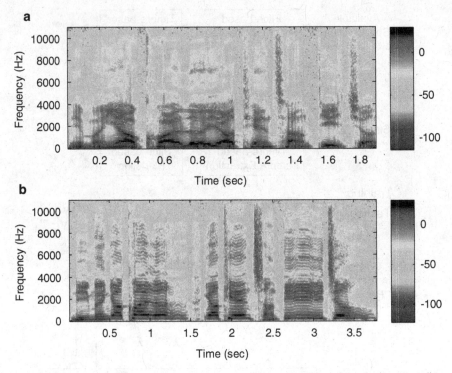

Fig. 3 (**a**) spectrogram of a speech utterance, (**b**) spectrogram of a singing recording produced by the person as that in (**a**), where (**a**) and (**b**) are based on the same lyrics: "/ni/ / man/ /iau/ /kuai/ /le/ /iau/ /tian/ /chang/ /di/ /jiou/"

weights, which are commonly estimated using Expectation-Maximization (EM) algorithm [21]. Prior to Gaussian mixture modeling, speech waveforms are converted frame-by-frame into MFCCs.

In the testing phase, the system computes the MFCCs $\mathbf{X} = \{\mathbf{X}_1, \mathbf{X}_2, \ldots, \mathbf{X}_T\}$ of an unknown test recording, and then evaluates the likelihood

$$
\begin{aligned}
&\Pr\left(\mathbf{X}\middle|\Lambda^{\mathrm{Speech}}\right)\\
&= \prod_{t=1}^{T}\sum_{k=1}^{K} w_k^{\mathrm{Speech}} \cdot \frac{1}{\pi^N \left|\mathbf{C}_k^{\mathrm{Speech}}\right|} e^{-\left(\mathbf{X}_t - \boldsymbol{\mu}_k^{\mathrm{Speech}}\right)' \mathbf{C}_k^{\mathrm{Speech}-1}\left(\mathbf{X}_t - \boldsymbol{\mu}_k^{\mathrm{Speech}}\right)},
\end{aligned}
\tag{3}
$$

where K is the number of mixture Gaussian components; w_k^{Speech}, $\boldsymbol{\mu}_k^{\mathrm{Speech}}$, and $\mathbf{C}_k^{\mathrm{Speech}}$ are the k-th mixture weight, mean, and covariance of GMM $\Lambda^{\mathrm{Speech}}$, respectively; and prime ($'$) denotes the vector transpose. Likewise, the likelihood $\Pr(\mathbf{X}|\Lambda^{\mathrm{Singing}})$ is computed in a similar way as Eq. (3).

3.2   Pitch-Based Feature Extraction

The most salient clue that makes singing different from speech is the melody, which mainly results from the variation of pitch. Singing usually involves a wider range of pitch than speech and hence it has a special pitch pattern that could be exploited to distinguish from speech. Because pitch is the reciprocal of fundamental frequency, a voice (speech or singing) recording can be viewed as a sequence of fundamental frequencies. We can then model the variations of the fundamental frequencies to characterize speech or singing voices. However, recognizing that the estimation of fundamental frequency is prone to numerical errors, we use MIDI note numbers instead of fundamental frequencies to explore the pitch information in voice recordings. The MIDI note numbers can be treated as the non-linear quantization of fundamental frequencies, and hence can absorb the numerical errors during the estimation of fundamental frequencies.

Let e_m, $1 \leq m \leq M$, be the inventory of possible notes in a voice recording. Our aim is to determine which among the M possible notes is most likely produced at each instant in a recording. We apply the strategy in [22] to solve this problem. As shown in Fig. 4, first, voice recording is divided into frames by using a P-length sliding Hamming window, with $0.5P$-length overlapping between frames. Every frame then undergoes a Fast Fourier Transform (FFT) with size J. Let $x_{t,j}$ denote the signal's energy with respect to FFT index j in frame t, where $1 \leq j \leq J$, and $x_{t,j}$ has been normalized to the range between 0 and 1. Then, the signal's energy on m-th note in frame t can be estimated by

$$x_{t,m} = \max_{\forall j,\ U(j)=n_m} x'_{t,j}, \tag{4}$$

and

$$U(j) = \left\lfloor 12 \cdot \log_2 \left(\frac{F(j)}{440} \right) + 69.5 \right\rfloor, \tag{5}$$

where $\lfloor \ \rfloor$ is a floor operator, $F(j)$ is the corresponding frequency of FFT index j, and $U(\cdot)$ represents a conversion between the FFT indices and the MIDI note numbers. By using the strategy of Sub-Harmonic Summation [23], we can determine the sung note in frame t by choosing the note number associated with the largest value of the "strength" accumulated for adjacent frames, i.e.,

$$Y_t = \operatorname*{argmax}_{1 \leq m \leq M} \sum_{b=-W}^{W} y_{t+b,m}, \tag{6}$$

and

$$y_{t,m} = \sum_{c=0}^{C} h^c x_{t,m+12c}. \tag{7}$$

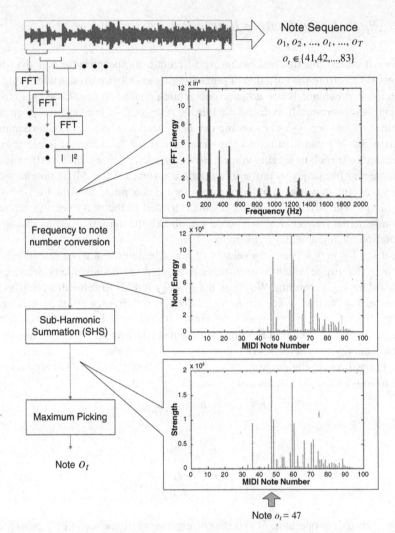

Fig. 4 Conversion of a waveform recording into a MIDI note sequence

where C is the number of harmonics considered, and h is a positive value less than 1 that discounts the contribution of higher harmonics. The result of summation in Eq. (7) is that the true note usually receives the largest amount of energy from its harmonic notes.

Further, the resulting note sequence is refined by taking into account the continuity between frames. This is done with median filtering, which replaces each note with the local median of notes of its neighboring $\pm W$ frames, to remove jitters between adjacent frames. In the implementation, the range of e_m is set to be $36 \leq e_m \leq 95$, corresponding to range from C2 to B6.

After each voice recording is converted into a note sequence, we use bigram model [24] to capture the dynamic information in the note sequence. The bigram model consists of a set of bigram probabilities and unigram probabilities. The bigram probabilities $\Pr(e_j|e_i)$, $1 \leq i, j \leq M$, accounts for the frequency of a certain note e_i followed by another note e_j, while the unigram probabilities $\Pr(e_i)$ accounts for the frequency of occurring a certain note e_i. It is assumed that speech and singing have their own pitch patterns that reflect in the frequency of occurrence of one or a pair of notes.

In the testing phase, the system computes the note sequence $\mathbf{Y} = \{Y_1, Y_2, \ldots, Y_L\}$ of an unknown voice recording, and then evaluate the likelihood:

$$\Pr\left(\mathbf{Y}|\lambda^{\text{Speech}}\right) = \Pr(Y_1) \cdot \prod_{t=2}^{L} \Pr\left(Y_t|Y_{t-1}, \lambda^{\text{Speech}}\right), \tag{8}$$

where λ^{Speech} is the bigram model of speech voice. Likewise, the likelihood $\Pr(\mathbf{Y}|\lambda^{\text{Singing}})$ is computed in a similar way as Eq. (7).

4   Experiments

4.1   Voice Data

The voice data used in this study involved two databases, one is TCC-300 and the other is collected by ourselves. The TCC-300 was used to establish the speech recognizer described in Sect. 2. The database collected by ourselves, denoted by DB, was used to train and test our speech/singing discrimination system.

In collecting database DB, we invited 30 male participants between the ages of 20 and 39 to produce vocal recordings. The 30 participants were separated into two groups, one contains 20 participants and the other 10. First, we asked each of the 20 participants in the first group to sing 30 passages of Mandarin pop songs using a Karaoke machine in a quiet room. All the passages were recorded at 22.05 kHz, 16 bits, in mono PCM wave. The Karaoke accompaniments were output to a headset and were not captured in the recordings. The duration of each passage ranges from 17 to 26 s. We denoted the resulting 600 recordings by DB-1-Singing. Next, we asked each of the 20 participants to read the lyrics of the 30 passages of Mandarin pop songs at a normal speed. All the read utterances were recorded using the same conditions as those in DB-1-Singing. The resulting 600 recordings were denoted as DB-1-Speech. The recordings in DB-1-Singing and DB-1-Speech were used to train our speech/singing discrimination system.

On the other hand, we asked each of the 10 participants in the second group to sing another 30 passages of Mandarin pop songs that are different from those in DB-1-Singing. The recording conditions were the same as those in DB-1-Singing. The resulting 300 recordings were denoted by DB-2-Singing. Then, each of the

10 participants was asked to read the lyrics of what they have sung at a normal speed. The resulting 300 recordings were denoted as DB-2-Speech. The recordings in DB-2-Singing and DB-2-Speech were used to evaluate the performance of our speech/singing discrimination system.

4.2 Experiment Results

4.2.1 Evaluation of the Speech-Recognition-Based Discrimination System

Our experiments were first conducted to examine the performance of the intuitive speech/singing discrimination system described in Sect. 2. Figure 5 shows the distributions of the likelihoods resulted by testing the recordings in DB-2-Speech and DB-2-Singing using the speech recognition system. We can see from Fig. 5 that a significant proportion of the likelihoods resulted from speech utterances are higher than those resulted from singing voices.

Table 1 shows the discrimination accuracy with respect to different values of threshold δ in Eq. (1), where the accuracy is defined by

$$\text{Accuracy (in \%)} = \frac{\text{Total number of correctly-classified recordings}}{\text{Total number of testing recordings}} \times 100\% .$$

We can see from Table 1 that the larger the value of threshold is set, the higher the accuracy of correctly determined singing recordings is obtained, but the lower the accuracy of correctly determined speech utterances is presented. A proper value of threshold is between −45,000 and −40,000. However, the best average accuracy obtained here ($\delta = -43,000$) is only 85.8 %, which leaves room to improve. Such results are not surprising, because Fig. 5 shows that there is a significant overlap between the distribution of the likelihoods resulted from speech and the distribution of the likelihoods resulted from singing.

Table 2 lists the accuracies of discriminating each individual subject's singing and speech recordings, where the threshold was set to −42,000. We can see from Table 2 that the system performs poorly in discriminating subject 2's voice, compared to the cases of other subjects. Further analysis found that subject 2 has a heavy accent so that the resulting likelihoods tend to be lower no matter he sings or speaks.

4.2.2 Evaluation of the Proposed Speech/Singing Discrimination System

Next, the performance of the proposed system was evaluated. In the timbre-based feature extraction, we computed 15 MFCCs and 15 delta MFCCs from the voice recordings, using a 30-ms Hamming-windowed frame with 15-ms frame shifts.

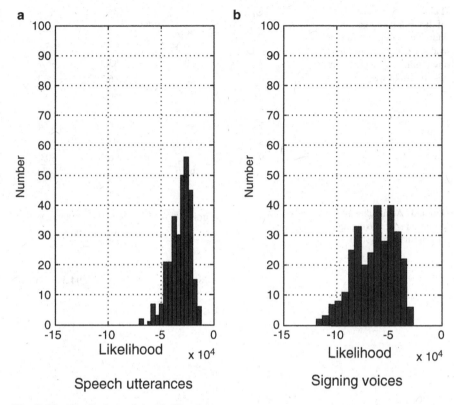

Fig. 5 The distributions of the likelihoods

Table 1 Accuracies (in %) of the intuitive speech/singing discrimination system for DB-2-Singing and DB-2-Speech

Threshold δ	Singing	Speech	Average
−75,000	32.3	100	66.2
−70,000	36.3	99.7	68.0
−65,000	43.3	99.3	71.3
−60,000	53.0	99.0	76.0
−55,000	60.3	96.7	78.5
−50,000	69.0	95.7	85.3
−45,000	81.0	89.7	85.3
−43,000	85.0	86.3	85.7
−42,000	87.0	84.7	85.8
−40,000	90.3	80.7	85.5
−35,000	96.3	67.0	81.7
−30,000	99.3	50.7	75.0
−26,500	100	36.0	68.0
−25,000	100	28.0	64.0

Table 2 Accuracies (in %) of discriminating each individual subject's singing and speech recordings using the intuitive system, where the threshold was set to −42,000

Subject	Singing	Speech	Average
1	86.7	86.7	86.7
2	80.0	53.3	66.7
3	90.0	83.3	86.7
4	83.3	86.7	85.0
5	86.7	86.7	86.7
6	86.7	93.3	90.0
7	90.0	86.7	88.4
8	93.3	93.3	93.3
9	83.3	76.7	80.0
10	90.0	100.0	95.0

Table 3 Accuracies of the proposed speech/singing discrimination system

α in Eq. (1)	Accuracy (%)
1.0	90.8
0.9	91.2
0.8	93.0
0.78	**94.3**
0.7	94.2
0.6	92.3
0.5	91.5
0.4	89.2
0.3	85.3
0.2	84.7
0.1	83.2
0.0	83.0

The FFT size was set to be 2048. The settings of framing and FFT were also used in the pitch-based feature extraction. In addition, the numbers of Gaussian densities were tuned to 128 to obtain the best discrimination results.

Table 3 shows the results obtained with the proposed speech/singing discrimination system. We can see from Table 3 that the speech/singing discrimination using timbre-based features solely (i.e., $\alpha = 1.0$) performs much better than that using pitch-based features solely (i.e., $\alpha = 0.0$). Despite the inferiority of the pitch-based sub-system, it can be observed from Table 4c that when combining the timbre-based and pitch-based features properly, i.e., $\alpha = 0.78$, the performance of the speech/singing discrimination can be improved noticeably from 90.8 % ($\alpha = 1.0$) to 94.3 %. Compared to the best accuracy of 85.6 % shown in Table 4a, it is clear that the proposed speech/singing discrimination system is superior to the intuitive speech-recognition-based discriminating system.

Table 4 lists the accuracies of discriminating each individual subject's singing and speech recordings using the proposed system. We can see from Table 4a that when using timbre-based features only, the system, in analogous to that in Table 1,

Table 4 Accuracies (in %) of discriminating each individual subject's singing and speech recordings

(A) Based on the timbre-based features only ($\alpha = 1.0$)

Subject	Singing	Speech	Average
1	90.0	93.3	91.7
2	63.3	83.3	73.3
3	96.7	93.3	95.0
4	93.3	90.0	91.7
5	93.3	86.7	90.0
6	96.7	93.3	95.0
7	93.3	96.7	95.0
8	90.0	90.0	90.0
9	96.7	100.0	98.3
10	96.7	80.0	88.3

(B) Based on the pitch-based features only ($\alpha = 0.0$)

Subject	Singing	Speech	Average
1	76.7	83.3	80.0
2	86.7	90.0	88.3
3	76.7	86.7	81.7
4	80.0	86.7	83.3
5	90.0	83.3	86.7
6	70.0	83.3	76.7
7	80.0	86.7	83.3
8	80.0	70.0	75.0
9	76.7	83.3	80.0
10	96.7	93.3	95.0

(C) Based on the combination of the timbre-based and pitch-based features ($\alpha = 0.78$)

Subject	Singing	Speech	Average
1	90.0	96.7	93.3
2	83.3	86.7	85.0
3	96.7	93.3	95.0
4	96.7	90.0	93.3
5	100.0	93.3	96.7
6	96.7	96.7	96.7
7	93.3	96.7	95.0
8	96.7	90.0	93.3
9	96.7	100.0	98.3
10	100.0	93.3	96.7

performs poorly in discriminating subject 2's voice, compared to the cases of other subjects. However, unlike the results in Table 1 that the intuitive system tends to falsely determine subject 2's speech recordings as singing, the proposed system using timbre-based features only tend to falsely determine subject 2's singing recordings as speech. The major reason is that subject 2 is not good at singing, which does not know how to modify their voices properly to make the singing melodious. As a result, the formant structures of his speech and singing are very similar, leading to the indistinguishableness for our system using the timbre-based features only. By contrast, we can see from Table 4b that the proposed system using only pitch-based features can handle subject 2's voices well, compared to that in Tables 2 and 4a. This implies that although subject 2's singing voice sounds like speech in terms of timbre, it differs significantly from speech in the pitch-level features. The results also indicate the importance of pitch-based features in discriminating speech and singing voices. The combined use of the timbre-based and pitch-based features complements each feature's advantages and disadvantages and hence obtains the better performance in Table 4c.

5 Conclusion

The technique of automatically discriminating speech from singing voices have been investigated. We proposed a discrimination approach based on both timbre and pitch feature analyses. In using timbre features, voice recordings are converted into Mel-Frequency Cepstral Coefficients and their first derivatives and then analyzed using Gaussian mixture models. In using pitch feature, we converted voice recordings into MIDI note sequences and then use bigram models to analyze the dynamic change information of the notes. Our experiments, conducted using a database including 600 test recordings from ten subjects, show that the proposed system can achieve 94.3 % accuracy for clean audio signals. In the future, we will study how the noises and signal distortions affect the performance of a speech/ singing discriminating system.

Acknowledgment This work was supported in part by the National Science Council, Taiwan, under Grants NSC101-2628-E-027-001.

References

1. S. Rosenau, An analysis of phonetic differences between German singing and speaking voices, in *Proc. 14th Int. Congress of Phonetic Sciences* (ICPhS), 1999
2. D. Gerhard, Computationally measurable differences between speech and song, Ph.D. dissertation, Simon Fraser University, 2003
3. J. Saunders, "Real-time discrimination of broadcast speech/music," in *Proc. IEEE Int. Conf. Acoustics, Speech, Signal Processing* (ICASSP), pp. 993–996, May 1996
4. E. Scheirer, M. Slaney, Construction and evaluation of a robust multi-feature speech/music discriminator, in *Proc. IEEE Int. Conf. Acoustics, Speech, Signal Processing* (ICASSP), pp. 1331–1334, Apr 1997

5. G. Williams and D. Ellis, "Speech/music discrimination based on posterior probability features," in *Proc. European Conf. Speech Commun. and Technology* (Eurospeech), pp. 687–690, Sept 1999
6. M. Carey, E. Parris, H. Lloyd-Thomas, A comparison of features for speech/music discrimination, *Proc. IEEE Int. Conf. Acoustics, Speech, Signal Processing* (ICASSP), 1999
7. K. El-Maleh, M. Klein, G. Petrucci, P. Kabal, Speech/music discrimination for multimedia applications, in *Proc. IEEE Int. Conf. Acoustics, Speech, Signal Processing* (ICASSP), 2000
8. W. Chou, L. Gu, Robust singing detection in speech/music discriminator design, in *Proc. IEEE Int. Conf. Acoustics, Speech, Signal Processing* (ICASSP), 2001
9. J. Ajmera, I. McCowan, H. Bourlard, Speech/Music segmentation using entropy and dynamism features in a HMM classification framework. Speech Comm. **40**, 351–363 (2003)
10. C. Panagiotakis, G. Tziritas, A speech/music discriminator based on RMS and zero crossings. IEEE Trans. Multimedia **7**(1), 155–166 (2005)
11. J. E. Muñoz-Expósito, S. Garcia-Galán, N., Ruiz-Reyes, P. Vera-Candeas, F. Rivas-Peña, Speech/Music discrimination using a single warped LPC-based feature, in *Proc. Int. Symp. Music Information Retrieval*, 2005
12. A. L. Berenzweig, D. P. W. Ellis, Locating singing voice segments within music signals, in *Proc. IEEE Workshop on Applications of Signal Processing to Audio and Acoustics*, pp. 119–122, 2001
13. L.R. Rabiner, A tutorial on Hidden Markov Models and selected applications in speech recognition. Proc. IEEE **77**(2), 257–286 (1989)
14. The Hidden Markov Model Toolkit (HTK) http://htk.eng.cam.ac.uk/
15. S.B. Davis, P. Mermelstein, Comparison of parametric representations for monosyllabic word recognition in continuously spoken sentences. IEEE Trans. Acoust. Speech Signal Process. **28** (4), 357–366 (1980)
16. The Association for Computational Linguistics and Chinese Language Processing (ACLCLP) http://www.aclclp.org.tw/use_mat_c.php
17. M.-Y. Hwang, X. Huang, Shared distribution Hidden Markov Models for speech recognition. IEEE Trans. Speech Audio Process. **1**(4), 414–420 (1993)
18. S.J. Young, P.C. Woodland, State clustering in HMM-based continuous speech recognition. Comput. Speech Lang. **8**(4), 369–384 (1994)
19. V. Digalakis, P. Monaco, H. Murveit. Genones: generalised mixture tying in continuous speech HMM-based speech recognizers. IEEE Trans. Speech Audio Process., **4**(4), 281–289 (1996)
20. D. Reynolds, R. Rose, Robust text-independent speaker identification using Gaussian mixture speaker models. IEEE Trans. Speech Audio Process. **3**(1), 72–83 (1995)
21. A. Dempster, N. Laird, D. Rubin, Maximum likelihood from incomplete data via the EM algorithm. J. R. Statist. Soc. **39**, 1–38 (1977)
22. H.M. Yu, W.H. Tsai, H.M. Wang, A query-by-singing system for retrieving karaoke music. IEEE Trans. Multimedia **10**(8), 1626–1637 (2008)
23. M. Piszczalski, B.A. Galler, Predicting musical pitch from component frequency ratios. J. Acoust. Soc. Amer. **66**(3), 710–720 (1979)
24. X. Huang, A. Acero, H. W. Hon, *Spoken Language Processing*, (Prentice Hall, 2001)

Exploring the Feature Selection-Based Data Analytics Solutions for Text Mining Online Communities by Investigating the Influential Factors: A Case Study of Programming CQA in Stack Overflow

Shu Zhou and Simon Fong

Abstract Community question answering (CQA) services accumulate large amount of knowledge through the voluntary services of the community across the globe. In fact, CQA services gained much popularity recently compared to other Internet services in obtaining and exchanging information. Stack Overflow is an example of such a service that targets programmers and software developers. In general, most questions in Stack Overflow are usually ended up with an answer accepted by the askers. However, it is found that the number of unanswered or ignored questions has increased significantly in the past few years. Understanding the factors that contribute to questions being answered as well as questions remain ignored can help information seekers to improve the quality of their questions and increase their chances of getting answers from the community in Stack Overflow. In this study, we attempt to identify by data mining techniques the relevant features that will help predict the quality of questions, and validate the reliability of the features using some of the state-of-the-art classification algorithms. The features to be obtained have to be significant in the sense that they can help Stack Overflow to improve their existing CQA service in terms of user satisfaction in obtaining quality answers from their questions.

Keywords Community question answering (CQA) • Classification • Feature section • Text analytics • Data mining

S. Zhou (✉)
Department of Product Marketing, MOZAT Pte Ltd, Singapore, Singapore
e-mail: suzyzhou@mozat.com

S. Fong
Department of Computer and Information Science, University of Macau, Macau SAR, China
e-mail: ccfong@umac.mo

© Springer International Publishing Switzerland 2016   49
P.C.K. Hung (ed.), *Big Data Applications and Use Cases*, International Series
on Computer Entertainment and Media Technology, DOI 10.1007/978-3-319-30146-4_4

1 Introduction

1.1 Background

The rapid growth of the Internet has changed the way people communicate. More people are increasingly relying on their distributed peer communities for information, advice, and expertise. In fact, internet services like public discussion forums, community-built encyclopedias (e.g., Wikipedia) and community question answering (CQA) sites (e.g., Yahoo! Answers, Answerbag,[1] Quora, etc.) are used globally by people for exchanging information and learning from each other. Of all these Internet services, CQA has recently gained much popularity among the general public for information seeking and knowledge sharing. In reality, it is estimated that the number of questions answered on CQA sites surpass the number of questions answered by library reference services [1].

CQA is defined as community services which allow users to post questions for other users to answer or respond [2]. It aims to provide community-based [3] knowledge creation services [4]. Compared to the previous keywords-based querying, CQA websites has been recognized as more precise [1] and trustworthy [5]. The reason is as opposed to traditional search engine such as Google, CQA provide a valuable alternative solution to information seeking for a number of reasons [6]. Firstly, the answers given by users with actual knowledge or experience are in no doubt more fruitful and foolproof for the questioner. CQA tends to be more efficient and useful to the answerers to get the information regarding particular questions asked by them rather than to go through a list of related documents. Secondly, CQA presents a centralized communication environment where it is possible to facilitate multiples answers from different perspectives and also allow the questioners to interact with the answerers for further clarifications. Thirdly, CQA provides an enticement for people to demonstrate their expertise and get recognized globally. This surely attracts the users to answer in order to be recognized as experienced ones.

Lately, CQA websites specifically in the programming context are gaining momentum among programmers and software developers [7]. This is because today's software engineering field involves a wide range of technologies, tools, programming languages, and platforms. Even for experienced developers, it can be difficult for them to be proficient and to keep up with the rapid growth of all the different technologies. CQA can therefore provide them with the environment for seeking help and advice from their distributed peers about technical difficulties that they face. In addition, software development has been described as knowledge intensive because it requires different areas of expertise and capabilities. For this reason, CQA can also play a role as knowledge management in this field [8].

---

[1] http://www.answerbag.com/

One of the most popular programming CQA website currently, Stack Overflow,[2] managed to capture compelling technical knowledge sharing among software developers globally [9]. From the perspective of practices, Stack Overflow is a place for people to post their programming or IT related questions for other people to provide answers [10]. After that, the questioners can select the most helpful answer and the question is considered solved. Registered members in Stack Overflow can vote on questions and also answers. The positive and negative votes show the helpfulness and quality of a question and answer. There is a reputation system in Stack Overflow, the members can increase their reputation in the website by participating in various activities like posting questions, answering, voting, posting comments, etc. With better reputations, they will obtain extra capabilities such as editing question/answers and closing a topic. From the perspective of theories, recently, many researches have been conducted to investigate this popular CQA website. For instance, the different online behaviors on Stack Overflow caused by user gender [11], the approaches of assigning new questions to Stack Overflow experts so as to facilitate the management process [12], the influence factors that could lead to the question deleted issues on Stack Overflow [13], and the trends of Stack Overflow [7]. All these practices and researches lead to the motivation in further improving the operations of CQA websites in terms of finding out which and why some questions are good in attracting replies and otherwise.

1.2 Objectives

This study aims to examine the predictors of ignored questions in a CQA service specifically those posted in Stack Overflow, by using data mining especially Text Analytics. Thus, there are two main objectives in this study.

Objective 1: The first objective is the identification of the crucial factors or features that affect the quality of the questions. The quality of the questions is divided into two classes: good and bad questions. In this specific context, good questions are defined as the questions that are solved by the community members. Contrarily, bad questions are defined as the ignored questions, which specifically mean the questions without any answers or comments from the online community for at least 3 months.

Objective 2: The second objective is to investigate the use of feature selection on classification models by combining the statistical approach and data mining approach for improving the accuracy of data mining algorithms, in classifying between good and bad questions. Feature selection techniques are also used to infer the importance of the features pertaining to the quality of questions in CQA.

---

[2] http://stackoverflow.com/

1.3 Justification

The high number of unanswered or ignored questions is a concern for CQA websites. Yang et al. [14] found out that of 76251 questions in Yahoo! Answers, among which 10424 (about 13.67 %) questions get no answers. Similarly, in Quora, another rapidly growing CQA website, 20 % of questions remain unanswered even though almost all questions were viewed at least by one user [15]. On the other hand, the Web data are crawled from Stack Overflow to investigate the number of ignored questions for the last few years to generate Figs. 1 and 2. In this context, an ignored question is defined as question that is without any answers or comments from the community for at least 3 months. From Fig. 1, there was a rapid growth in the number of ignored questions in Stack Overflow from the beginning of Stack Overflow in 2009–2014. If the ignored questions were not managed properly, the number of ignored questions would keep increasing exponentially resulted from the increasing users registering to Stack Overflow in the future. Similarly, Fig. 2 shows that the percentage of ignored question also increase over the years. To control the growth, it would be important for Stack Overflow to understand the factors that contribute to low quality questions and introduce a mechanism that helps reduce the number of ignored questions. Thereby, the mechanism can lead to a better management of the CQA site and to help users increase their chances of getting answers from their questions.

Most of the previous study focused on investigation of high quality answers in CQA, with the anticipation to improve the quality of user generated contents of

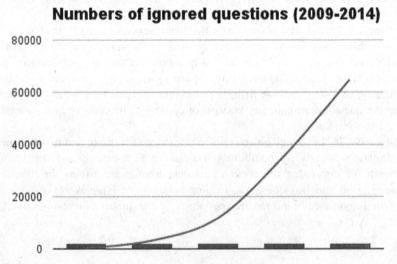

Fig. 1 Number of ignored questions each year. (Source: crawled data from the website stackoverflow.com)

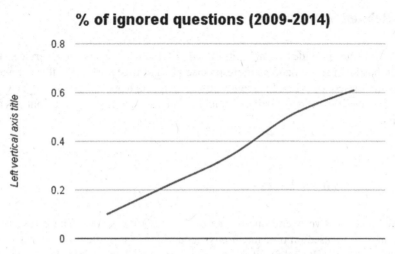

Fig. 2 Percentage of ignored questions each year. (Source: crawled data from the website stackoverflow.com)

CQA websites in the future. However, not many researchers focused on the quality of the questions. Low quality questions often lead to bad answers whereas high quality questions usually receive good answers [16]. Thus, we would argue that the quality of the questions is one of the main influences to the low quality answers in CQA websites. *"Questions are never indiscreet, answers sometimes are."* a quote by Oscar Wilde, suggested that a question might be asked poorly or incorrectly if there are no desirable answers to the question. Therefore in this study, the authors will attempt to identify the factors that influence the selection of high and low quality questions in a CQA service specifically questions related to programming in Stack Overflow.

For further justification, identifying the quality of question in CQA service is significant for a number of other reasons. Firstly, high quality questions can actually promote the development of the CQA community. This is because high quality questions will attract more authentic expert users to share their knowledge and experience, eventually further enhancing the knowledge base of the CQA community. The users can therefore gain more value from the CQA community. Secondly, low quality questions hinder the service quality of CQA websites. For example, low quality questions, such as posting advertisements as questions, are eyesores for the users and will highly reduce the overall user experience. Lastly, question quality can aid question searching in CQA. The accuracy of question retrieval and question recommendation in CQA services can be improved if the system can take advantage of the high quality questions to understand their meaning from the natural language.

2   Related Works

CQA websites provides community-based [3] knowledge creation services [4], which has been recognized as more precise [1] and trustworthy [5] than previous keywords-based querying. In recent years, researchers have started to analyze CQA websites on different perspectives, mainly on the users, user generated contents and the features of CQA.

2.1   Research on Users

Firstly, studies have been done on the users in CQA websites. These researches have mainly focused on user intentions, gender issue, user attention, user activity, and user typology. Based on different user intentions, Chen et al. [3] have proposed the taxonomy that categorizes the questions on CQA websites into three types: objective questions (posed by users so as to get factual knowledge), subjective questions (posed by users so as to get opinions or experiences), and social questions (posed by users so as to establish social interactions). Vasilescu et al. [11] conducted a quantitative study of online communities and found out that users' gender differences leading to different online behavior. This study have claimed that men contribute vast majority contents, and earned more reputation by participating than women on Stack Overflow. Wang et al. [15] have suggested that users are connected by three networks, namely topics, social networking and questions on CQA websites, and have pointed out that heterogeneity is the key success factor in directing users' attention and activities into small popular questions. Dror et al. [17] have studied the churn prediction in new users of CQA websites by crawling users' personal information, activity data and the data on social interaction. Similarly, Lai and Kao [18] have claimed that both users' expertise and also users' activities are crucial criteria for question routine. Anderson et al. [4] have found out that users can be divided into answers and voters, and have studied how users' community activities that affect the answers in CQA websites.

2.2   Research on User-Generated Contents

Secondly, studies have been done on the user-generated contents in CQA websites, researches had mainly focused on questions, answers and the pairs of question-answer. Many research were conducted on answers. Blooma et al. [19], Nasehi et al. [10], Cai and Chakravarthy [6], Shah and Pomerantz [1] had analyzed the quality of answers in CQA and the factors that will affect their quality. Besides quality issue, the categorizing issue of answers had also emerging. Miao et al. [20]

had studied on new answer categories that had not been concluded in the existing category hierarchy, and proposed two modeling methods to solve this problem.

On the other hand, researches on questions were emerging. Suzuki et al. [21] and Li et al. [2] had analyzed the questions in CQA, Singh and Visweswariah [22] had studied the question classifications of CQA website, Quan and Wenyin [23] analyzed the attractiveness of questions. Riahi et al. [12] had focused on assigning new questions to experts who got the most suitable expertise in Stack Overflow. Similarly, Xuan et al. [24] had also proposed topic cluster for experts narrowing down the domain expertise, and combined with latent links for experts ranking in specific topic, so as to solve the expert find problem. Furthermore, Barua et al. [7] had studied the trends and topics on CQA website specifically in Stack Overflow, Correa and Sureka [13] had focused on the deleted questions on Stack Overflow, and they proposed that all four categories (users' profile, community generated, question content and syntactical style) would lead to the question-deleted issue. Although this model was one of the earliest prediction model that focused on poor quality question of Stack Overflow, but the accuracy was only reported as 66 % and it seemed a lot of further work to be conducted in this field.

Apart from that, the research on similarity analysis of question-answer pairs in CQA had also been popular. Wang et al. [25] had proposed the ranking algorism to find the best answer by utilizing the relationships between questions and answers. Pera and Ng [26] had introduced a CQA refinement system based on analyzing 4,000,000 pair of questions-answers crawdad from Yahoo! However, Chen et al. [5] figured out that focus solely on textual similarities would fail in detecting commercial answers in CQA websites, hence, they had proposed an effective detecting algorism that involves more context indexes (answering pattern and answerer's reputation track).

2.3   Research on Functionality of CQA Websites

Thirdly, studies had been done on the features in CQA websites. Both functionalities and non-functionalities of CQA websites had been explored. In terms of functionalities of CQA websites, Mamykina et al. [9] had studied the design features of successful CQA websites. Whereas Danescu et al. [27] and Hong et al. [28] studied the voting and reputation system of CQA, Souza et al. [29] and Li et al. [30] studied the routing of questions to appropriate answerers in CQA. In order to improve users' searching accuracy and efficiency, Tang et al. [31] developed an answer summary system to replace existing lists of similar queries. Zhang et al. [32] had suggested a mobile multimedia functionality that could be used in CQA websites, and the authors had claimed that supported by identifying mobile screenshots, matching these instances and retrieving candidate answers, the question asking process could be effective facilitated.

In terms of the non-functionalities of CQA websites, the characteristic of communities of CQA websites had attracted intense research attentions.

Zhang et al. [33] had proposed a unified framework to examine the typology of community structures in CQA websites. Shachaf [34] had regarded the collaborations in CQA websites as an enabler of better services. However, Fichman [35] had defined the popularity as higher user participation, and had reported the unclear correlations between website popularity and answer quality. Chua and Balkunje [36] had measured the system usability issues and provided general recommendations of improving usability features for CQA websites.

Based on the extensive literature review, it is suggested that the past works on CQA had been quite fruitful, and many research had already contributed a lot of insights to this topic. On the one hand, all achievements had provided the authors with adequate inspirations. On the other hand, since the management of CQA website is a dynamic problem that contains multiple-roles, it is found that previous research mainly focused on one side of the problem. As we argued previously, the importance of questions have attracted emerging attentions. However, past works had mainly concentrated on one side of questions, for instance, the classification or attractiveness of questions, or the approaches to assigning questions to experts, or some specific type of questions like deleted ones and etc. But the distinctions between different types of questions had not been clearly articulated. In another word, the possible influence factors of questions had been identified, but the comparisons between how these factors perform in different types of questions and the causes of different performances have not been taken care of. Therefore, we would like to investigate the comparisons between good quality questions and bad quality questions so as to contribute more from a new perspective.

3 Methodology

Stack Overflow's data is used for this study due to the popularity of Stack Overflow among programmers globally. Stack Overflow is one of the largest community question-answering sites for questions related to programming. In addition, they are rich in metadata such as user's reputation that are suitable to be used for the study. Stack Overflow had been used in many existing studies (e.g.: [10, 37]).

3.1 Dataset

This study focuses on Java solely in Stack Overflow, to keep balance of both macro and micro research perspectives. From the macro perspective, Java is the most popular programming language on average. According to Tiobe[3] Programming Community Index (Fig. 3), a measure of popularity of programming languages,

---

[3] http://www.tiobe.com/index.php/content/paperinfo/tpci/index.html

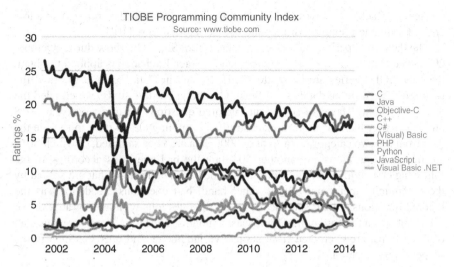

Fig. 3 Tiobe Programming Community Index (Source: Tiobe, April 2014)

Table 1 Number of questions on SO (Source: crawled data from the website stackoverflow.com)

Popular language	Number of tagged questions	Number of ignored questions
Java	456748	8463
C	103461	557
C++	217951	1896

Java has been the lingua franca and long-term favored in the past decade and, without no doubt, gets the highest average ratings in popularity from 2002 to 2014. From the micro perspective, based on data collected from Stack Overflow (Table 1), Java-related questions are the most tagged and the most ignored, with 456748 and 8463 respectively, which are extremely superior compared to other top two popular languages, C (103461 and 557) and C++ (217951 and 1896).

Our investigation is centered about questions that have been answered and unanswered on Stack Overflow. Previous researches pay more attention on either high-quality answers [19] or the pairs of question-answer [10]. It is estimated that investigation on the questions in CQA service are seriously underestimated or even neglected. However, questions actually generate great value for CQA. In order to compensate for this research gap, this study aims to focus on questions in CQA service. Data from Stack Overflow are considered suitable for examining the predictors of questions for three causes. Firstly, practically, the numbers of both solved and ignored questions of Stack Overflow are soaring continually from 2009 to 2014. In order to deal with this serious challenge in Stack Overflow, a practical solution is highly expected. Secondly is the richness data available on Stack Overflow. Large number of data from both kinds of questions could be served to make comparisons. Hence, the causes behind could be mined out. Thirdly is the accessibility. Free services of Stack Overflow (unlike Expert Exchange[4]) enable data retrieval at a low cost, so valuable previous work could also be referred (e.g. [10]).

The data for experimentation are collected from Stack Overflow during October 2014. The Data Explorer[5] service provided by Stack Exchange is applied to obtain the data. SQL queries are be written and executed in Data Explorer to crawl the required data from the database of Stack Overflow. For this study, we crawled the data with the tag 'Java' of solved and ignored questions starting from year 2008 onwards. After that, disproportionate stratified sampling are be used to sample the data from the two categories. A total of 3000 data are to be sampled, of which 50 % are the good questions and another 50 % are the bad questions according to the following criterion. Good questions are defined as the questions that are solved by the community members. On the other hand, bad questions are defined as the ignored questions, which specifically mean the questions without any answers or comments from the community for at least 3 months. The terms, good questions and bad questions, are exempted from subjective judgments and only confined in the scope of this research.

4 Feature Identification

This section presents a literature review to identify the features used for this study. In summary, the authors have identified 24 features that are used for classifying the quality of the questions in CQA from the literatures. The features are divided into two main categories: metadata features and content features; and four sub-categories. Table 2 shows a summary of all the features identified from the literatures. The detailed explanations of the features are given in the sub-sections below.

4.1 Metadata Features

Metadata is data that describes the raw data, which abstracts basic information about data. The main purpose of metadata is to facilitate in the identification and retrieval of relevant information, in which also known as resource discovery. In the context of question in CQA, metadata can refer to the category of the question, the time and date of creation, the creator of the question and other available information that describe the question. Additionally, there are also metadata that describe about the users such as their personal information and reputation in the CQA site.

---

[4] http://www.experts-exchange.com/
[5] https://data.stackexchange.com/

Table 2 Features for characterizing high-quality questions.

Category	Sub-category	Features
Metadata features	Asker's user profile	Reputation [37–41]
		Days since join [16, 41]
		Upvotes [16, 37]
		Downvotes [39]
		Upvotes/Downvotes [39]
		Questions asked [14, 37, 39–41]
		Answers posted [14, 37, 39–41]
		Answers posted/questions asked [41]
	Question	Time [14, 39, 41]
		Day [14, 39]
Content features	Textual features	Tags [16]
		Title length [37, 39–41]
		Question length [14, 37, 39–41]
		Code snippet [37]
		Wh word [40, 41]
	Content appraisal	Completeness [37]
		Complexity [16, 37]
		Language error [16]
		Presentation [37]
		Politeness [14, 37]
		Subjectivity [2, 14]

In classification, metadata features are defined as features that can be obtained directly from the metadata to be used as predictors, without the need to perform further complicated extractions on the features. In classifying the quality of questions in CQA, the metadata that describe the questions and the askers of the questions are commonly used [14, 39]. Only the information on the metadata available at question time are used because the objective of the study is to predict the quality of the question, when the questions are first posted by the users. The metadata features in the study were divided into two main sub-categories: the asker's user profile and questions. Below are the descriptions of the identified features.

4.1.1 Asker's User Profile

This metadata information is related to the users who were asking questions, which may include their personal information as well as the information obtained from their online activities performed on the website. The metadata features about the askers used are: reputation of the askers, days since the first day of joining data, upvotes, downvotes, the ratio of upvotes to downvotes, number of questions asked, number of answers posted and lastly the ratio of answers responded to the questions asked. One of the reasons in including the metadata features from the askers' user profile is that they offer information about the background and involvement of the askers in a particular CQA site. Experienced users are more familiar with the CQA services as well as the community while new users probably wonder what to ask and how to ask [14]. In addition, users are also able to assess the quality of the questions and answers posted by a particular user by giving positive or negative votes, the information can be utilized to find out the overall quality of the information provided by the askers in the past. Furthermore, this set of features about the askers is used as predictors of high quality questions because they are readily available at the time when the questions were posted. A description of these metadata features from the askers' user profile is given below:

1) **Reputation**. The stature of the askers in the CQA site [37–41].
2) **Days since join**. The total number of days since the askers joined the CQA site [16, 41].
3) **Upvotes**. The total number of positive votes of the questions and answers from the askers by other users in the past [16, 37].
4) **Downvotes**. The total number negative votes of the questions and answers from the askers by other users in the past [39].
5) **Upvotes/Downvotes**. The ratio between the total number positive votes and the negative votes of the questions and answers from the askers by other users in the past [39].
6) **Questions asked**. The total number of questions the askers asked in the past [14, 37, 39–41].
7) **Answers posted**. The total number of answers the askers posted in the past [14, 37, 39–41].
8) **Answers posted/questions asked**. The ratio between the total number of question asked and the total number of answers posted [41].

4.1.2   Questions

In CQA services, metadata that describe about the questions posted can also be found. Two important metadata features on the questions that determine whether the questions will be answered are the time and day when the questions were posted. The chances of the questions quickly being answered are largely affected by the number of users that are active online at the moment when the questions are posted. Therefore, the authors use the features time and the day of the week when the questions were posted as predictors in this study. However, due to the periodic nature of time and day, the authors modified the features during the feature extraction process so that they are more appropriate to be used in classification. Each feature is transformed to a dual; the novel approach is explained in the feature extraction section of this paper.

1) **Time**. The time of the day when the questions were posted by the askers [14, 39, 41].
2) **Day**. The day of the week when the questions were posted by the askers [14, 39].

4.2   Content Features

In the context of questions in CQA, content features are defined as the metrics that track intrinsic and extrinsic content quality of the questions. Content features are divided into two sub-categories, textual features and content appraisal. Specifically, textual features are defined as the intrinsic quality metrics related to tangible features of the text in the questions. Textual features can be automatically generated using a sequence of procedures and they are usually done using computer programs. On the other hand, content appraisal features are defined as extrinsic quality metrics related to intangible features of the content in the questions. Content appraisal features require human expert judgment in ranking the content of the questions. Intuitively, these types of features are used in the classification of the quality of questions in CQA given that the content of the questions are primarily textual in nature.

4.2.1   Textual Features

From the literatures, the authors have identified five textual features that are useful in classification of the quality of questions in CQA. The features are: tags, title length, question length, code snippet and whether the titles prefix with the question letters 'Wh'. Tags is the number of tags (or category) of the questions, a question may be generalized by one or more tags. However in this study, the questions contain the 'Java' tag alone or along with other tag(s). Title length and question length are the number of word counts computed from the textual content of the title and from the questions respectively. The textual features from the content of the questions are described below:

1) **Tags**. The number of tags or categories the questions is associated with [16].
2) **Title length**. The number of words in the title of a question [14, 39, 41].
3) **Question length**. The number of words in the content of a question [14, 37, 39–41].
4) **Code snippet**. Whether the content of the questions contain code snippet(s) [37].
5) **Wh word**. Whether the title of a question starts with any one of these 'wh' question words: "what", "when", "where", which", "who", "whom", "whose", "why", and "how" [40, 41].

4.2.2   Content Appraisal

The inclusion of content appraisal features in this study motivated by Asaduzzaman et al. [37], where they incorporate a series of extrinsic features to analyze the unanswered questions in CQA. In addition, there are researches on the way people making judgment on the quality of information in CQA (e.g.: [42]) and the theoretical quality measures created are utilized in the study. The content appraisal features used in the study to classify the quality of questions are: completeness, complexity, language error, presentation, politeness, and question subjectivity. A description of the six content appraisal features identified from the literatures is given below:

1) **Completeness**. [37].
2) **Complexity**. The degree of difficulty of the questions [16, 37].
3) **Language error**. The degree of grammar and typing errors made by the askers in the content of the questions [16].
4) **Presentation**. The format, clarity and writing style used to present the questions to ensure readability [37].
5) **Politeness**. The courtesy and sincerity shown in content of the questions by the askers [14, 37].
6) **Subjectivity**. Subjective questions are those asking for answers with private states, e.g. personal interests, opinions, judgments; on the other hand, objective questions require authoritative information [2, 14].

5   Data Preprocessing

Data preprocessing is a series of steps to be performed on the raw dataset before constructing an effective classification model. Data preprocessing is important for three reasons. First, many raw data from the real world cannot be applied straight into the classification algorithms without any proper transformation over the data, for example: the raw textual content in the dataset. Second, raw data may contain many irrelevant information and those information need to be filtered out during preprocessing. Third, the value range of the features needs to be normalized and standardized. This is because the wide variation of value ranges in the raw data is likely to affect the significance of the representations of each feature during the classification process. In this study, the data preprocessing steps include: feature extraction, feature normalization and feature selection. Each of the data preprocessing steps is explained in the sub-sections below.

5.1   Feature Extraction

Feature extraction is an essential pre-processing step in data mining of transforming the raw dataset into a representation set of meaningful features, which involves simplifying the large and redundant raw dataset in order to generate a significantly smaller set of features to accurately describe the raw dataset. The feature extraction process for the dataset is automated by executing custom-developed Python scripts. In the study, the three sub-categories of features that require automated extraction are: the asker's user profile, metadata features of the questions as well as the textual features from the content of the questions. In addition to that, content appraisal features from the content of the questions require manual extraction, which is the expert judgment from human.

The features from the users' asker profile (reputation, upvotes, downvotes, questions asked, and answers posted) that the authors crawled are inconsistent as most of them are crawled over a long period after the questions were asked. The features may not represent the experience of the askers in Stack Overflow at the particular time when the questions were asked. Therefore, for the purpose of our study, the values of these features with the assumption that the values increase linearly in time are estimated and adjusted. The formula used is shown in Eq. (1) where x is the value of the feature and x' is the estimation of the value at the time when the question was asked.

$$x' = \frac{(x)}{(current\_date - join\_date)} * (question\_date - join\_date) \qquad (1)$$

The metadata features of the questions are the time of the day and day of the week the questions were posted by the askers. However, due to the cyclical nature of the time and day, it is impossible to apply them directly for classification without further extraction. This is because there is no meaning in the ranking of time and day value. Most classification algorithms define hypotheses of distinguishing different classes with a linear separator in a two dimensional data feature or a hyper plane in a higher dimensional data feature. For example, Fig. 4 shows a simple example of the day feature (from 1: Monday to 7: Sunday) used directly without any extraction, demonstrated using two classes: positive and negative. It is impossible to perform a linear classification in the given dataset. In order to solve this problem of the cyclical features like time, Yang et al. [14], in their study of predicting unanswered questions in CQA, had attempted to split the time into 24 different features, each to represent an hour of a day. However, this approach will generate additional 24 features causing the dataset to become unnecessarily sparse with

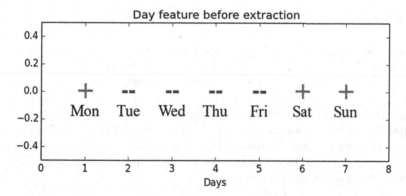

Fig. 4 Periodic feature before extraction

Table 3 *Sine* and *cosine* functions for periodic feature extraction

Periodic features	*sine* function	*cosine* function
Time 1–24 h	$\sin(2\pi * time/24)$	$\cos(2\pi * time/24)$
Day 1 (Monday) to 7 (Sunday)	$\sin(2\pi * day/7)$	$\cos(2\pi * day/7)$

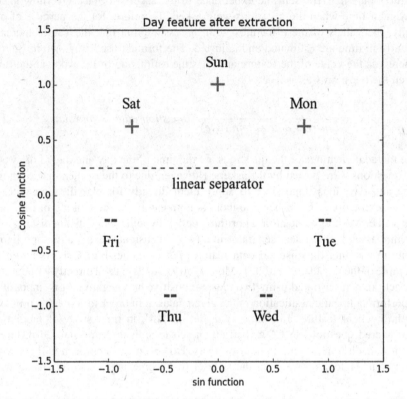

Fig. 5 Periodic feature after extraction

many zeroes. Therefore in the study, a novel approach is applied which is similar to an approach introduced by Bishop [43] for solving this problem. It is done by expanding each periodic feature into a pair of features using *sine* and *cosine* functions, so that each periodic feature is now represented in a two-dimensional space. This way, classification algorithms can perform linear separation correctly in distinguishing the classes: positive and negative. The equations for the *sine* and *cosine* functions to extract the time and day features are shown in Table 3. Figure 5 shows the example of the day feature after extraction and a linear line is able to separate the two different classes.

Some of the textual features from the content of the questions are extracted by utilizing NLTK[6] (Natural Language Toolkit) module. NLTK is a free open source Python module, with a broad-coverage natural language toolkit that provides a simple, extensible, uniform framework [44]. NTLK is widely used in academic research and teaching. The authors mainly use the tokenization function implemented in NLTK for the feature extraction from textual content. Tokenization is a process of separating a stream of text into individual words, which are also known as tokens. For the dataset, the textual content of the title and questions are tokenized into separated words. This is done so that the number of words or length of the title and questions can be calculated more efficiently to extract the required features.

As for the evaluation of the content appraisal features from the content of the questions, expert judgments from human are used as proxies for the users' judgments of the questions. Human experts are used for evaluation of the content appraisal because automatic analysis of appraisal approach is still under extensive research and there is still room for improvement [45]. From previous research, Rieh and Danielson [46] and Suryanto et al. [47] used similar techniques in their CQA studies. More specifically in the study by Suryanto et al. [47], content quality based on usefulness, readability, sincerity, readability and objectivity are rated by independent evaluators.

In the study, a team of expert users with the background of computer science helped to qualitatively evaluate the questions in terms of the six content appraisal features identified, they are: completeness, complexity, language error, presentation, politeness, and question subjectivity. Because of the nature of questions in Stack Overflow which are programming related questions and only questions with Java tags are crawled, the human evaluators invited possess post-graduate degrees to information technology and they have experience in Java programming. Given their relevant academic and professional background, they are able to offer reliable judgment on the content appraisal of the questions in Stack Overflow.

Hence, it is crucial to ensure their degree of agreement in order to confirm the consistency of their judgment. Cohen's kappa coefficient is utilized to measure the inter-rater agreement between the two evaluators. Initially, each evaluator is given 180 questions for a start, which consist of 90 bad questions (without any answers) and 90 good questions (with at least one accepted answer by the askers). The average kappa coefficient was calculated to be 0.765 before continuing the evaluations of the content appraisal on the complete dataset (Appendix 1 shows the complete calculation of the average kappa coefficient). This suggests that there is a high degree of agreements between both evaluators and the content appraisal features rated by them are of high quality and consistency.

---

[6] http://www.nltk.org/

5.2 *Feature Normalization*

Feature normalization is a method used to standardize the value range of the features of the raw dataset. In classification, feature normalization is an important step because the range of values of raw data varies widely. If the scales for different features are widely different, some classification algorithms may not work correctly. Ensuring standardized values among all the features implicitly weights all features equally in their representation of the dataset. In addition, normalization may improve the accuracy and efficiency of classifications algorithms like support vector machine (SVM), logistic regression, artificial neural networks and k-nearest neighbor [48].

Among all the normalization methods available, min-max normalization is one of the best methods in rescaling the values of raw data to be used in classification [49]. In the study, the authors normalized the values of all the features by adopting the min-max normalization method to rescale the value range of every feature. Min-max normalization performs a linear transformation on the original raw data to a value range of 0–1. The formula of the min-max normalization is shown in Eq. (2), where x is the original value and x' is the normalized value, whereas max (x) and min(x) are the maximum and minimum values in the feature. After the min-max normalization process, decimal value ranging from 0 to 1 are obtained for all the features. As a result every normalized feature is comparable to each other in terms of its representation to the dataset.

$$x' = \frac{x - \min(x)}{\max(x) - \min(x)} \tag{2}$$

5.3 *Feature Selection*

Feature selection is the process of selecting a subset of relevant features from all the features available for use in the construction of classification models. The objective of feature selection is to determine the best or good enough combination of features that improves or maintains the accuracy of classification over selecting every single feature available. Feature selection techniques are often used with dataset of many features and comparatively few samples, like the dataset in this study. In building a classification model, feature selection techniques provide three main advantages. First, the interpretability of the classification model is greatly improved. This is because a simpler model with few predictive features can be easily translated to human's understanding compared to a complex model which consist of a large number of features, and to understand their influence in the classification task [50].

Second, the time used for training the classification model is significantly reduced. This is especially true for a dataset with a large number of samples, because most classification algorithms train faster with fewer amounts of data. Third, feature selection may reduce over-fitting of the classification models. Over-fitting occurs when a classification model is too complex with a high number of features, which may contain redundant data or noise. The over-fitting model may make prediction with high accuracy on the training dataset (over-fitting the dataset) but generally having poor accuracy on new dataset not known beforehand. Reduction of features using feature selections produces less redundant data and therefore less chances for the classification model to make prediction based on noise and irrelevant data.

In order to select the most relevant and significant features in the dataset, the authors adopted two different approaches, namely the machine learning approach and statistical approach. Blooma et al. [19] also combine the two approaches with the help of SPSS software in their study to identify the most significant features in the prediction high quality answers in CQA. First, for the machine learning approach, the logistic regression classification algorithm is utilized with its L1 regularization parameter enabled to filter out the irrelevant features. Using L1 regularization, the logistic regression algorithm becomes extremely insensitive to the presence of irrelevant features, causing many logistic regression coefficients of the features to become zero [51]. Therefore, those features with zero coefficients are natural candidates as irrelevant features and should be ignored during classification.

Second, in order to get a more solid set of most relevant features, the Analysis of variance (ANOVA) F-test, a statistical hypothesis testing is also adopted. In the study, both approaches of feature selection are combined: machine learning and statistical approach to single out a set of features that is relevant, statistically significant and reliable, before applying them into some state-of-the-art classification algorithms (which are introduced in the next section) for the prediction of good and bad questions.

6 Classification

This section explains about the classification algorithms, the validation approach and the evaluation metrics used in this study. The validation and evaluation process are done to ensure that the features that are identified and selected are useful and reliable in classifying the good and bad questions in this study.

6.1 Classification Algorithms

In this study, classification algorithms are used to investigate the usefulness of the identified features to predict good and bad question in Stack Overflow. The performance of the popular classification algorithms are investigated: logistic regression, support vector machine (SVM), decision tree, naïve Bayes and

k-Nearest Neighbors. These algorithms are implemented in the computing platform called Scikit-learn.[7] Scikit-learn is a free open source Python module integrating a wide range of state-of-the-art machine learning algorithms, with the emphasis on ease of use, performance, documentation completeness and API consistency [52]. In addition, Scikit-learn is very popular and widely used among academic as well as commercial researchers. The classification algorithms used are explained below.

- **Logistic regression**: Logistic regression applies the maximum likelihood estimation after transforming the features into a logistic regression coefficient, the natural log of the odds on whether the feature occurs. In this study, the logistic regression classification algorithm is applied with its L1 regularization parameter enabled in the feature selection process as it was found to be insensitive to the presence of irrelevant features [51].
- **Support vector machine (SVM)**: SVM is considered as one of the best classification algorithm for many real world tasks, mainly due to its robustness in the presence of noise in the dataset used for training, and also high reported accuracy for many cases. In addition, one of the advantages of SVM is the ability to perform non-linear classification using kernel trick. However, in this study, the linear version of SVM is used so that comparison can be made with other linear classification algorithms like logistic regression and naïve Bayes, in addition to preventing over fitting of the classification on the dataset.
- **Decision tree**: The classification and regression tree CART algorithm of the decision tree implemented in the Scikit-learn module are used. One of the benefits of using decision tree for classification is the ease of interpretability of the models and results. However, if there are irrelevant features in the training data, decision tree algorithm can create overly complex trees used for classification and causing over fitting (do not generalize the training data to unknown new data). Because of using cross-validation technique (refer to the next sub-section), which is able to surface the over fitting problem in classifications models, the comparison can be done between the performance of decision tree of using complete set of features along with the smaller set of features obtained from feature selection.
- **Naïve Bayes**: One of the advantages of naïve Bayes is that it requires less training data to perform a classification compared to other algorithms. Its main disadvantage is that it cannot learn the interactions between the features, because a particular feature is assumed to be unrelated to other features, as mentioned earlier. In addition, naïve Bayes can suffer from oversensitivity to redundant or irrelevant features [53]. However, this shortcoming of naïve Bayes is utilized to verify that the feature selection step is actually successful in getting rid of the irrelevant features, by comparing the performance of naïve Bayes using

---

[7] http://scikit-learn.org/

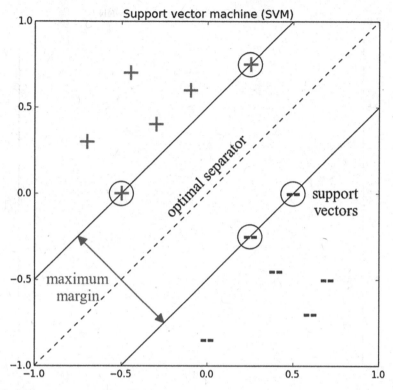

Fig. 6 Support vector machine (SVM)

complete set of features along with the smaller set of features obtained from feature selection.

- **K-Nearest Neighbors (k-NN)**: In the classification or testing phase, k is a user-defined constant, and a data point is classified by a majority vote of its neighbors, the class assigned is the class most common among its k nearest neighbors. Please see Fig. 6. The classification is highly depending on the number of nearest neighbor, k. Figure 7 below illustrate the k-NN with different setting of k, if $k = 3$, the new data point (green question mark in the figure) will be classified as positive, whereas if $k = 5$, the class will be negative. Euclidean distance is a commonly used distance metric to find out the k nearest neighbors of a data point in the data space [54]. For the dataset, we found that $k = 55$ gives us the optimal classification results.

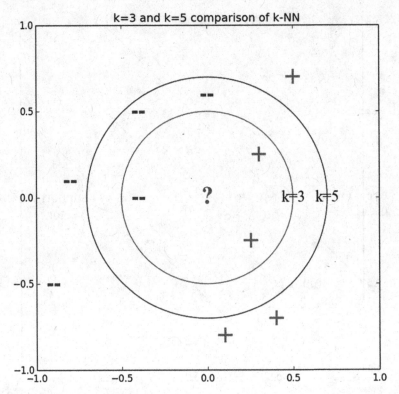

Fig. 7 $k = 3$ and $k = 5$ comparison of k-NN

6.2 Cross-Validation

Cross-validation is a statistical approach used to evaluate classification algorithms
by dividing the dataset into two main segments: one larger segment that is used for
learning or training a classification model and the other usually smaller segment is
used to validate the model. In cross validation, every segments of the dataset must
cross over each iteration of testing so that each segment has the chance of being
tested.

The commonly used cross-validation approach is k-fold cross-validation,
Kohavi [55] recommended using a stratified tenfold cross-validation where $k = 10$
and he indicated that stratification in cross validation is better in terms of bias and
variance when compared to the normal cross-validation. In cross-validation with
stratified sampling, each fold contains roughly the same percentage of samples of
each class as the complete dataset. This is done to ensure that each fold is a
reasonably satisfactory representation of the whole dataset. In the experiment, the
stratified tenfold cross-validation approach was used with the help of evaluation
metrics that are discussed in the next sub-section.

6.3 Evaluation Metrics

Two evaluation metrics are adopted in validating the performance of the classification, the two evaluation metrics are: accuracy and area under the receiver
operating characteristic (ROC) curve. In classification, accuracy is used to measure
of the performance of binary classification test, the correctness of the algorithm in
identifying or excluding a condition; the accuracy is the fraction of correctly
classified results (both true positives and true negatives) of the overall results.
The formula for accuracy is shown in Eq. (3), where TP is true positives: the
number of positive classes that are classified as positives and TN is the true
negative: the number of negatives classes that are classified as negatives. In the
study, both positive class (questions with an accepted answer by the asker) and
negative class (questions that are completely ignored) are equally important classes
to be considered in the evaluation of the classification performance. Therefore, the
evaluation metric: accuracy is used because it considers both true positives and true
negatives in the measurement, unlike precision measure that only take the true
positives into account.

$$accuracy = \frac{TP + TN}{TP + FP + FN + TN} \tag{3}$$

In addition to accuracy, the area under the ROC curve (AUC) is also used as an
evaluation metric for a reliable comparative study. ROC is a curve that represents
the performance of a classification model with the true positive rate (TPR) and false
positive rate (FPR) when the discrimination threshold is varied. The TPR is the
fraction of correct positive results to all the positive samples, whereas FPR is the
fraction of incorrect positive results to all the negative samples. An ROC curve is a
two-dimensional representation of the performance of a classification model. Similarly, AUC, the calculated area under the ROC curve, can be used to measure the
performance of classification models. The AUC is statistically useful in the sense
that the AUC is equivalent to the probability that the classification model will rank a
positive class higher than a negative class that is randomly chosen. From previous
research, AUC is found to be a better evaluation metric than accuracy in terms of
statistical consistency and discrimination [56, 57]. Therefore, AUC measure apart
from accuracy is also incorporated in order to ensure that the features used for the
classification of good and bad questions are useful and reliable.

7 Results and Discussion

The results and discussion of this study are presented into two sub-sections: feature
selection and classification. The final outcome of the results of the feature selection
is a set of features that are relevant and carry significance to the classification of

good and bad questions. On the other hand, the results of the classification include the performances (accuracy and AUC) of the classification algorithms in predicting good and bad questions using the complete set of features as well as the features obtained from the feature selection step. The details of the results and discussion of the feature selection and classification are explained thoroughly in the following sub-sections.

7.1 Feature Selection

Table 4 shows the results of feature selection, obtained from logistic regression with L1 regularization and the ANOVA F-test for all the features identified from the literatures. The features are divided into two main categories: metadata features and content features, and each category is further divided into their respective

Table 4 Coefficient and p-value in feature selection

Category	Sub-category	Feature	Coefficient from logistic regression (not equal to zero)	p-value from F-test (less than 0.05)
Metadata features	Asker's user profile	Reputation	0.000	0.559
		Days since join	−2.197	0.000
		Upvotes	0.830	0.333
		Downvotes	0.618	0.140
		Upvotes/ Downvotes	2.307	0.042
		Questions asked	2.233	0.173
		Answers posted	0.000	0.910
		Answers posted/ questions asked	0.000	0.183
	Question	Time (*sine*)	−0.253	0.016
		Time (*cosine*)	0.305	0.000
		Day (*sine*)	−0.318	0.023
		Day (*cosine*)	0.266	0.050
Content features	Textual features	Tags	−1.522	0.000
		Title length	−1.419	0.000
		Question length	−4.359	0.000
		Code snippet	−0.736	0.000
		Wh word	0.513	0.000
	Content appraisal	Completeness	2.658	0.000
		Complexity	−4.099	0.000
		Language error	−0.008	0.361
		Presentation	0.000	0.968
		Politeness	−0.547	0.004
		Subjectivity	0.197	0.000

sub-categories (as discussed in the feature identification section of this paper). In the Table, the coefficient from logistic regression as well as the p-value from F-test is listed for all the individual features. Features with zero coefficients from the L1 regularized logistic regression are usually irrelevant features and should be ignored during classification [51]. For a feature to be relevant and significant in the classification of good and bad questions, the absolute value of the coefficient must be non-zero and the p-value must be lower than a threshold of significant level, 0.05. Furthermore, from the results in Table 4, the features can be broken down into three major groups of features according to their association to the classification task, namely: positively associated features, negatively associated features and lastly irrelevant features. Each group of the features is discussed below.

Features that are positively associated have coefficient values of more than zero and p-values of less than 0.05: this means that with a higher value in the coefficient, the higher the association of the features to good questions (questions with an accepted answer by the asker) and the less association to bad questions (questions that are completely ignored). From the asker's user profile features, only one feature is found to be positively associated to good questions: upvotes/downvotes. This probably means that the quality of the questions asked in Stack Overflow depends on the quality of the contents (both questions and answers) posted by the askers previously, with high number of upvotes and low number of downvotes. Moreover, it appears that two content appraisal features are found to be positively associated to good questions, they are: completeness and subjectivity. This basically means that users in Stack Overflow prefer to answer questions that are that clear and understandable with reasonable amount of information provided by the askers, as well as questions that request for opinions from different perspectives. Furthermore, the time feature from the metadata of the questions is found to be positively associated for the *cosine* function but negatively associated for the *sine* function, this interesting finding is discussed in the following sub-section. Lastly, from the textual features, wh word feature is found to be positively associated. This means that the titles of the questions that prefixed with a question word are more likely to receive answers from the community. The positively associated features from the highest relevance and significance to the least relevance (listed in decreasing value of the coefficient) are shown in the first column of Table 5.

On the other hand, features that are negatively associated have coefficient values below zero and p-values of less than 0.05: this means that with a lower value in the coefficient, the more the features' association to good questions and the less association to bad questions. It is found that some features from the sub-categories of textual features, content appraisal features are negatively associated to good questions. The textual features include: tags, title length, question length and whether the questions contain code snippet(s). The content appraisal features that are negatively associated to good questions are: complexity and politeness. The negatively association of complexity feature basically means that the users in Stack Overflow prefer to answers questions which are simple. Politeness is found to be least relevant among the negatively associated features to good

Table 5 Three groups of features from feature selection

Positively associated features (from most relevant to least)		Negatively associated features (from most relevant to least)		Irrelevant or not significant features	
1	Completeness	1	Question length	1	Reputation
2	Upvotes/Downvotes	2	Complexity	2	Upvotes
3	Wh word	3	Days since join	3	Downvotes
4	Time (*cosine*)	4	Tags	4	Questions asked
5	Subjectivity	5	Title length	5	Answers posted
		6	Code snippet	6	Answers posted/ questions asked
		7	Politeness	7	Day (*cosine*)
		8	Day (*sine*)	8	Language error
		9	Time (*sine*)	9	Presentation

question, this probably means that the users do not really care whether the askers are polite or sincere when asking questions. It is also worth noting that the day and the time feature with the *sine* function is also negatively associated to good questions. The negatively associated features from the most relevance and significance to the least relevance (listed in increasing value of the coefficient) are shown in the second column of Table 5.

Nevertheless, the irrelevant features are those features that are useless in the classification of good and bad questions. All the irrelevant features have coefficient values of zero or the *p*-value are no less than 0.05, suggesting a lack of association to the classification of good and bad questions. Some of them are found in asker's user profile and the metadata of the questions, as well as the content appraisal features obtained from the questions. From the features in the asker's user profile sub-category, it is found that most of them do not have any impact on whether the subsequent questions asked will get good answers, the irrelevant features are: reputation, upvotes, downvotes, questions asked, answers posted and answers posted/questions asked. In addition, the *cosine* function of the day feature does not affect whether the questions will get any answers. Lastly, the content appraisal features that are irrelevant include: language error and presentation. This essentially means that the overall look and feel of the questions does not affect a user's decision to answer the questions. The list of irrelevant features is populated in the last column of Table 5.

Among all the identified relevant features from feature selection step, it is, also interesting to report that the textual features are found to be the most relevant sub-category of features, the specific features that are the most relevant to the classification of good and bad questions include (from the most relevant to the least): question length, tags, title length, code snippet and wh word. This is followed by the sub-category of content appraisal features, which include (from the most relevant to the least): complexity, completeness politeness and subjectivity. The third most relevance sub-category of features is from the asker's user profile.

Among all the eight features from the asker's user profile, only days since join and upvote/downvotes are found to be useful. Finally, the sub-category of features that is found to be the least relevance is the features from the questions' metadata, which are the time and day the questions are asked.

7.2   Classification

The validation of the performance of classification is used to verify the usefulness and reliability of the identified features to predict good and bad questions in Stack Overflow. It can also be utilized to investigate whether the feature extraction step done earlier produces a smaller set of highly relevance and significance features, which can be used more effectively for classification compared to using the complete set of features.

Table 6 shows the average accuracy and AUC from the stratified tenfold cross-validation for all the classification algorithms used, containing both the average and AUC without feature selection (using the complete set of features) and with feature selection. The complete set of results of every fold of the cross-validation as well as the ROC curves can be found in Appendix 2 and 3 located at the end of this paper. The value of the accuracy and AUC has a maximum value of 1 if the prediction of good and bad questions from the classification model is 100 % correct, and a minimum value of zero if all the predictions are wrong. For a binary classification task in the study, the value of accuracy or AUC for a random guess is 0.5, which means that the classification model is useless (performs worse than a random guess) if either the value accuracy or AUC falls under 0.5.

There are three important information that can be depicted from the results of the classification performance in Table 6. First, it is found that all the classification algorithms perform reasonably well in the prediction of good and bad questions, better than a random guess. Without the feature selection, the overall accuracy is found to be ranging from 0.574 (naïve Bayes) to 0.735 (logistic regression). Whereas for the AUC, it is found to be ranging from 0.759 (naïve Bayes) to 0.816 (logistic regression and SVM). This basically means that it is a feasible option to make use of the identified features to classify good or bad questions in Stack Overflow.

Table 6 Average accuracy and AUC from tenfold cross-validation

Algorithms	Without feature selection		With feature selection	
	Accuracy	AUC	Accuracy	AUC
Logistic regression	0.735	0.816	0.735	0.813
SVM	0.734	0.816	0.735	0.813
Decision tree	0.728	0.780	0.732	0.784
Naïve Bayes	0.574	0.759	0.712	0.777
k-NN	0.694	0.763	0.698	0.763

Secondly, the overall performance of the classification improves by replacing the features with a smaller set of features obtained from the feature selection step. With the inclusion of feature selection, the lowest accuracy actually improves to a 0.698 (k-NN) and the highest accuracy stays the same at 0.735, whereas the lowest AUC increases to 0.763 (k-NN). Among all the classification algorithms, the performance of naïve Bayes improves significantly with feature selection. This is because as mentioned earlier, naïve Bayes is sensitive to redundant or irrelevant features [53]. Therefore, this essentially means that the feature selection step successfully determines a subset of highly relevant and significant features, which serves a better representation of the dataset compared to using all the original features.

Thirdly, two classification algorithms, namely: logistic regression and SVM are found to have the best overall performance both in terms of accuracy and AUC, when compared to other algorithms. This is expected because these classification algorithms represent some of the best performing supervised learning methods in the current age [58].

8 Discussion

From the results in the previous sub-section, three characteristics of the community in CQA, specifically in Stack Overflow can be observed. Firstly, the community in Stack Overflow prefers to answer simple and understandable questions, which is in agreement with the findings from Asaduzzaman et al. [37]. From the results of feature selection, lower number of word count in the questions, lower complexity, higher completeness and fewer tags (categories) lead to a higher chance of the questions to be answered. Questions are easily understandable when they are concise with relatively small word count in the question and reasonable amount of information provided by the askers. The few tags imply that the question is very specific and probably only require the answerers to answer with only certain scopes of knowledge.

Secondly, questions which are asked after evening and before mid-night, or towards the end of the week or during the weekends have a higher chance of being answered, with the assumption that most users are located in the same time zone as Stack Overflow. From the result, the time feature in the *sine* function is negatively associated to good questions and the *cosine* function is positively associated. Therefore, the rough estimation of the time is from 6 p.m. in the evening to 12 mid-night. Figure 8 shows questions are more likely to end up with an accepted answer if they are asked within that time frame in the green region. For the day feature, it was found that *sine* function of the feature is negatively associated and the *cosine* function is statistically insignificant. Figure 9 shows the rough estimation of the days in a week; if questions are asked on those days, they are more likely to get an accepted answer, compared to other days. This suggests that users in Stack Overflow consist of working professionals and they are more active in answering

Time feature after extraction

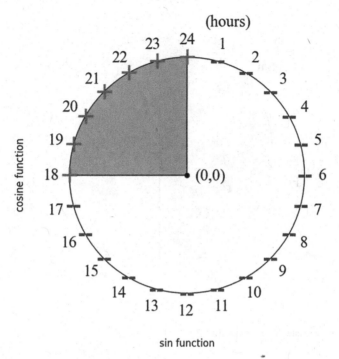

Fig. 8 Time frame associate to good questions

questions off working hours (after evening and weekends). However, the time and day features are found to be not highly relevant among the relevant features partly due to the influence of different time zone of the users in Stack Overflow.

Thirdly, the experience level of the askers in Stack Overflow is found to be less important in determining the quality of the questions. Most of the features of the users' asker profile are found to be irrelevant features in identifying the quality of the questions. Interestingly, the number of days since the users joined Stack Overflow is found to be negatively associated to good questions. A user can be asking good questions and get some acceptable answers without requiring much prior member experience on Stack Overflow. In addition, the only feature from users' asker profile that is found to be positively associated is up votes/down votes. Users that consistently posted high quality content (high agreements and low disagreements from other users in terms of questions and answers) will, in the future, are likely to ask high quality questions that ended up with acceptable answers.

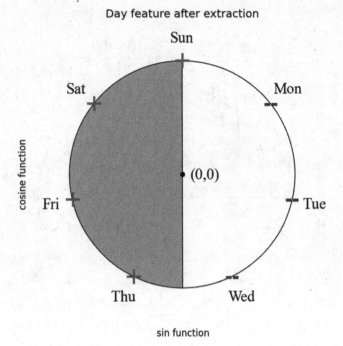

Fig. 9 Days associated to good questions

9   Conclusion

This article describes a research framework and anticipated efforts on classifying between the good questions (questions that contain at least an accepted answer by the askers) and bad questions (questions that are completely ignored by the community) in CQA, specifically in the context of Stack Overflow. The analysis processes are investigated and the crucial steps of data mining and knowledge discovery from data in the problem of questions' quality classification are studied, which include specialized feature extraction process, feature selection process and the exploration of some of the state-of-the-art classification algorithms which are popularly used in data mining community.

The outcome of this study covers computational techniques for quantitatively finding the important features that are useful in the classification of good and bad questions. The features that are revealed from this study come from the metadata of the askers' user profile and questions, as well as from the contents of the questions, which include textual features and content appraisal features. In addition to that, the identified features are relevant, significant and reliable because they have gone through the process of feature selection to get rid of irrelevant and statistically insignificant features, along with the performance evaluation of classification process to ensure that the selected set of features are reliable when it comes to the real task of classifying between good and bad questions. The challenges, future research direction and the significance are discussed in the sub-sections below.

9.1 Challenges and Future Research

There are three challenges associated with this study. Firstly, the previous work is only done on one category (also known as tag in Stack Overflow) of questions, the authors specifically focus on the questions about Java programming language due to pragmatic reasons and as a preliminary approach in generalizing to other categories of CQA forums. However, the problem with the approach is that we have not fully taken advantage of the wide range of users' metadata (which are all the details in their user profiles) in Stack Overflow. Therefore, in the study, the features from the asker's user profile are reported may not be so highly relevant in the classification of good and bad questions. For similar future research, more refined categories of questions should be included and also we should identify more features that can be found in a certain category to help in the classification tasks (e.g.: [41]).

Secondly, when predicting the quality of a question, the user does not consider the previously asked similar or exactly same questions that are solved or unsolved. Information about the previously asked similar questions can be useful in classifying whether the newly asked question whether it is good or bad. This is because questions that are similar will have identical quality [40]. Therefore, future research should investigate ways to identify similar questions and the relevant features that can be extracted from them.

Thirdly, the extraction of content appraisal features requires judgment from human expert, which is highly labor intensive and inefficient due to the manual intervention. Because content appraisal features are found to be quite relevant in the classification task, future research should probe deep into this problem and explore techniques of automatic content appraisal extraction from the content of questions in CQA. For example, Taboada and Grieve [45] had presented some method for analyzing appraisal from text automatically. This will highly enhance and speed up the future research in the area of CQA because of less reliance on the slow manual extraction of content appraisal features.

Based on the identified factors of SO, future research is expected to be conducted to solve boarder questions. Specifically, both qualitative and quantitative explorations to management solution of online communities should be further conducted. Besides, data from other reputable online communities such as Yahoo! Answers, Answerbag, Quora are expected to be tested on for further validation of the data analytic methods. By leveraging on both efforts, the comprehensive framework for the management of online communities will be built on top of the modern text analytic computational model which we experimented in this study.

9.2 Significance of the Study

It is found that the outcome of the study would have significant benefits to the stakeholders of the forum as explained below. Firstly, more comprehensive research for researchers in the area of CQA. For a long time, the importance of the questions posed on CQA websites are underestimated or even neglected. So the management of questions in CQA websites has always been a missing part in solution. Fortunately, this study aims to fix this problem by comparing the features of good and bad questions, and revealing the important factors that influence the questions. As a result, more reasonable research within CQA service domain is expected to provide a more comprehensive solution.

Secondly, better experiences for the users of CQA. This study would help users to formulate questions in a more intelligent approach that will not be ignored easily in CQA. To increase their chances of getting answers, users with questions would be educated to organize thoughts and articulate appropriately based on the identified factors. Hence, the posed question would be attractive enough to encourage decent answers and comments in CQA timely. As a result, the questions are more likely to be addressed in a short time, and user experiences in the community would be enhanced greatly. To this end, even question templates and/or guidelines could be devised based on the findings of the analytical work.

Thirdly, value added for CQA owners especially Stack Overflow. With the knowledge from the study, CQA owners are able to provide better CQA services for the public by introducing an automatic system to predict the quality of a newly posted question. This way, if the question is predicted that it will probably not getting any answers from the public, the asker of the question will be prompted to revise the questions with suggestion of improvement given, based on the outcomes of the predictive model. As such similar unsuccessful questions could be avoided to be posted by the same users again. In this way, storage space will not be wasted on questions that are likely to be ignored by the public. Moreover, CQA owners can also take advantage on active time and day period of the users. For example, the users are encouraged to post questions during the period when most users are active so that the questions are more likely to end up being answered. On the other hand, long-term value is expected for the CQA service. It is known that the value of CQA websites is generated by both content consumption and content creation [10]. High quality questions will lead to high quality answers. With no doubts, the more high-quality contents would be created, the more high-quality contents are consumed. Apart from that, high-quality contents would be stored and distributed for future reference, perhaps as FAQ or newsletters as useful knowledge. Thus, CQA websites can help improve the question behavior of the posters, which translate to value that could be continuously added to the websites in a long run.

Appendix 1. Inter-Rater Agreement for Content Appraisal Features

Completeness (between evaluator 1 and 2)
Kappa value $= 0.768$

Table 7 Evaluator 1 & 2 on Completeness

Completeness		Evaluator 2				
		1	2	3	4	5
Evaluator 1	1	4	0	0	0	0
	2	1	21	0	0	0
	3	3	11	38	1	0
	4	0	3	1	59	5
	5	0	0	3	3	27

Completeness (between evaluator 1 and 3)
Kappa value = 0.707

Table 8 Evaluator 1 & 3 on Completeness

Completeness		Evaluator 3				
		1	2	3	4	5
Evaluator 1	1	4	0	0	0	0
	2	1	18	3	0	0
	3	3	2	39	9	0
	4	0	0	3	61	4
	5	0	4	1	8	20

Completeness (between evaluator 2 and 3)
Kappa value = 0.781

Table 9 Evaluator 2 & 3 on Completeness

Completeness		Evaluator 3				
		1	2	3	4	5
Evaluator 2	1	5	0	3	0	0
	2	3	22	0	7	3
	3	0	0	42	0	0
	4	0	1	1	61	0
	5	0	1	0	10	21

Complexity (between evaluator 1 and 2)
Kappa value = 0.796

Table 10 Evaluator 1 & 2 on Complexity

Complexity		Evaluator 2				
		1	2	3	4	5
Evaluator 1	1	7	4	2	0	0
	2	3	29	5	0	0
	3	0	4	68	4	0
	4	0	0	0	43	4
	5	0	0	0	0	7

Complexity (between evaluator 1 and 3)
Kappa value = 0.726

Table 11 Evaluator 1 & 3 on Complexity

Complexity		Evaluator 3				
		1	**2**	**3**	**4**	**5**
Evaluator 1	**1**	6	5	2	0	0
	2	6	27	4	0	0
	3	1	8	63	4	0
	4	0	1	3	42	1
	5	0	0	0	0	7

Complexity (between evaluator 2 and 3)
Kappa value $= 0.836$

Table 12 Evaluator 2 & 3 on Complexity

Complexity		Evaluator 3				
		1	**2**	**3**	**4**	**5**
Evaluator 2	**1**	6	0	0	4	0
	2	0	34	3	0	0
	3	1	5	69	0	0
	4	5	0	0	42	0
	5	1	2	0	0	8

Language error (between evaluator 1 and 2)
Kappa value $= 0.703$

Table 13 Evaluator 1 & 2 on Language error

Language error		Evaluator 2				
		1	**2**	**3**	**4**	**5**
Evaluator 1	**1**	136	6	2	0	0
	2	4	16	5	2	0
	3	0	0	7	0	0
	4	0	0	0	2	0
	5	0	0	0	0	0

Language error (between evaluator 1 and 3)
Kappa value $= 0.780$

Table 14 Evaluator 1 & 3 on Language error

Language error		Evaluator 3				
		1	**2**	**3**	**4**	**5**
Evaluator 1	**1**	131	7	5	1	0
	2	2	25	0	0	0
	3	0	0	7	0	0
	4	0	0	0	2	0
	5	0	0	0	0	0

Language error (between evaluator 2 and 3)
Kappa value $= 0.749$

Table 15 Evaluator 2 & 3 on Language error

Language error		Evaluator 3				
		1	2	3	4	5
Evaluator 2	1	130	7	1	2	0
	2	0	21	1	0	0
	3	2	2	10	0	0
	4	1	2	0	1	0
	5	0	0	0	0	0

Presentation (between evaluator 1 and 2)
Kappa value = 0.729

Table 16 Evaluator 1 & 2 on Presentation

Presentation		Evaluator 2				
		1	2	3	4	5
Evaluator 1	1	3	0	0	0	0
	2	1	12	1	0	0
	3	0	1	58	2	0
	4	0	0	6	64	6
	5	0	4	5	7	10

Presentation (between evaluator 1 and 3)
Kappa value = 0.703

Table 17 Evaluator 1 & 3 on Presentation

Presentation		Evaluator 3				
		1	2	3	4	5
Evaluator 1	1	3	0	0	0	0
	2	2	9	0	3	0
	3	0	2	56	3	0
	4		0	6	65	5
	5	0	3	7	5	11

Presentation (between evaluator 2 and 3)
Kappa value = 0.858

Table 18 Evaluator 2 & 3 on Presentation

Presentation		Evaluator 3				
		1	2	3	4	5
Evaluator 2	1	3	0	0	1	0
	2	1	9	0	7	0
	3	1	0	69	0	0
	4	0	5	0	67	1
	5	0	0	0	1	15

Politeness (between evaluator 1 and 2)
Kappa value = 0.752

Table 19 Evaluator 1 & 2 on Politeness

Politeness		Evaluator 2				
		1	2	3	4	5
Evaluator 1	1	62	8	5	0	0
	2	2	44	5	0	0
	3	0	0	30	2	0
	4	0	1	6	7	3
	5	0	0	0	0	5

Politeness (between evaluator 1 and 3)
Kappa value = 0.696

Table 20 Evaluator 1 & 3 on Politeness

Politeness		Evaluator 2				
		1	2	3	4	5
Evaluator 1	1	60	6	7	2	0
	2	5	45	1	0	0
	3	1	4	27	0	0
	4	0	4	2	4	7
	5	0	0	0	0	5

Politeness (between evaluator 2 and 3)
Kappa value = 0.806

Table 21 Evaluator 2 & 3 on Politeness

Politeness		Evaluator 3				
		1	2	3	4	5
Evaluator 2	1	57	2	2	0	3
	2	4	49	0	0	0
	3	2	8	35	0	1
	4	3	0	0	6	0
	5	0	0	0	0	8

Subjectivity (between evaluator 1 and 2)
Kappa value = 0.778

Table 22 Evaluator 1 & 2 on Subjectivity

Subjectivity		Evaluator 2				
		1	2	3	4	5
Evaluator 1	1	6	2	6	0	0
	2	3	33	3	0	0
	3	0	4	35	3	0
	4	0	2	6	57	0
	5	0	0	0	1	19

Subjectivity (between evaluator 1 and 3)
Kappa value = 0.751

Table 23 Evaluator 1 & 3 on Subjectivity

Subjectivity		Evaluator 3				
		1	2	3	4	5
Evaluator 1	1	3	2	9	0	0
	2	2	28	7	2	0
	3	0	6	33	3	0
	4	0	0	0	65	0
	5	0	0	0	2	18

Subjectivity (between evaluator 2 and 3)
Kappa value = 0.848

Table 24 Evaluator 2 & 3 on Subjectivity

Subjectivity		Evaluator 3				
		1	2	3	4	5
Evaluator 2	1	4	0	1	3	1
	2	0	36	0	5	0
	3	1	0	46	3	0
	4	0	0	2	58	1
	5	0	0	0	3	16

Overall average kappa value = **0.765**

Table 25 Overall average Cohen's kappa coefficient for the evaluation of content appraisal features

Content appraisal feature	Evaluator 1 & evaluator 2	Evaluator 2 & evaluator 3	Evaluator 1 & evaluator 3	Average kappa coefficient
Completeness	0.768	0.781	0.707	0.752
Complexity	0.796	0.836	0.726	0.786
Language	0.703	0.749	0.780	0.744
Presentation	0.729	0.858	0.703	0.763
Politeness	0.752	0.806	0.696	0.751
Subjectivity	0.778	0.848	0.751	0.792
Average kappa coefficient	0.754	0.813	0.727	**0.765**

Appendix 2. Accuracy and AUC from Tenfold Cross-Validation

Table 26 Accuracy and AUC from tenfold cross-validation for logistic regression

Logistic regression	Without feature selection		With feature selection	
	Accuracy	AUC	Accuracy	AUC
Fold-1	0.730	0.800	0.753	0.803

(continued)

Table 26 (continued)

Logistic regression	Without feature selection		With feature selection	
	Accuracy	AUC	Accuracy	AUC
Fold-2	0.743	0.817	0.740	0.815
Fold-3	0.750	0.819	0.733	0.814
Fold-4	0.733	0.830	0.740	0.824
Fold-5	0.767	0.829	0.763	0.826
Fold-6	0.743	0.832	0.747	0.830
Fold-7	0.737	0.836	0.730	0.829
Fold-8	0.750	0.848	0.757	0.845
Fold-9	0.700	0.760	0.707	0.753
Fold-10	0.697	0.784	0.680	0.781
Average	**0.735**	**0.816**	**0.735**	**0.813**

Table 27 Accuracy and AUC from tenfold cross-validation for SVM

SVM	Without feature selection		With feature selection	
	Accuracy	AUC	Accuracy	AUC
Fold-1	0.727	0.800	0.743	0.805
Fold-2	0.727	0.814	0.733	0.817
Fold-3	0.750	0.819	0.733	0.815
Fold-4	0.747	0.830	0.747	0.824
Fold-5	0.767	0.829	0.760	0.826
Fold-6	0.733	0.825	0.737	0.822
Fold-7	0.747	0.836	0.743	0.829
Fold-8	0.743	0.847	0.760	0.844
Fold-9	0.703	0.761	0.703	0.754
Fold-10	0.697	0.788	0.687	0.784
Average	**0.734**	**0.816**	**0.735**	**0.813**

Table 28 Accuracy and AUC from tenfold cross-validation for decision tree

Decision tree	Without feature selection		With feature selection	
	Accuracy	AUC	Accuracy	AUC
Fold-1	0.743	0.777	0.733	0.775
Fold-2	0.757	0.807	0.743	0.791
Fold-3	0.720	0.789	0.740	0.797
Fold-4	0.767	0.806	0.777	0.824
Fold-5	0.717	0.780	0.737	0.792
Fold-6	0.723	0.788	0.733	0.787
Fold-7	0.743	0.800	0.743	0.811
Fold-8	0.703	0.756	0.700	0.758
Fold-9	0.693	0.747	0.693	0.749
Fold-10	0.710	0.744	0.720	0.750
Average	**0.728**	**0.780**	**0.732**	**0.784**

Table 29 Accuracy and AUC from tenfold cross-validation for naïve Bayes

Naïve Bayes	Without feature selection		With feature selection	
	Accuracy	AUC	Accuracy	AUC
Fold-1	0.663	0.775	0.703	0.792
Fold-2	0.523	0.758	0.733	0.791
Fold-3	0.567	0.805	0.730	0.792
Fold-4	0.557	0.733	0.733	0.775
Fold-5	0.557	0.780	0.693	0.766
Fold-6	0.543	0.777	0.757	0.804
Fold-7	0.587	0.770	0.727	0.786
Fold-8	0.543	0.767	0.723	0.799
Fold-9	0.640	0.709	0.647	0.719
Fold-10	0.563	0.709	0.677	0.738
Average	**0.574**	**0.759**	**0.712**	**0.777**

Table 30 Accuracy and AUC from tenfold cross-validation for k-NN

k-NN	Without feature selection		With feature selection	
	Accuracy	AUC	Accuracy	AUC
Fold-1	0.647	0.727	0.670	0.752
Fold-2	0.707	0.773	0.697	0.771
Fold-3	0.707	0.749	0.717	0.770
Fold-4	0.707	0.779	0.690	0.761
Fold-5	0.697	0.792	0.703	0.776
Fold-6	0.770	0.797	0.753	0.805
Fold-7	0.697	0.756	0.723	0.765
Fold-8	0.747	0.806	0.720	0.798
Fold-9	0.613	0.720	0.647	0.714
Fold-10	0.650	0.727	0.657	0.720
Average	**0.694**	**0.763**	**0.698**	**0.763**

Appendix 3. ROC Curves from Tenfold Cross-Validation

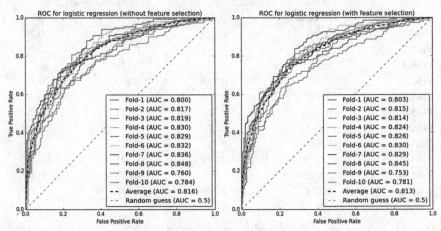

Fig. 10 ROC curves for logistic regression

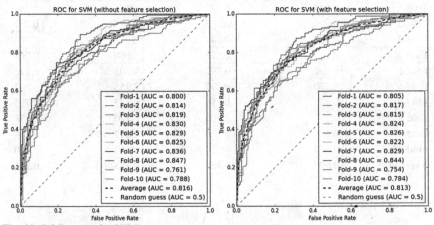

Fig. 11 ROC curves for SVM

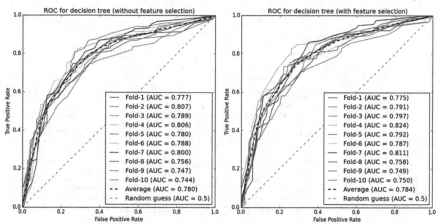

Fig. 12 ROC curves for decision tree

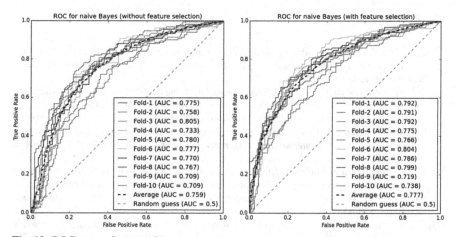

Fig. 13 ROC curves for naïve Bayes

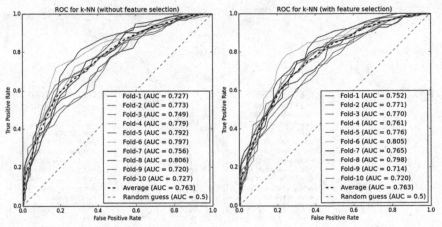

Fig. 14 ROC curves for *k*-NN

References

1. C. Shah, J. Pomerantz, Evaluating and predicting answer quality in community QA, in *Proceedings of the 33rd international ACM SIGIR conference on Research and development in information retrieval*, (2010), pp. 411–418
2. B. Li, Y. Liu, A. Ram, E. V. Garcia, E. Agichtein, Exploring question subjectivity prediction in community QA, in *Proceedings of the 31st annual international ACM SIGIR conference on Research and development in information retrieval*, (2008), pp. 735–736
3. L. Chen, D. Zhang, L. Mark, Understanding user intent in community question answering, in *Proceedings of the 21st international conference companion on World Wide Web*, (2012), pp. 823–828
4. A. Anderson, D. Huttenlocher, J. Kleinberg, J. Leskovec, Discovering value from community activity on focused question answering sites: a case study of stack overflow, in *Proceedings of the 18th ACM SIGKDD international conference on Knowledge discovery and data mining*, (2012), pp. 850–858
5. C. Chen, K. Wu, V. Srinivasan, R. K. Bharadwaj, The best answers? think twice: online detection of commercial campaigns in the CQA forums, in *Proceedings of the 2013 IEEE/ACM International Conference on Advances in Social Networks Analysis and Mining* (ACM, 2013), pp. 458–465
6. Y. Cai, S. Chakravarthy, Predicting Answer Quality in Q/A Social Networks: Using Temporal Features (2011)
7. A. Barua, S.W. Thomas, A.E. Hassan, What are developers talking about? An analysis of topics and trends in Stack Overflow. Empir. Software. Eng. **19**(3), 619–654 (2014)
8. C. Treude, O. Barzilay, M. A. Storey, How do programmers ask and answer questions on the web?: Nier track, in Software Engineering (ICSE), 2011 33rd International Conference, (2011), pp. 804–807
9. L. Mamykina, B. Manoim, M. Mittal, G. Hripcsak, B. Hartmann, Design lessons from the fastest q&a site in the west, in *Proceedings of the SIGCHI conference on Human factors in computing systems*, (2011), pp. 2857–2866
10. S. M. Nasehi, J. Sillito, F. Maurer, C. Burns, What makes a good code example?: A study of programming Q&A in StackOverflow, in Software Maintenance (ICSM), 2012 28th IEEE International Conference, (2012), pp. 25–34

11. B. Vasilescu, A. Capiluppi, A. Serebrenik, Gender, representation and online participation: a quantitative study of Stackoverflow, in International Conference on Social Informatics (2012)

12. F. Riahi, Z. Zolaktaf, M. Shafiei, E. Milios, Finding expert users in community question answering, in *Proceedings of the 21st international conference companion on World Wide Web*, (ACM, 2012), pp. 791–798

13. D. Correa, A. Sureka, Chaff from the Wheat: Characterization and Modeling of Deleted Questions on Stack Overflow. (2014). arXiv preprint arXiv:1401.0480

14. L. Yang, S. Bao, Q. Lin, X. Wu, D. Han, Z. Su, Y. Yu, *Analyzing and Predicting Not-Answered Questions in Community-based Question Answering Services*, (AAAI, 2011)

15. G. Wang, K. Gill, M. Mohanlal, H. Zheng, B. Y. Zhao, Wisdom in the social crowd: an analysis of quora, in *Proceedings of the 22nd international conference on World Wide Web, 1341-1352. International World Wide Web Conferences Steering Committee*, (2013)

16. E. Agichtein, C. Castillo, D. Donato, A. Gionis, G. Mishne, Finding high-quality content in social media, in *Proceedings of the international conference on Web search and web data mining*, (2008), pp. 183–194

17. G. Dror, D. Pelleg, O. Rokhlenko, I. Szpektor, Churn prediction in new users of Yahoo! answers, in *Proceedings of the 21st international conference companion on World Wide Web*, (ACM, 2012), pp. 829–834

18. L. C. Lai, H. Y. Kao, Question Routing by Modeling User Expertise and Activity in cQA services, in The 26th Annual Conference of the Japanese Society for Artificial Intelligence, (2012)

19. M.J. Blooma, D.H.L. Goh, A.Y.K. Chua, Predictors of high-quality answers. Online Inform. Rev. **36**(3), 383–400 (2012)

20. Y. Miao, C. Li, J. Tang, L. Zhao, Identifying new categories in community question answering archives: a topic modeling approach, in *Proceedings of the 19th ACM international conference on Information and knowledge management*, (ACM, 2010), pp. 1673–1676

21. S. Suzuki, S. I. Nakayama, H. Joho, Formulating effective questions for community-based question answering, in *Proceedings of the 34th international ACM SIGIR conference on Research and development in Information Retrieval*, (2011), pp. 1261–1262

22. A. Singh, K. Visweswariah, CQC: classifying questions in CQA websites, in Proceedings of the 20th ACM international conference on Information and knowledge management, (2011), pp. 2033–2036

23. X. Quan, L. Wenyin, Analyzing Question Attractiveness in Community Question Answering. Modern Advances in Intelligent Systems and Tools **431**, 141–146 (2012)

24. H. Xuan, Y. Yang, C. Peng, An expert finding model based on topic clustering and link analysis in CQA website. J. Network Inform. Secur. **4**(2), 165–176 (2013)

25. X. J. Wang, X. Tu, D. Feng, L. Zhang, Ranking community answers by modeling question-answer relationships via analogical reasoning, in *Proceedings of the 32nd international ACM SIGIR conference on Research and development in information retrieval*, (ACM, 2009), pp. 179–186

26. M. S. Pera, Y. K. Ng, A community question-answering refinement system, in *Proceedings of the 22nd ACM conference on Hypertext and hypermedia*, (ACM, 2011), pp. 251–260

27. C. Danescu, G. Kossinets, J. Kleinberg, L. Lee, How opinions are received by online communities: a case study on amazon.com helpfulness votes, in *Proceedings of the 18th international conference on World wide web*, (2009), pp. 141–150

28. L. Hong, Z. Yang, B. D. Davison, Incorporating participant reputation in community-driven question answering systems, in Computational Science and Engineering, 2009. CSE'09. International Conference, 4, 475–480, (2009)

29. C. Souza, J. Magalhães, E. Costa, J. Fechine, Routing Questions in Twitter: An Effective Way to Qualify Peer Helpers, in *Web Intelligence (WI) and Intelligent Agent Technologies (IAT), 2013 IEEE/WIC/ACM International Joint Conferences*, (2013), 1, pp. 109–114

30. B. Li, I. King, M. R. Lyu, Question routing in community question answering: putting category in its place, in *Proceedings of the 20th ACM international conference on Information and knowledge management*, (2011), pp. 2041–2044

31. Y. Tang, F. Li, M. Huang, X. Zhu, Summarizing similar questions for chinese community question answering portals, in Information Technology and Computer Science (ITCS), 2010 Second International Conference on (2010), pp. 36–39, IEEE
32. W. Zhang, L. Pang, C. W. Ngo, FashionAsk: pushing community answers to your fingertips, in *Proceedings of the 20th ACM international conference on Multimedia*, (ACM, 2012), pp. 1345–1346
33. Z. Zhang, Q. Li, D. Zeng, Evolutionary community discovery from dynamic multi-relational CQA networks, in Web Intelligence and Intelligent Agent Technology (WI-IAT), 2010 IEEE/WIC/ACM International Conference on, (2010), vol. 3, pp. 83–86. IEEE
34. P. Shachaf, Social reference: toward a unifying theory. Libr. Inf. Sci. Res. **32**(1), 66–76 (2010)
35. P. Fichman, A comparative assessment of answer quality on four question answering sites. J. Inform. Sci. **37**(5), 476–486 (2011)
36. A.Y. Chua, R.S. Balkunje, The outreach of digital libraries: a globalized resource network, in *Comparative evaluation of community question answering websites* (Springer, Berlin Heidelberg, 2012), pp. 209–218
37. M. Asaduzzaman, A. S. Mashiyat, C. K. Roy, K. A. Schneider, Answering questions about unanswered questions of stack overflow. in *Proceedings of the Tenth International Workshop on Mining Software Repositories* (IEEE Press, 2013), pp. 97–100
38. E. Agichtein, Y. Liu, J. Bian, Modeling information-seeker satisfaction in community question answering. ACM T. Knowl. Discov. D. **3**(2), 10 (2009)
39. J. Bian, Y. Liu, D. Zhou, E. Agichtein, H. Zha, Learning to recognize reliable users and content in social media with coupled mutual reinforcement, in *Proceedings of the 18th international conference on World wide web* (ACM, 2009), pp. 51–60
40. B. Li, T. Jin, M. R. Lyu, I. King, B. Mak, Analyzing and predicting question quality in community question answering services, in *Proceedings of the 21st international conference companion on World Wide Web* (ACM, 2012), pp. 775–782
41. Y. Liu, J. Bian, E. Agichtein, Predicting information seeker satisfaction in community question answering, in *Proceedings of the 31st annual international ACM SIGIR conference on Research and development in information retrieval*, (ACM, 2008), pp. 483–490
42. M. Bovee, R.P. Srivastava, B. Mak, A conceptual framework and belief-function approach to assessing overall information quality. Int J. Intell. Syst. **18**(1), 51–74 (2003)
43. C.M. Bishop, *Pattern Recognition and Machine Learning*, 1st edn. (Springer, New York, 2006), p. 740
44. S. Bird, NLTK: the natural language toolkit, in *Proceedings of the COLING/ACL on Interactive presentation sessions* (Association for Computational Linguistics, 2006), pp. 69–72
45. M. Taboada, J. Grieve, Analyzing appraisal automatically, in *Proceedings of AAAI Spring Symposium on Exploring Attitude and Affect in Text (AAAI Technical Re# port SS# 04# 07)*, (Stanford University, CA, 2004), pp. 158q161, AAAI Press
46. S.Y. Rieh, D.R. Danielson, Credibility: a multidisciplinary framework, in *Annual review of information science and technology*, ed. by B. Cronin (Information Today, Medford, NJ, 2007), pp. 307–64
47. M.A. Suryanto, E.P. Lim, A. Sun, R.H.L. Chiang, Quality-aware collaborative question answering: methods and evaluation, in *Proceedings of the WSDM '09 Workshop on Exploiting Semantic Annotations in Information Retrieval*, (ACM Press, New York, NY, 2009), pp. 142–151
48. J. Han, M. Kamber, J. Pei, *Data mining: concepts and techniques* (Morgan Kaufmann, San Francisco, 2006)
49. L.A. Shalabi, Z. Shaaban, B. Kasasbeh, Data mining: a preprocessing engine. J. Comput. Sci. **2**(9), 735 (2006)
50. I. Guyon, A. Elisseeff, An introduction to variable and feature selection. J. Mach. Learn. Res. **3**, 1157–1182 (2003)
51. A. Y. Ng, Feature selection, L 1 vs. L 2 regularization, and rotational invariance, in *Proceedings of the twenty-first international conference on Machine learning*, (2004, ACM), pp. 78
52. F. Pedregosa, G. Varoquaux, A. Gramfort, V. Michel, B. Thirion, O. Grisel, E. Duchesnay, Scikit-learn: machine learning in Python. J. Mach. Learn. Res. **12**, 2825–2830 (2011)

53. C. A. Ratanamahatana, D. Gunopulos, Scaling up the naive Bayesian classifier: Using decision trees for feature selection (2002)
54. K. Weinberger, J. Blitzer, L. Saul, Distance metric learning for large margin nearest neighbor classification. Adv. Neural Inf. Process. Syst. **18**, 1473 (2006)
55. R. Kohavi, A study of cross-validation and bootstrap for accuracy estimation and model selection. IJCAI **14**(2), 1137–1145 (1995)
56. A.P. Bradley, The use of the area under the ROC curve in the evaluation of machine learning algorithms. Pattern Recogn. **30**(7), 1145–1159 (1997)
57. J. Huang, C.X. Ling, Using AUC and accuracy in evaluating learning algorithms. IEEE Trans. Knowl. Data Eng. **17**(3), 299–310 (2005)
58. R. Caruana, A. Niculescu-Mizil, An empirical comparison of supervised learning algorithms, in *Proceedings of the 23rd international conference on Machine learning* (ACM, 2006), pp. 161–168
59. Y. Chen, R. Dios, A. Mili, L. Wu, K. Wang, An empirical study of programming language trends. Software IEEE **22**(3), 72–79 (2005)
60. M. Frické, D. Fallis, Indicators of accuracy for answers to ready reference questions on the internet. J. Am. Soc. Inform. Sci. Technol. **55**(3), 238–245 (2004)
61. C. W. Hsu, C. C. Chang, C. J. Lin, A practical guide to support vector classification (2003)
62. J.R. Landis, G.G. Koch, The measurement of observer agreement for categorical data. Biometrics **33**(1), 159–174 (1977)
63. K.A. Neuendorf, *The content analysis guidebook* (Sage Publications, Thousand Oaks, CA, 2002)
64. H. Zhang, The optimality of naive Bayes. A A **1**(2), 3 (2004)

Temporal Event Tracing on Big Healthcare Data Analytics

Chin-Ho Lin, Liang-Cheng Huang, Seng-Cho T. Chou, Chih-Ho Liu, Han-Fang Cheng, and I-Jen Chiang

Abstract This study presents a comprehensive method for rapidly processing, storing, retrieving, and analyzing big healthcare data. Based on NoSQL (not only SQL), a patient-driven data architecture is suggested to enable the rapid storing and flexible expansion of data. Thus, the schema differences of various hospitals can be overcome, and the flexibility for field alterations and addition is ensured. The timeline mode can easily be used to generate a visual representation of patient records, providing physicians with a reference for patient consultation. The sharding-key is used for data partitioning to generate data on patients of various populations. Subsequently, data reformulation is conducted as a first step, producing additional temporal and spatial data, providing cloud computing methods based on query-MapReduce-shard, and enhancing the search performance of data mining. Target data can be rapidly searched and filtered, particularly when analyzing temporal events and interactive effects.

Keywords Big medical data • NoSQL • Temporal event analysis • Shard • Data mining • Medical record

1 Introduction

Considering five pillars of healthcare outcome policy priorities: (1) Improving quality, safety, efficiency and reducing health disparities; (2) Engaging patients and families in their health; (3) Increasing the coordination of care; (4) Improving the health of the population; and (5) Ensuring patient privacy and security protection for personal health information [1], an sophisticated information technology

C.-H. Lin (✉) • L.-C. Huang • S.-C.T. Chou
Department of Information Management, National Taiwan University, Taipei, Taiwan, Republic of China
e-mail: d95725005@ntu.edu.tw; d95725010@ntu.edu.tw; chou@ntu.edu.tw

C.-H. Liu • H.-F. Cheng • I.-J. Chiang
Institute of Biomedical Engineering, National Taiwan University, Taipei, Taiwan, Republic of China
e-mail: drliu@mail2000.com.tw; 109657@ntuh.gov.tw; ijchiang@ntu.edu.tw

© Springer International Publishing Switzerland 2016
P.C.K. Hung (ed.), *Big Data Applications and Use Cases*, International Series on Computer Entertainment and Media Technology, DOI 10.1007/978-3-319-30146-4_5

has engaged in effort to adopt and implement eligible electronic health records. In practice, medical records are maintained to support patient care assessments and related decisions, legitimate medical practice reports, healthcare institution management and planning, and clinician and nurse education. In addition, medical records serve as the primary sources for studies investigating the enhancement of medical care and health [2, 3]. However, medical data must be rapidly processed, preserved, acquired, analyzed, and used to ensure its contribution to public health promotion.

The rapid development of science and medical technology has yielded rapid and effective methods for verifying, detecting, preventing, and treating diseases. This phenomenon has generated big healthcare data, specifically (1) a rapid accumulation in the number of medical records; (2) increased number of medical evaluation factors (e.g., items investigated during laboratory, biochemical, and genetic tests); (3) diverse data types (e.g., texts and numerals, diagrams, tables, images, and handwritten documents); and (4) difficulties processing and managing data. Combined, these aspects of big data delay response times and increase costs. Using a traditional relational database management system (RDBMS) conserves storage space, avoids repeated data, and supports complex table structures, enabling users to engage in various queries [4]. However, the use of big medical data is increasingly prevalent and previous relational model methods adopted to ensure data efficiency and consistency (e.g., categorizing medical records in various tables or databases) can no longer be used to effectively collect and analyze data. Thus, a bottleneck negatively affects the system performance level, hindering the data compilation process. Although RDBMS is advantageous regarding storage space conservation and data quality, it cannot efficiently be used to manage or ensure the meaningful use of big medical data.

NoSQL (not only SQL) has become increasingly popular [5], and scholars have indicated that it exhibits more advantages compared with RDBMS. However, research regarding the use of NoSQL in big medical data remains nascent; thus, various vital and urgent research concerns must be addressed. In this study, methods involving NoSQL structural approaches were proposed for rapidly processing, preserving, acquiring, analyzing, and using big medical data. Currently, a big medical data environment that can rapidly expand and be used to effectively process accumulated health records is required. In addition to using cloud computing to rapidly analyze relevant medical records and assess patient conditions, medical researchers can incorporate empirical data (PubMed) to produce evidence-based clinical guidelines, providing references for physician diagnoses and treatments. Consequently, scholars can rapidly compile various data types for use in analyses and mining (i.e., tracing and analyzing temporal events) to facilitate medical research on the interactions and relationships among disease-inducing factors.

The proposed method is divided into three parts based on the model-view-controller (MVC) design pattern. Part 1 represents the model (M), which adopts the NoSQL data platform and a patient-driven data format design and partitions the data based on the sharding-key into distributed environments to build highly efficient data cubes for Big Data analytics. Part 2 denotes view (V), which employs a Web-based user interface. The search input interface can accept combined search conditions, such as diseases, drugs, population characteristics, and temporal sequences, and displays the search results by using various statistical distribution charts and data tables. Individual patient records are presented using a visual timeline. Finally, Part 3 is the controller (C), which involves a data-reconstruction algorithm that converts original relational data model into NoSQL data. It provides additional temporal information through data reformulation, in cloud computing environment to use query-MapReduce-shard to improve the performance of search. To verify this method, we performed a prototype system test by using the MongoDB database platform [6] and produced related programs. The data comprised information from Taiwan's National Health Insurance Research Database (NHIRD) for 2010; the sample involved one million people over 15 years and 1,175,186,752 medical records [7]. We successfully imported the data to the test platform and all functions passed the test. In addition to demonstrating the advantages of NoSQL, the empirical results indicated that the query-MapReduce-shard approach enhanced the performance by more than tenfold. Regarding temporal event tracing and analysis, superior performance was observed in medical record search and display, as well as in complex data mining.

2   Related Work

The Taiwanese Health Insurance program comprises 23 million people [8], and more than one million new medical records are generated each day. In addition to these records, other data, such as insurance claim data, as well as clinical data, patient records, empirical literature, and medical images are accumulated over time, yielding a considerable amount of data that cannot be quantified. Similar situations have occurred in numerous fields such as social media, customer behaviors, and sensing devises. Big data has become a concept typically described using the 3Vs (volume, variety, and velocity). Simply expressed, big data is large volumes of versatile data that require high temporal effectiveness to retrieve, analyze, process, and store. This cannot be achieved in a limit time by using current database query software tools. For example, RDBMSs experience the following problems: (1) the SQL JOIN syntax must be used to perform cross-table queries. However, when data volumes accumulate, JOIN causes a performance bottleneck; and (2) the pre-designed schema architecture generally impedes field updates, particularly when involving vast data volumes. Updates require redefining schema, which potentially disturbs the relational logic within the database or even changes the data format. For example, when Twitter sought to modify a data field, 2 weeks were required to perform an alter table command that would change the definition of an existing data table. Such a situation severely influences data collection and analysis. Traditional data warehouse or intelligent analytic systems are adept at handling structured data, but not semi-structured (e.g., XML, logs, click-streams, and RFID tags) and unstructured data (e.g., Web pages, email, multimedia, and instant messages). These systems will be unable to cope with the rapidly increasing data volumes of the present day.

Numerous researches have focused on designing relevant strategies and suggesting a future direction for databases [9, 10]. Furthermore, enterprises have developed NoSQL databases according to their application needs. For example, Amazon developed Dynamo [11], Google established Big Table [12], and Facebook proposed Cassandra [13]. Compared with traditional relational database systems, NoSQL systems break the restrictions of schema fields, providing schema-less data storage. NoSQL has become widespread in recent years, and more than 150 types of NoSQL databases are used for various applications and purposes [5]. Studies have confirmed the advantages of using NoSQL compared with traditional relational databases [14–18], such as its flexibility of data design, system performance level, storage capacity, scalability, and low cost. Integrating the NoSQL database architecture with a cloud platform enables MapReduce distributed computing. In addition, NoSQL can expand horizontally; it can dynamically expand new database nodes and the old nodes automatically copy the data to the new nodes to balance the data access loads between them [19, 20]. Thus, common database partitioning procedures, whereby databases are normalized, tables are segmented, data are copied, and application links are manually specified, are rendered superfluous.

In contrast to relational databases, no fundamental theory exists for non-relational databases; thus, a universal data modeling technique is lacking. Non-relational databases can be categorized as key-value, column-oriented, document-oriented, and graph databases [5, 21]. Considering the distinct types and diversity of healthcare data, the temporal sequence characteristics, and the continuously increasing number of data items, document-oriented and column-oriented NoSQL databases are most suitable for constructing healthcare analytic databases. During data searching and mining analysis, it is often necessary to change, recompile, and recombine the data. To verify or refute hypotheses, various arms must frequently be combined for comparative analysis. Temporal and spatial information is typically a crucial factor in such analyses; however, time and space are often separated, rendering the visual representation of search results extremely difficult when collecting and analyzing healthcare data. This problem must be resolved. After careful consideration and based on our previous study [22], we employed cloud computing as the foundation of our long-term research and plans, collecting, archiving, analyzing, and visually presenting the obtained data to establish a mining and knowledge-based big healthcare data service platform.

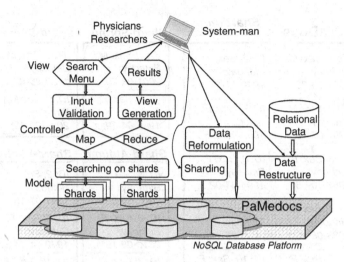

Fig. 1 Overall operational architecture of the proposed methods

3 Methods

The paper proposes methods and overall operational architecture are presented in Fig. 1. In the present section, the MVC design pattern is used to explain the architecture in three steps.

3.1 Model Layer

To respond to the increasing variety and velocity of healthcare data, we compiled all healthcare data of each patient into separate documents called patient-driven medical documents (PaMeDocs). Each patient has an independent PaMeDoc. PaMeDocs are used in document-oriented databases and their basic elements are key-value pairs such as (Birthday, "2013-12-31") where "Birthday" is the key and "2013-12-31" is the value. The key is used for identification and is unique within a PaMeDoc; thus, it cannot be repeated. The value can be arbitrary data. One PaMeDoc can contain another PaMeDoc, forming a tree structure; thus, the medical data of individual patients can form a tree. The PaMeDoc tree structure features height and horizontal growth, which facilitates the rapid retrieval and flexible expansion of data, rendering the structure suitable for use in big healthcare data.

PaMeDocs are a type of highdimensional data that can be concentrated to specific dimensions or perspectives by using sharding to form the patient data of a specific population (Fig. 2). Sharding is a type of horizontal partitioning and is highly expandable, increasing the level of search performance [23, 24]. When data are partitioned into multiple small shards, these shards become individually

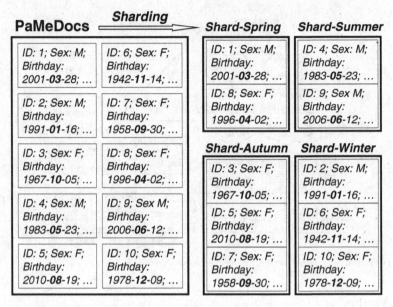

Fig. 2 The data were divided into season shards according to birthday

searchable. Multiple shards can be combined using MapReduce [25] to conduct parallel computing and provide increased operating speed. The key-value pair is the basic elements of PaMeDocs, thus deeming it suitable for use in key-based sharding. Sharding-keys can be formed using one or several key fields, where the value of the sharding-key is the basis for the sharding of data and can be a single value or a range of values. Using the birthday example, which involved a yyyy-mm-dd format, the year (yyyy), month (mm), month and year (yyyy-mm), or a certain time frame can be used to produce shards comprising populations of various ages or those born in various seasons. However, only meaningful shards improve search performance; thus, the data characteristics and query purpose must be considered when selecting suitable sharding-keys and values. For example, if disease codes are used as sharding-keys, the code arrangements can be used to determine the values.

The PaMeDoc storage platform can use an existing NoSQL database, preferably the document-oriented type (e.g., MongoDB). PaMeDocs can easily be expressed using the JSON (JavaScript Object Notation) [26] or BSON (binary-encoded serialization of JSON-like documents) [27] data formats. If other NoSQL platform types are used, the data format can be converted to import the PaMeDocs into the database.

In addition to being a NoSQL database, this model has the advantages of PaMeDocs and sharding, enabling clinicians to rapidly view all relevant records for the present patient (data are collected in the same PaMeDoc). Thus, medical institutions can easily and efficiently manage and exchange patient medical records in a schema-less manner. PaMeDocs also exhibit a superior performance in complex searching and filtering of data (e.g., data on the interactive effects among diseases, drugs, and treatments) and temporal analysis, because the search is ultimately conducted within the same PaMeDoc.

3.2   View Layer

A Web-based user interface was adopted. The interface receives user requests and displays the results. Shared standards such as Ajax (asynchronous JavaScript and XML) [28] and D3.js (just D3 for data-driven documents) [29] can be used for page rendering technology. As described in Sect. 3.1, various diseases, drugs, populations, and temporal sequence characteristics can be used to form complicated query request conditions (Fig. 3). Based on the PaMeDoc and shard design, Ajax and D3.js can be used to easily render various statistical distribution charts and data tables, specifically the timeline visual representation of individual patient records.

3.3   Controller Layer

In this subsection, the approach used for restructuring the data into a PaMedoc is described. In addition, data reformulation, shading and using MapReduce, and conducting targeted queries and searches are explained.

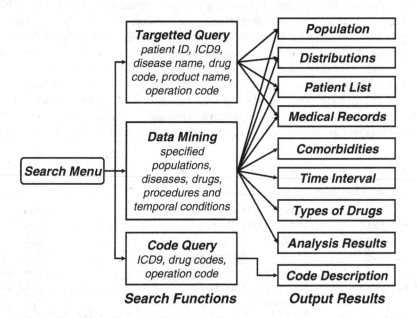

Fig. 3 The web-based search functions and results

1) *Restructuring Relations to PaMeDocs*: When attempting to restructure medical records, which are stored in the tables of a relational database, into PaMeDocs, the clinical operations of hospitals must first be understood. At a patient's first consultation, the hospital collects the demographic information of the patient, which is stored in the patient data table (ID). In clinics, the physician records outpatient prescriptions and treatments; each time the patient attends a clinic for treatment, multiple new medical orders (drug prescriptions and medical examination sheets) may be issued. Medical operations of inpatient and outpatient care and pharmacies generate various data tables, which are mutually concatenated using primary keys (PK) and foreign keys (FK). Therefore, when restructuring these data into patient PaMeDocs, the basic information can be acquired from the ID table, after which the PK-FK relationship is determined to obtain the target data from the linked data tables. This recursive procedure continues until all patient PaMeDocs have been completed, as shown by the Restructure() algorithm. In practice, redundant keys or duplicated fields in the data tables are deleted during restructuring to conserve storage space.

2) *Temporal and Spatial Data Reformulation*: Temporal and spatial data are vital factors in event analysis but these data may not be obtained directly from the existing data. By analyzing past research related to the NHIRD, we found that obtaining data regarding the patient age and year of seeking medical advice, patient residential area, drug type, days of drug use after a single hospital/clinic visit, total days of drug use, duration of medical history, and the time interval between the occurrence of diseases, requires additional processing or computation. However, when the data volume is substantial, additional processing and computation may require a prolonged duration, rendering waiting impossible. Therefore, additional processing and computation of these factors can be performed in advance based on the currently known data (Table 1), and new fields and collections can be generated and saved for immediate access in future research, eliminating the need for recomputation.

3) *Using MapReduce and sharding-key for targeted queries and searches*: When performing conditional searches, MapReduce uses the sharding-key to perform a targeted query, enhancing the search and computing performance. Because the information is dispersed in various shards, when the user searches the

Table 1 Newly added data items and generating methods

Newly added key fields	Computing methods	Property
FUNC_AGE	*FUNC_DATE-ID_BIRTHDAY*	*Numerical*
FUNC_YEAR	*FUNC_DATE(YYYY)*	*Time*
Residential_Area	*AREA_NO_I*	*Category*
Drug_Category	*Searching drug classification table*	*Category*
Drug_Use_Day	*Total_QTY/Drug_Use × Drug_Fre*	*Numerical*
Total_Drug_Use_Day	*SUM(Drug_Use_Day)*	*Numerical*
Disease_History	*CURRENT_DATE -FIRST_ FUNC_DATE*	*Time*
Interval_Diseases	*FIRST_ FUNC_DATE_D2 -FIRST_ FUNC_DATE_D1*	*Time*

information, the query conditions are mapped to the corresponding sharding-key and parallel searching is conducted on the corresponding shard. Finally, all search results are compiled (Reduce). For example, Fig. 2 shows the field birthday, which is used as a sharding-key for sharding; the data table is separated into four-season shards, where birthdays yyyy-(02, 03 and 04)-dd for spring; yyyy-(05, 06 and 07)-dd for summer; yyyy-(08, 09 and 10)-dd for autumn; and yyyy-(11, 12 and 01)-dd for winter. When searching the number of people of each season, search and computation can be performed directly in the corresponding shard.

```
Restructure ( )
 tt <- construct all tables as a tree exhibiting a root ID;
 for each tuple in table ID
  pomedoc <- Sub_restruct(tuple, tt);
 return all;
Sub_restruct(tuple, tt)
 doc <- new pomedoc();
 (doc.keys, doc.values) <- tuple
 for each subtt in tt.subtrees {
  doc1 <- new pomedoc();
  for each tuple1 in table subtt and tuple1.FK == tuple.PK
   doc1.subdocs++ <- Sub_restruct(tuple1, subtt);
  doc.subdocs++ <- doc1;
 } return doc;
```

4   Results and Discussion

The experiment material was gathered from the 2010 Taiwanese NHIRD, which contained all the medical data of one million people randomly sampled from the 2010 Registry for Beneficiaries of the NHIRD. The NHIRD data were then serially connected to all medical data retrieved between 1996 and 2010, yielding 1,175,186,752 medical records. The data were separated into seven types of documents: registry for beneficiaries (ID), ambulatory care expenditures by visits (CD), inpatient expenditures by admissions (DD), expenditures for prescriptions dispensed at contracted pharmacies (GD), details of ambulatory care orders (OO), details of inpatient orders (DO), and details of prescriptions dispensed at contracted pharmacie (GO). All documents were connected using a key value. Legal access to these data can only be gained for research purposes, and an access application must be filed. Basic information about the patients is contained within the ID document, however this document does not contain patient names, and the addresses are only indicated by area. The encrypted ID numbers are used as key values to connect to other detail documents.

MongoDB 2.2.0 was used as the database platform and the experiment equipment comprised a Windows 7 server involving four core CPUs, 16 GB of memory, and 3 TB of storage. We used Apache, PHP, Java, Ajax, D3.js, and the Google Chrome browser as tools to design and produce related components and programs (e.g., data restructure and reformulation, BSON-format PoMeDocs, data importation, search and MapReduce, and Web page). After completion, all PaMeDocs were successfully imported into MongoDB and the diagnostic, drug, and operation codes were used as sharding-keys to establish corresponding shards and complete related function tests.

To filter and view the results of various combined conditions, we designed a Web-based search function (Fig. 3), which consists of three parts: (1) targeted query. Users can input a patient ID, ICD code or disease name, drug code or component, product name, or operation code to retrieve population proportion and distribution charts in accordance with the search conditions; (2) data mining. Data mining can be conducted on specified populations, diseases, drugs, procedures and temporal conditions to produce population distribution charts, statistics regarding comorbidities, the time interval between two query conditions, types of drugs taken, and statistical analysis results; and (3) code description. Descriptions of various codes can be searched. The search results of targeted queries and data mining also list patient information and medical records.

The sharding-key evaluation involved using patients with diabetes as query targets and three methods: (1) a direct search without shards; (2) search using system-defined shards; and (3) search using user-defined shards. Using these methods yielded 88,601 diabetic patients from the total population of one million. The search duration for Methods 1, 2, and 3 were 791.969, 50.142, and 20.466 s, respectively. This demonstrates that sharding considerably enhances the search performance. Specifically, when users define the shards, the performance increased 40 times. Inconvenient key value settings can be avoided using system-defined shards; however, if users can set an appropriate value, the search performance is further enhanced. According to our previous experience and analyses of NHIRD research plans, researchers and physicians most commonly explore diseases, drugs, and operation procedures, making these items suitable sharding-keys. Nevertheless, the acquisition of appropriate key values requires careful analysis to ensure that shards effectiveness is maximized.

The temporal event tracing and analysis was conducted by using the case study that "taking the drug Januvia might cause acute pancreatitis in diabetic patients" as an example [30]. We used the data mining function of the system and set four data-filtering conditions: diabetic population, acute pancreatitis, Januvia, and chronological order of occurrences. The system generated various related statistical charts for researchers to reference, including population distribution charts of various aspects, statistics on chronic complications, time interval between the occurrence of two specific diseases (Fig. 4), drug type statistics, and days of drug use. Table 2 shows the statistical analysis results generated by the system. The odds ratio value was 1.626, verifying that the results corresponded to the warning statement. In practice, analysis is often performed gradually, extensively, and repeatedly. By

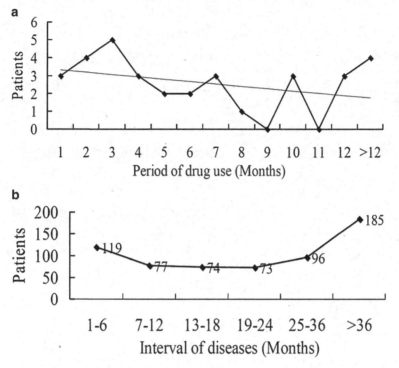

Fig. 4 Statistical charts: (**a**) day of drug Januvia use; (**b**) Interval between acute pancreatitis and diabetes mellitus

Table 2 Statistical analysis results

Diabetes mellitus		Acute pancreatitis		Sum
		Yes	No	
Drug Januvia	+	32	2,830	2,862
	−	592	85,147	85,793
Total		624	87,977	88,601
Odds Ratio		1.626		

contrast, the proposed method involving PaMeDocs, temporal information, and query-MapReduce-shard can rapidly yield results by focusing the data and conducting parallel searches based on filtering conditions. In addition, filtering conditions can be set for new drugs or specific populations, and the system can perform periodic automatic statistical analyses, providing a monitoring function.

The system visually represents the medical records of individual patients on a timeline. In Fig. 5, each point represents a medical record, and the point colors represent categories. The points may be expanded to reveal detailed content on diagnosis, operations, medical orders, and drugs. The filtering conditions can be set to show the desired records (Fig. 5). Visual representations of patient cases are produced using Ajax and D3.js; specifically, when patent information is compiled

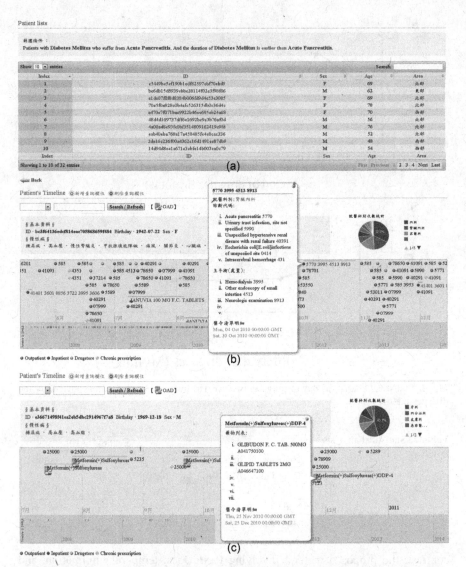

Fig. 5 Timelime representation to medical records, where (**a**) patient lists; (**b**) one patient's all medical records; and (**c**) desired records of the patient

in PaMeDocs, the visual representation is particularly rapid and simple. In practice, physicians can use the system as a reference for making diagnoses by tracing patient medical histories and using the data to elucidate their current situations. Furthermore, this information can provide a health care reference for family physicians and patients.

5 Conclusion

Although no fundamental theory or universal data modeling technique existed for use in NoSQL databases, their strong expansibility and flexibility enabled abandoning relational data model for a novel cloud database. When adopting a NoSQL storage architecture, processing, storing, accessing, and analyzing big healthcare data must be rapid in order for meaningful use to be possible and public health promotion to be achieved. Based on NoSQL, this study proposed a PaMeDoc data tree structure, in which the tree features height and horizontal growth. This facilitated rapid storage and flexible expansion, rendering the proposed structure suitable for managing big healthcare data. Regarding management, using PaMeDocs can overcome the schema differences between various medical institutions, enabling flexible field alteration and addition. Concerning treatment, using PaMeDocs simplifies the timeline visual representation of patient medical history and provides references for physicians in clinics. For the research analysis, we used sharding-keys to perform data partition on the PaMeDocs, generating patient information for various populations. Data reformulation was performed in advance to generate temporal and spatial information, facilitating analyses of temporal events and interactive effects. We used cloud computing combined with query-MapReduce-shard to enhance the search performance of data mining. Although the experimental data volume was not big, the proposed methods were all verified during the test, and their superior level of performance was particularly evident when searching and analyzing temporal events.

References

1. W. Hersh et al., Health-care hit or miss? Nature **470**, 327–329 (2011)
2. M. Porta, J.M. Last, *A dictionary of epidemiology* (Oxford University Press, New York, 2008)
3. M.A. Musen, J.H. Bemmel, *Handbook of medical informatics* (Bohn Stafleu Van Loghum, Houten, 1999)
4. E.F. Codd, A relational model of data for large shared data banks. Commun. ACM **13**(6), 377–387 (1970)
5. NoSQL Databases, Available: http://www.nosql-database.org/
6. 10gen. MongoDB, http://www.mongodb.org/
7. National Health Insurance Research Database, Available: http://nhird.nhri.org.tw/en/index.htm
8. National Health Insurance Administration, Available: http://www.nhi.gov.tw/english/index.aspx
9. P.A. Bernstein et al., Future directions in DBMS research - the Laguna Beach Participants. ACM SIGMOD Record. **18**(1), 17–26 (1989)
10. A. Silberschatz, S. Zdonik, Strategic directions in database systems—breaking out of the box. ACM Comput. Surv. **28**(4), 764–778 (1996)
11. G. DeCandia et al., Dynamo: amazon's highly available key-value store. ACM SIGOPS **41**(6), 205–220 (2007)

12. F. Chang et al., Bigtable: a distributed storage system for structured data, ACM T. Comput. Syst., **26**(2), art. 4, (2006)
13. A. Lakshman, P. Malik, Cassandra: a decentralized structured storage system. ACM SIGOPS **44**(2), 35–40 (2010)
14. N. Jatana, S. Puri, M. Ahuja, I. Kathuria, D. Gosain, A survey and comparison of relational and non-relational database, Int. J. Eng. Res. Tech., **1**(6), (2012)
15. R. Cattell, Scalable SQL and NoSQL data stores. ACM SIGMOD Record. **39**(4), 12–27 (2010)
16. M. Stonebraker, SQL databases v. NoSQL databases. Commun. ACM **53**(4), 10–11 (2010)
17. A.B.M. Moniruzzaman, S.A. Hossain, NoSQL database: new era of database for big data analytics – classification, characteristics and comparison. Int. J. Database Theor. App. **6**(4), 1–14 (2013)
18. I. Lungu, B.G. Tudorica, The development of a benchmark tool for NoSQL databases. Database Syst. J. **4**(2), 13–20 (2013)
19. J. Pokorny, NoSQL databases: a step to database scalability in web environment. Int. J. Web Inform. Syst. **9**(1), 69–82 (2013)
20. M. Ward, NoSQL database in the cloud: MongoDB on AWS, Amazon Web Services, 2013
21. J. Han, E. Haihong, L. Guan, J. Du, A survey on NoSQL databases, Int. Conf. on Pervas. Comput. and Appl. (ICPCA), IEEE Press, Oct 2011, pp. 363–366, doi: 10.1109/ICPCA.2011.6106531
22. C.H. Lin, P.H. Tseng, L.C. Huang, Y.J. Oyang, M.S. Wu, S.C. Chou, A multi-level cloud-based virtual health exam system on health cloud. J. Med. Biol. Eng. **33**(4), 373–379 (2013)
23. A. Pavlo, C. Curino, S. Zdonik, Skew-aware automatic database partitioning in shared-nothing, parallel OLTP systems, ACM SIGMOD, pp. 61–72, May 2012
24. Y. Liu, Y. Wang, Y. Jin, Research on the improvement of MongoDB auto-sharding in cloud environment, IEEE ICCSE, pp. 851–854, July 2012
25. J. Dean, S. Ghemawat, MapReduce: simplified data processing on large clusters. Commun. ACM **51**(1), 107–113 (2008)
26. JSON, Available: http://www.json.org/
27. BSON, Available: http://bsonspec.org/
28. J.J. Garrett, *Ajax: a new approach to Web applications* (Adaptive Path, CA, 2005)
29. D3.js, Available: http://d3js.org/
30. FDA Januvia Tablet, Available: http://www.fda.gov/Safety/MedWatch/SafetyInformation/Safety-RelatedDrugLabelingChanges/ucm121926.htm

Unstructured Data, NoSQL, and Terms Analytics

Richard K. Lomotey and Ralph Deters

Abstract Today's high-dimensional data, which is mostly unstructured, makes data patterns discovery (a.k.a. data mining) challenging and difficult for services engineers. Unstructured data mining deviates from existing information extraction methodologies that have been previously put forward due to the fact that recent data formation and storage has no standard schema; and the data is heterogeneous. At the storage level, the NoSQL database has been proposed as a preferred technology to accommodate the high-dimensional data, and the technology has received significant enterprise adoption. At the technology level, the query style of NoSQL databases differ from schema-based storages such as the RDBMS. Currently, there is lack of tools, technologies, and methodologies that can aid the community to support data patterns discovery in the big data epoch. Previously, an *Analytics-as-a-Service (AaaS)* framework is proposed for terms mining in document-based NoSQL systems. In this chapter, we provide comprehensive views about the performance of several algorithms that have been employed to achieve the topics and terms mining tasks. This chapter is a reproduction of several proposed algorithms which can enable the software engineering community to realize what has been done regarding the enhancement of accuracy of terms mining form document-based NoSQL systems.

Keywords Bernoulli algorithm • Association rule • Big data • Analytics-as-a-Service (AaaS) • Unstructured data • Data mining • Hidden Markov Model • Apriori • Optimistic search • Pessimistic search • Parallel search

R.K. Lomotey (✉)
Information Sciences and Technology, The Pennsylvania State University - Beaver, 15061 Monaca, PA, USA
e-mail: rkl5137@psu.edu

R. Deters
Department of Computer Science, University of Saskatchewan, Saskatoon, Canada, S7N 5C9
e-mail: deters@cs.usask.ca

© Springer International Publishing Switzerland 2016   109
P.C.K. Hung (ed.), *Big Data Applications and Use Cases*, International Series on Computer Entertainment and Media Technology, DOI 10.1007/978-3-319-30146-4_6

1 Introduction

The enterprise landscape today is considered data-driven due to the enormous opportunities it presents. This era is described as the advent of "Big Data" [1]. The era has presented data accessibility more easily for enterprises and third parties at minimal cost. Big Data actually has no clear definition as of now but has been explored as: big transaction data (i.e., exponential increase and diversity in the volume of transaction data), big interaction data (i.e., increase in open data such as social media and device data), and big data processing (i.e., increasing processing demand on high-dimensional data) [2]. However, in our work, we shall explain the area from the concept of the 5V model (illustrated in Fig. 1) as an extension to the 3V model that the IBM researchers proposed earlier in [3].

Volume (the era of size): Truly, the content of digital assets in the modern era has increased astronomically over the last 3 years. The success of online power houses such as social media forums has led to the generation of huge user content. It is reported that Twitter alone generates 12 Terabytes of data daily [4], with similar quantum of data or higher being generated from other forums. Thus, the consideration of data size is shifting from Terabytes to Zettabytes. The fact that enterprises are also transforming their paper-based transactions to digital transactions further contributes to increase in volume.

Variety (the era of unstructured data): The data being generated is coming from multiple sources and comes in heterogeneous formats such as multimedia, text, blogs, emails, sensors, etc. Furthermore, the data has no schema which is shifting the focus from structured and semi-structured data storage to entirely unstructured data.

Fig. 1 The concept of big data

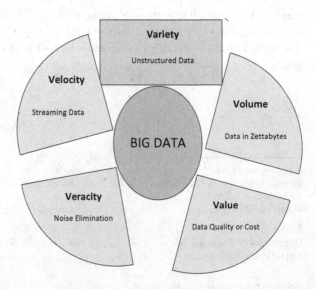

Velocity (from batch data to streaming data): The rate at which the data is being generated is very fast which has shifted our focus from data sets (batch) to streaming data.

Value (cost associated with data): While the data is being generated, collected, and analyzed from different quarters, it is important to state that today's data has some costs. The data itself can be a "commodity" that can be sold to third parties for revenue. Moreover, understanding the cost or value of the data can aid in budget decision making regarding storage cost of the data. For instance, is it worth it to spend six million US dollars on infrastructure cost to keep data that is worth one million dollars?

Veracity (the era of data pollution that needs cleansing): There is the need to check the accuracy of the data by eliminating the noise through methodologies such as data pedigree and sanitization. This is to ensure data quality.

In this chapter, we put together methodologies that have been proposed to tackle the issues of "Variety". The variety in the era of big data is necessitated as a result of the rise of unstructured data. The ever-growing data comes in multiple formats which poses challenge for data mining. This is because existing data mining techniques have been designed for schema-oriented and structured data storages. Analytics-as-a-Service (AaaS) [5] is therefore becoming a promising area which involves the studies of unstructured data mining.

We highlight a proposed terms mining AaaS tool that aids enterprise consumers to perform topics and terms mining from unstructured data silos. Specifically, document-based NoSQL storages are researched. The chapter reproduced several search algorithms that have been previously proposed by the authors in [31, 33, 36, 37] such as the: Bernoulli algorithm, Hidden Markov Model, Pessimistic Search, Optimistic Search, and Apriori. Results from pilot tests using training dataset have also been reproduced. The pessimistic and optimistic search methodologies are time efficient in very large distributed storage systems. This is because the data provider can decide on which sources to search for data or which sources not to search. The limitation however is that, the accuracy of the result can be affected drastically since the user can be wrong in the determination of data sources. The two-class Bernoulli model also shows high accuracy in terms of double-keyword artifacts in comparison to other algorithms such as the HMM. The pros and cons of the various algorithms are discussed further in the chapter.

The remaining sections are organized as follows. Section 2 expounds on unstructured data and in Sect. 3, the progress made at mining textual contents, the emergence of Analytics-as-a-Service (AaaS), and our research motivation are discussed. Sections 4, 5, 6, and 7 describe the implemented AaaS framework and the various terms analytic algorithms. The evaluation of the various algorithms, discussions, and findings of the proposed AaaS tool is carried out in Sect. 8. The chapter concludes in Sect. 9 with an overview of the aim, proposed design of the analytics tool, contributions, and future directions.

2 Unstructured Data and NoSQL

The heterogeneity in data (i.e., "Variety") arises because today's data economy encompasses all enterprises. Though it may appear that the data is in silos (e.g., social media information vs. corporate data), there are new opportunities that can be created when all of these data can be analysed. These opportunities are beneficial for end-users, enterprise consumers, services providers, and prosumers. For instance, online social analytics tools can aid security agencies to determine criminal communities while advertising agencies can re-align products and services towards more demand-driven audience based on social media analytics.

However, the potential opportunities that we seek and desire is hampered by the nature of the data, which is unstructured. The current view of variety is illustrated in Fig. 2 for brevity.

- Data Heterogeneity: The data is represented in varying formats (documents, multimedia, emails, blogs, websites, textual contents, etc.)
- Schema-less: The data has no specific structure because there is no standardization or constraints placed on content generation.
- Multiple Sources: The data is from diverse sources (e.g., social media, data providers such as Salesforce.com, mobile apps, sensors, etc.)
- Varying API Types: The data requires multiple APIs to aggregate data from the multiple sources; and the APIs are not standardized nor have SLAs.

In order to capture data, taking the above points into consideration, the NoSQL [6] database has been proposed. This style of storage has received significant enterprise adoption due to the fact that it supports schema-less, semi-structured, and structured data storage. Moreover, some accommodate textual and file attachments (e.g., CouchDB). Also, there are some of the NoSQL storages that stores only files such as DropBox, MEGA, Amazon S3, and so on. The NoSQL platforms that

Fig. 2 Variety in today's data

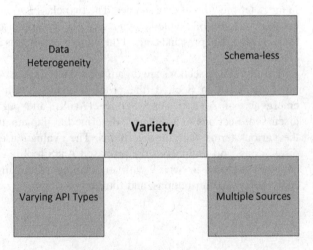

support actual data (e.g., MongoDB, Google Bigdata, etc.) allow the users to store data in formats such as JSON, XML, or other textual formats.

Furthermore, the fact that graphing methodologies have achieved significant success in [7] and [8], emerging NoSQL databases have adapted the idea to ensure efficient query and infrastructure support.

Despite the efforts being made to deploy NoSQL databases, there are still challenges. It is important to note that while NoSQL storages have aided the accommodation of unstructured data, the analytics of the data is an entirely different issue.

The problem is that, these NoSQL databases are products of different vendors so their query styles vary. Moreover, in order to aggregate the data from all of these sources, a mashup service has to be deployed which presents the researcher with two problems. Firstly, multiple APIs has to be studied and secondly, the returned data from the individual data silos are in different structures [6]. Further, the querying of the individual data sources can be time consuming and computationally demanding.

These problems will be explained in detail when we discuss the motivation of our work. In the next section, we highlight the field of Analytics-as-a-Service and how this has become important in the era of big data.

3 Unstructured Data and Analytics

3.1 Analytics-as-a-Service

IBM Research has identified AaaS as an area that can offer business value [5]. This is because AaaS is able to aid in the transformation of unstructured data into business creation ventures. In this regard, IBM pushed for the creation of an AaaS platform that can aid end-users and companies to submit their data (in either structured or unstructured format) for analytics purposes. This platform as depicted in Fig. 2 is meant to reduce the financial burden on companies from maintaining in-house data analysts; the same view is shared by EMC [9]. As an on-going work, IBM has identified the following hurdles that must be overcome in order for the AaaS to materialize: Definitions of Service Level Agreements, Quality of Service monitoring methodologies, pricing, unstructured data manageability, and business processes (models).

Another major enterprise player in the AaaS platform services deployment is SAS [10]. The AaaS service provided by SAS is based on predictive analytics which enables customers to quickly access solutions to their business problems.

Sun et al. [11] propose an AaaS framework as an extension to a Software-as-a-Service (SaaS) that enables enterprises to access data analytics as services. While focusing on multi-tenancy, the authors propose an SLA customization methodology which supports multiple analytics capability demands of tenants. Their architecture details how the virtual servers are constructed to accept the data input from the users. The servers that perform the actual analytics are referred to as scoring servers.

Deepak et al. [12] also detail the architectural design of their proposed AaaS platform which is cloud-hosted. Users are facilitated to upload files and data over a web interface which is the means of interacting with the system. Uploaded files are pushed to the analytics engines which comprise SPSS, R, SAS, Cluto, and WEKA. This type of AaaS platform requires technologies from other providers as well and the analyzed result is stored in data systems such as oracle, DB2, and file systems.

Regarding data analytics, frameworks are constantly being developed for different style of data and enterprise needs. Currently, the following tools exist as reproduced from [13]:

- *Statistical analysis* (e.g., SPSS, SAS, Quantum, EasySample)
- *Scientific computation* (e.g., Matlab, Scilab, GNU Octave)
- *Machine learning toolkits* (e.g., WEKA, KNIME)
- *Textual analysis* (e.g., GATE, StatSoft, AeroText, SAS Text Miner)
- *Video analysis* (e.g., OpenCV, Pelco)

  Image analysis (e.g., Aperio PRECISION)

3.2   The Open Issues

Analytics-as-a-Service is in its infancy though it is receiving much attention from major enterprise players recently. There are companies that provide such services and expect the enterprise consumers to pay (similar to the utility-based Software as a Service cloud model). The problem however is that companies are compelled to submit their data to third parties for analytics; and this can be detrimental to data privacy for some companies. Moreover, there are not many open source projects on AaaS which means companies have to build their in-house tools for analytics.

However accuracy, time effectiveness and reliability of the tools can be are major issue.

In this chapter, we build a terms analytics tool specifically for terms mining from unstructured data sources. The focus is on document-style NoSQL storage though the tool can be applied to any other form of storage. In order to achieve this goal, there is the need to also understand the intricacies of unstructured data mining. Unfortunately, unstructured data mining is equally a fairly new area which is yearning for research attention. In the next section, we present an overview of the area on unstructured data mining and how applicable some concepts can be to our work. On the whole, most of the methodologies are based on Natural Language Processing (NLP) which is inherited from Artificial Intelligence, Linguistics, and Ontological Semantics [14–16].

3.3 Unstructured Data Mining

Without data mining, we cannot deduce any meaning out of the high-dimensional data at our disposal. As already posited, existing data mining techniques which are well-advanced have been designed to work with schema-oriented databases which are structured [17]. However, these existing techniques are no longer relevant to the modern challenges of information extraction. To enhance the data mining process, scientist in both the academia and industry are beginning to explore the best methodologies that can aid in the unstructured data mining process; especially in the context of textual data mining. As a result, we have witnessed some methodologies such as: Information Retrieval algorithms based on templates [18], Association Rules [19, 20], Topic tracking and topic maps [21], Term crawling (terms) [22], Document Clustering [23], Document Summarization [24], Helmholtz Search Principle [39], Re-usable Dictionaries [25], and so on. Since our focus is on terms and topics extraction, these are discussed further for the reader's better understanding.

3.4 Terms Extraction

Terms extraction unlike topics publishing focuses on establishing a network of associative relationships between terms [21]. A typical example is the presence of concurrent terms in a World Wide Web (WWW) document. The main benefit of term mining is that, it optimizes the search space vector thereby reducing processing time [26, 27]. Term crawling for example aims at indicating the relevance of information gathered in an unstructured document by showing the interdependencies between the terms.

The work by Feldman et al. [27] extended on the Knowledge Discovery in Databases (KDD) by shifting from topic tracking and word tagging to term identification in unstructured documents. The authors push for term normalization based on lemmas with corresponding part-of-speech tags such as stock/N, market/N, annual/Adj, interest/N, and rate/N where N is a noun and Adj is an adjective. A proposal for term extraction module is put across which is primarily responsible for the labelling of extracted terms from a particular textual document. Overall, the term extraction module performs Linguistic Pre-processing, Term Generation, and Term Filtering. What is also important to highlight in the work of Feldman et al. [27] is that, the authors provide a score test based on relevance in the document using the following techniques: Deviation-Based Approach—calculate the frequency of a term in the document based on the relative standard deviation; Statistical Significance Approach—to test the significance of the relative frequency variation of a term; and Information Retrieval Approach—using the maximal term frequency-inverse document frequency (tf-idf) to assign a score for information retrieval. The work further explores the option of building a taxonomy constructor based on terms. The use of taxonomy constructors facilitates the search for specified terms which have association rules in an optimal time rather than searching through an entire document.

There are other ways of finding terms such as the conversion of terms into a vector space and calculating the cosine distance between the search terms [28]. The idea is to understand the size of the cosine distance, the frequency of the search term, and the document correspondent.

One of the areas that terms are dominant to a software process is Online Analytic Processing (OLAP) applications [22]. Furthermore, based on term occurrences as central root, a star-like architecture can be established using the following child dependencies: time, location, term, document, and category [29]. In a star-like architecture, the idea is to determine the occurrences of a specified term based on the listed dependencies.

Also, as the computing landscape is venturing into the adaptation of methodologies from related and non-related fields, term extraction can be a very optimal approach to perform some of the time consuming tasks. For example, there is enough room to explore terms applicability to traceability, readability of bugs, maintainability, and so on. As an extension on Table 1, terms extraction can be challenging due to linguistic issues. For instance, similar words in different languages can mean different things and even similar written words in the same language can mean different things. This problem is also present in topic mining scenarios.

Table 1 The analysis Od the extracted term for Hemophilia

| | Bernoulli model | | | | Hidden Markov Model | |
| | Single-term | | Two-term | | | |
	One-word (%)	Two-words (%)	One-word (%)	Two-words (%)	One-word (%)	Two-words (%)
True positive	88.30	80.06	100.00	99.87	92.34	77.41
False positive	9.06	11.33	0.33	1.24	4.75	14.56
True negative	89.12	81.01	99.97	99.84	95.77	85.54
False negative	16.70	21.45	4.19	9.11	4.60	24.81
Precision	90.69	87.60	99.67	98.77	95.11	84.17
Recall (sensitivity)	84.10	78.87	95.98	91.64	95.25	75.73
Specificity	90.77	87.73	99.67	98.77	95.27	85.45
Accuracy	87.32	83.09	97.79	95.07	95.26	80.54
F1 score	87.27	83.01	97.79	95.07	95.18	79.73

3.5   Topics

Topic tracking is generally employed to recommend subjects of interest to a user. Most online subscription systems (e.g., hotel booking, flight, news articles, etc.) are based on topics methodologies where keywords are extracted from users' subscription to form a basis for the users' interests [21, 30]. Based on these keywords, a mechanism of grouping the related keywords (called Lexical Chaining) can be employed to extract subsequent published messages [21].

Topic Maps (ISO/IEC 13250:2003) on the other hand focuses on the representation and knowledge interchangeability in a repository [21]. Topic maps deal with the following elements (commonly referred to as TAO) as representations: topics—refer to the entities being referred to which are mainly names, events, application component and modules etc.; associations—graphical links between the topics of interest; occurrences—refers to the relevant linkages of the information to topics. Abramowicz et al. [21] researched on the automation of topic map creation and outline four procedures which can be adopted such as: subject recognition, information extraction and preparing, RDF modeling, and mapping RDF model into a topic map. The basic idea is that the information extraction is initialized after the topic of interest is identified. Information Extraction at this point from the unstructured data source can be done by exploring other techniques such Natural Language Processing and Shallow Text Mining. RDF models are triples of the format subject (e.g., resources), property (e.g. property type of the subject), and value (e.g., URL). RDF models label the corresponding objects to topics in a map and their occurrences and associations. However, mapping RDF model into a topic map has various processing procedures to follow which include One-time Processing, Repeated Processing, and Continuous Processing [21].

Based on the background works and the general lack of tools in the area of mining terms in document-based NoSQL systems, the authors have proposed several algorithms in previous works. In this chapter, we reproduced some of the works and this aids the reader to understand the different dynamics from a single source. This can further aid enthusiastic researchers to extend on what we have accomplished and come up with further innovative research perspectives.

In the next section, we copied the design of a proposed AaaS tool in [31].

4   The Architecture of the AaaS Platform

The architectural proposal of the Analytics-as-a-Service (AaaS) framework is illustrated graphically in Fig. 3. The entire architecture is categorized into three layers namely:

- the view layer,
- the analytics layer, and
- the storage layer

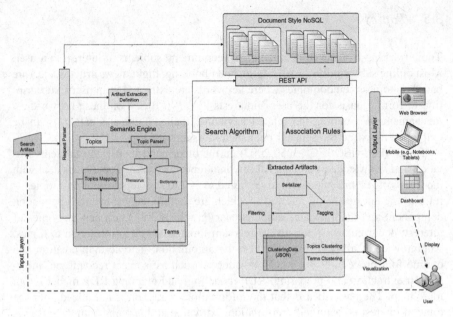

Fig. 3 The architectural design of the AaaS Platform

The architectural design incorporates the case of remote search requirements as well as localization of the search. By remote search, we mean the data source can be located in a different environment and accessible over a network. Localization can be achieved where the search dashboard is installed directly on the same environment as the data source.

In the upcoming sections, the various components are discussed based on the process execution flow as well as the algorithms for the search criteria.

4.1 The Search Execution Flow

The view layer represents a dashboard which allows the user to enter the topics and terms to be mined.

This is the *output/input layer* where the user is enabled to interact with the system. This layer is designed to be deployed on heterogeneous devices such as mobile devices, desktop (including browser), and dashboard.

When the search term is specified from the input layer, the request is sent to the entry point on the analytics layer which is designated as the *Request Parser*. At this point, the specified term is treated as the search artefact. Further, the user has to specify the link to the data source at this point which facilitates the request parser to guarantee that the search task can be carried out. Without the specification of the link (which can be a URL over an HTTP protocol), the system will not perform the data extraction task. Once the initial requirements are met, the search artefact is sent to the analytics layer for *Artefact Extraction Definition*. The importance of this component is to differentiate topics from terms, and to further determine the exact requirement of the user. Specifically to this work, we are focusing on extracting single word terms as well as two word terms. For example, single word terms may be heart, disease, psychiatry, etc.; while two word terms may include heart disease, psychiatry medication, etc. The successful decoding of the search term activates the *Semantic Engine* component where the analytics framework tries to understand the terms to be extracted.

Initially, we consider the artefact specified by the user as *Topics*. This aids us to do the traditional information retrieval task which focuses on extracting the exact artefacts specified by the user. This approach also suggests that when a user specifies an artefact, we look for the exact keyword. However, to perform intelligent terms analytics, there is the need to accommodate the concepts of synonyms, antonyms, parts of speech, and lemmatization as proposed by [20]. Thus, the topics are sent to the *topics parser* to check the meaning of the specified artefact. There are two layers that are designed to check the meanings of the artefacts, the *Dictionary* and the *Thesaurus*. The dictionary contains standard keywords, their meanings, and their antonyms. The thesaurus is the component that contains jargons that otherwise are not found in the standard dictionary. This is important for situations where the analytics is done in certain technical domains such as the medical field. The thesaurus can be updated by the specific domain that is adopting the framework for the analytics task. This further makes the proposed analytics framework highly adaptable and agile. When the artefact is reviewed by the topic parser by looking through the thesaurus and dictionary, the *topics mapping* task is enabled. The mapping tasks include the organization of the specified artefact and possible synonyms as may be found in the semantic engine. The expected artefact and the newly found keywords from the dictionary and the thesaurus is categorize as *Terms*. For instance, when searching for the artefact haemophilia, the terms formation can be formulated as:

{"Hemophilia" : "Bleeding Disorder"}
{"Hemophilia" : "Blood Clotting"}
{"Hemophilia" : "Pseudohemophilia"}
{"Hemophilia" : "Hemogenia"}

The successful formation of the terms leads to the activation of the *Search Algorithm* component. The algorithms we proposed are discussed in the later section. The search algorithm component is also linked to the main data source where the data is stored. Using the CouchDB [1] framework for instance, the data source can be accessible over REST API. Primarily, the search algorithm interfaces the data source through the HTTP GET method. The data source which is document style stores the data following the JSON format.

---

[1] http://couchdb.apache.org/

Each of the Ids shown in the figure above is a specific document that contains JSON data. In our framework, the documents are extracted and written in a flat text file. This aids us to easily read through the entire storage repository regardless of the number of documents.

The extracted terms are then reviewed to determine the association between the terms. We apply association rules based on the similarities and diversity of the extracted terms. Then, we employ the *Filtering* methodology to remove the pollutants (or noise) from the data. In most instances, the extracted artifacts are bound to contain keywords that appear valuable but are not actually relevant to the term mining tasks (e.g., antonyms, or similar written words but mean different things). The next task is *Tagging* which is applied to the filtered data. Tagging is employed to determine the existing relationship between the filtered data and how they are connected to the user specified artifact. At this stage, the *Serializer* component checks the format of the categorized data for visual presentation. The data must be modelled in JSON format before it can be parsed to the visual display. Once the *data clustering* is done in JSON, the output is sent to the visualization layer.

5   The Bernoulli Model

More details of the Bernoulli Model can be found in [31]. The Bernoulli model is applied to the flat database that contains the aggregation of all the documents structures from the database. From the specified terms to be extracted, we can establish the following base relationships:

$K \subset Dic$

$T \subset Db$

to mean that the specified keyword (K) is a subset of the vocabularies in the dictionary/thesaurus (Dic), and the constructed terms (T) from the semantic engine is a subset of the dataset in the database (Db). In a situation where there are no vocabularies similar (i.e., absence of synonyms or antonyms) in the Dic, then $K = T$. Also, it is practical to get into situations where K is not found at all in the dictionary and we treat this case also as $K = T$.

From the process execution flow in the previous section, the search algorithm is activated only when the terms have been formulated so, the Bernoulli model applies to T and the Db components. The characteristics of T can be defined as follows:

$T = \{t1, t2, t3, t4, \ldots, tn\}$

To mean that T can contain a list of several artefacts that are related to the specified term (described earlier as topics) and in the least, $T = \{t1\}$ to mean that the specified term has no related keywords. Thus, $T = \emptyset$ is not supported because this is an indirect way of saying that there is nothing specified to be searched.

The existence of T in the data source is represented as 1 and the non-existence of T in the data source is represented as 0. In this work, we are focusing on supporting the extraction of single word terms and two word terms. We describe the first case as "Single-Term" Bernoulli space and the latter as "Two-Term" Bernoulli space.

The single-term Bernoulli space is applicable to search terms that contain single words and meet the true positive (TP) criteria. The two-term Bernoulli space is more efficient for cases where T is a list of both antonyms and synonyms. It is important to state that there are instances where the two-term Bernoulli model is the preferred especially when the specified artefact has conflicting meanings. For example, when looking for "Contract", the result can be related to "acquire" as in the case of disease or "agreement" as in the case of pact.

In order to perform a reliable search, the Bernoulli Model proposed by Gu et al. [32] is adopted. The authors' work is a good reference source for further reading.

5.1   The Bernoulli Space

The Bernoulli model is good for the determination of terms occurrences in the data source rather the Hidden Markov Model which focuses on frequency of terms. The "Single-Term" Bernoulli space is denoted as $\bar{b} = [b_1, b_2, b_3, \ldots, b_n]$ where b_i is a Boolean value of 1 to mean that the term t_i is present in a single document storage within the storage source. Thus, the single-term Bernoulli space for a single document (d) can be denoted as Eq. (1):

$$p(d) = \prod_{i=1}^{|\bar{b}|} p(t_i)^{b_i} (1 - p(t_i))^{1 - b_i} \tag{1}$$

Where $p(t_i)$ is the probability that a term t_i is in existence in a particular document. The difficulty with the document style NoSQL database is that, it is difficult to treat the entire data source as a single layer as in the case of RDBMS storages. Rather, every single document is considered as a single storage layer. Thus, the existence of terms T in an entire document NoSQL (d_T) will be represented as Eq. (2):

$$p(d_T) = \sum_{1}^{n} \left(\prod_{i=1}^{|\bar{b}|} p(t_i)^{b_i} (1 - p(t_i))^{1 - b_i} \right) \tag{2}$$

The existence of terms in an entire document is represented as the sum of all the occurrences of ti in the single documents. Furthermore, the probability of the occurrences of terms $p(t_i)$ is formulated as Eq. (3):

$$p(t_i) = \frac{number\ of\ single\ documents\ containing\ t_i}{total\ number\ of\ documents} \tag{3}$$

The representation of the "Two-Term" Bernoulli space extends on the single-term space. The Two-terms can be represented as:

$$\bar{b} = \left[\langle b_i, b_j \rangle, \ \ldots \langle b_n, b_m \rangle\right]$$

Where $i \neq j$ and $< b_i, b_j >$ assumes the value of 0 or 1 to indicate the occurrence of the terms $< t_i, t_j >$ in a particular document.

Next, there is the need to design a working model for the proposed Bernoulli space based on the data source available. Two working models are proposed which we discuss below as Single-Term Bernoulli model and Two-Term Bernoulli model.

5.2   Single-Term Bernoulli Model

This model is designed to work with terms that are found within the true positive set in the document. This model is designed for cases where the terms are related through synonyms or any positive association between the terms. This set is denoted as A. Thus, the chances/probability that a term t_i belong to A can be denoted as $p(t_i/A)$. So, for a given set of terms in the positive set, the single-term Bernoulli model is formulated as shown in Eq. (4):

$$p(d|A) = \prod_{i=1}^{|\bar{b}|} p(t_i|A)^{b_i} \left(1 - p(t_i|A)\right)^{1 - b_i} \tag{4}$$

Then, normalization is achieved based on the size of the positive set within the document as shown below in Eq. (5).

$$p_{norm}(d|A) = p(d|A)^{1/|d|} \tag{5}$$

The parameter $|d|$ represents the existing number of terms in the document. Finally, the topics clustering which is done based on ranking follows the score below as shown in Eq. (6).

$$Rank(A|d) = p(A|d) \propto p_{norm}(d|A) \tag{6}$$

5.3   The Two-Term Bernoulli Model

This model is designed for search criteria that contains both synonym and anonym list of topics in a single set of terms. This requires that we design two sets which are true positive sets and true negative sets. The negative set is designed to eliminate negative terms from the search result. Though this model is most relevant for two word terms, it is applicable to one word terms as well. While the probability of having a term t_i in the true positive set is defined as $p(t_i|A)$, the existence of t_i in a true negative set is $p(t_i|B)$. Since we have already defined the positive set in Eq. (4), the negative set is defined below in Eq. (7).

$$p(d|B) = \prod_{i=1}^{|\bar{b}|} p(t_i|B)^{b_i} \left(1 - p(t_i|B)\right)^{1 - b_i} \qquad (7)$$

The extracted terms are then ranked following the classification ratio based on the Bayes' Rule as shown below in Eq. (8):

$$Ratio(A|d) = \frac{p(A|d)}{p(B|d)} \propto \frac{p(d|A)}{P(d|B)} \qquad (8)$$

6 Hidden Markov Model

In today's data economy, there are instances where the data is located in several databases. One technical issue is the fact that NoSQL storages (e.g., CouchDB) relies on map/reduce rather than RDBMS queries. There are also instances where cross database queries are not supported. Hence, the second major algorithm that is copied in this chapter, from [33], is the proposed Hidden Markov Model (HMM) with the specific aim of traversing several databases in a graph setting. Previously, Scheffer et al. [34] attempted to use the HMM to solve textual mining tasks on the Web. From Fig. 3, we model the NoSQL databases as interlinked nodes where the existence of terms across the databases is treated as a relationship. In graph databases, the concept is about nodes and their relationships. However, in the non-graph NoSQL databases, such relationships don't exist across products so the relationship we portray in Fig. 4 only means that the terms we are interested in extracting exist on those data sources. For example, the node represented as N can contain the artifact "Hemophilia" but the dependent terms may be scattered on the nodes denoted as D. This means there is a relationship between the N node and the D nodes. By observing the NoSQL storages, it is obvious we can model the terms extraction as a state transition flow; which makes the Hidden Markov Model a perfect fit. In this case, we found the tutorial presented by Mukherjee and Mitra [35] particular useful though the authors focused on a different application domain (Bioinformatics). We adopt the methodology the authors presented and this forms the basis and the highlight of the formal model shown in this section. The question is, how do we transition from the initial state through the other nodes until we get to the final state and return the result? Here, a state refers to a NoSQL source.

Fig. 4 Term linkages in several NoSQL

NoSQL Storages

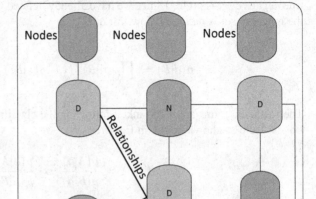

The start state can be specified by the user as any of the NoSQL nodes. Given a term A on a particular node, the conditional probability that the term or its dependency keywords B exist(s) on other nodes can be expressed as:

$$f_{A|B} = \frac{f_{A,B}(a_i, b_j)}{f_B(b_j)}$$

However, the condition of the existence of terms can be independent and random which follows that:

$$f_{A|B}(a_i, b_j) = f_A(a_i) \times f_B(b_j)$$

Considering a sequence of reproducible terms and their dependencies, let us have a sequence of random variables $A_0, A_1, \ldots, A_n$ having values in a set $S = s_1, s_2, \ldots, s_n$. Then the sequence is Markov Chain if $\forall n \geq 1$, and $j_0, j_1, \ldots, j_n \in S$, we have:

$$P(A_n = j_n \mid A_0 = j_0, \ldots, A_{n-1} = j_{n-1}) = P(A_n = j_n \mid A_{n-1} = j_{n-1})$$

The next step is to define an Observable Random Process (ORP) which defines a finite state space of available NoSQL nodes $N = n_1, \ldots, n_K$, such that the two states

S and N can contain the same or different number of tuple arguments. The condition that there will be an outcome E from the data silos is then defined as:

$$Outcome = e_j(k)_{j=1, k=1}^{J, K}$$

where ej(k) ≥ 0 and $\sum_{k=1}^{K} e_j(k) = 1$

The third property is the Conditional Independence (CI). The CI assumes that the outcomes are conditionally independent for the NoSQL state sequence. For a sequence of states $j_0, j_1, \ldots, j_n$, the probability of the sequence $o_0, o_1, \ldots, o_n$ can be expressed as:

$$P\left(B_o = o_0, \ldots, B_n = o_n \mid A_0 = j_0, \ldots, A_n = j_n, E\right) = \prod_{l=0}^{n} e_{jl}(l)$$

We then define a joint probability based on the terms and states $o_0, o_1, \ldots, o_n$ and $j_0, j_1, \ldots, j_n$ as:

$$P(B_0 = o_0, \ldots, B_n = o_n, A_0 = j_0, \ldots, A_n = j_n; T, E, \pi(0))$$
$$= P(B_0, \ldots, B_n / A_0, \ldots, A_n, E) \times P(a_0, \ldots, A_n, T, \pi(0))$$

$$= \pi_{j_0}(0) \times \prod_{l=0}^{n} e_{j_l} \times \prod_{l=1}^{n} pj_{l-1}|_{j_l}$$

The total sum of all possible NoSQL nodes in the entire graph network results into:

$$P(B_0, \ldots, B_n; T, E, \pi(0)) = \sum_{j_0=1}^{J} \cdots \sum_{j_n=1}^{J} \pi_{j_0}(0) e_{j_0}(0) \prod_{l=1}^{n} p_{j_l-1}|_{j_l} e_{j_l}(l)$$

At this point, the HMM model is exponential so we have to improve on the algorithm in order to make the model linear. This is achieved by splitting the above equation into forward/backward recursion. From the last equation above, we can re-write a new equation as:

$$L_N = P(B_0, B_1, \ldots, B_n; \lambda) = \sum_{j=1}^{J} \alpha_n(j) \times \beta_n(j)$$

The forward variable α is defined formally as:

$$\alpha_n(j) = P\big(B_0 = o_0, \ B_1 = o_1, \ \ldots, \ B_n = o_n \ \big| \ A_n = j\big)$$

Consequently, the backward variable is defined as:

$$\beta_n(j) = P\big(B_{n+1} = o_{n+1}, \ \ldots, \ B_N = o_N \ \big| \ A_N = j\big)$$

From the two variables, the recursion relations can be written as:

$$\sum_{i=1}^{J} \alpha_n(i) \times p_{i\big|j} \times e_j(o_{n+1}) = \left[\sum_{i=1}^{J} \alpha_n(i) \times p_{i\big|j}\right] \times e_j(o_{n+1})$$

and

$$\beta_n(j) = \sum_{i=1}^{J} e_i(o_{n+1}) \times \beta_{n+1}(i) \times p_{j\big|i}$$

Since the two recursive equations have a computational complexity of $O(n^2)$, the model in a given state i at a specified time t given a sequence of given terms o and a model λ can be formalized as:

$$P\big(A_t = i\big|o, \ \lambda\big) = \frac{\alpha_i(t)}{\beta_i(t)}$$

This final equation reduces the exponential complexity of traversing all the nodes in search of the terms to be extracted and the dependency keywords into a linear complexity. The next algorithm to discuss is the Apriori model.

7 Apriori

The Apriori technique is reproduced from [36]. The proposed terms analytic framework has a *Search Log* that keeps the record of the frequency of the keywords being searched. This is a disk storage that can grow in size so we use ranking based on the frequency of hits to prioritize which records to keep. When the storage is growing out of proportion, less frequently searched keywords (i.e., less prioritized keywords) are deleted.

The proposed Apriori model is a unique algorithm that combines two algorithms on association rule and Bayesian inference. First, the association rule is designed so that we can determine the presence of frequency of terms, T in the database Db. Since the Apriori model is designed to naturally align with transactional databases, we considered every search within a document as a transaction as well as cross documents. Further, we model every pile of document (illustrated in Fig. 4) as a row, identical to RDBMS systems.

In the association rule, the proportion of documents (i.e., transactions) in the entire database that contain T, known as the support, and denoted as $supp(T)$ can be defined simply as:

$$supp(T) = \frac{Number\ of\ documents\ containing\ T}{Total\ number\ of\ documents}$$

The support methodology enables the proposed framework to crawl the entire Db (i.e., every level of append document) to determine the frequency of occurrences of T. Further, there is the need to determine the probability that within the set of term T of keywords, $t1,\ t2,\ \dots,\ tn$, the occurrence of a keyword and other keywords truly exists. This is known as confidence and denoted $conf(t1 \Rightarrow t2)$, and it is relevant for the situations when $T \neq \{t1\}$. This is represented as:

$$conf(t1 \Rightarrow t2) = \frac{supp(t1 \wedge t2)}{supp(t1)}$$

In this case, the confidence is calculated within the term set T rather than the entire Db. The performance of the methodology is then measured as the ratio of the target response and the average response. This is represented as:

$$perf(t1 \Rightarrow t2) = \frac{supp(t1 \wedge t2)}{supp(t1) \cdot supp(t2)}$$

The $perf()$ function focuses on the individual keywords that form the set T. However, the same function is what is employed to determine the success ratio of terms being extracted from the entire Db. This is due to the fact that the keyword extraction is happening at two stages; looking for the appropriate associations between the keywords in the semantic engine and the existence of the keywords in the entire document Db.

The association rule as of now solves one part of the problem, which is the issue of the determination of the frequency of occurrence of terms. Also, we have found the relationships between the keywords that comprise the set of terms. The set of terms are basically the expected keyword, and other artifacts such as synonyms and antonyms that are found in the dictionary and/or thesaurus. In order to facilitate a reliable search based on reasoning, we explored the option of the inference rule. This is to aid us perform the data mining based on historical searches that have been tagged as success hits. Thus, the Bayesian inference is adopted based on the probability formula:

$$P(T_p|T_n) = \frac{P(T_n|T_p) \cdot P(T_p)}{P(T_n)}$$

Where T_p is the previous terms that return some acceptable result and T_n is the existence of new keywords in T that can affect the previous state. This is known as new evidence which is not used when performing the prior T. The evidence of the inference rule is then estimated based on the formula:

$$p(T|\propto) = \int_\oslash [p(T|\oslash)p(\oslash|\propto)]d\oslash$$

We are able to re-calculate the new conditional probability (a.k.a., posterior probability) based on this new evidence as shown in the formula:

$$p(\oslash|T, \propto) = \frac{p(T|\oslash)p(\oslash|\propto)}{p(T|\propto)} \propto p(T|\oslash)p(\oslash|\propto)$$

Where $\oslash$ is a vector parameter of the keywords t in the set of T, $\propto$ is the parameter of the prior distribution that determines expected future searches. This is aimed at predicting future searches that will contain the same T or variations to T.

The combination of the association rule and the inference methodology in the design of the Apriori model enhanced the accuracy of the search as evidenced in the experiments in the evaluation section. The next section explains the other search methodologies that are designed.

8 Directed Graph Methodologies

This approach is reproduced from [37]. In this section, we employ the directed graph approach to implement four search algorithms namely the: linear search, parallel search, pessimistic search, and optimistic search. The search algorithm is applied directly to the unstructured data source based on the user's search preferences. The proposed algorithms are explored in order to examine the best methodology that meets our need; especially, optimization of information extraction time. Thus, the AaaS framework is built following the *directed graph* approach.

Hence, the search methodologies determine the depth of the unstructured data and traverse the layers from top to bottom. For example, considering a pile of documents in CouchDB that have linkages as in Fig. 5, for each methodology, the extraction process starts from the root which is node 1.

Searching through node 1 shows that there are existing external links that are nodes 2, 3, and 4. The search then continues with each child node of the root until every node is visited. Also, with the directed graph, we adopt the hyperlink search

Fig. 5 Directed graph

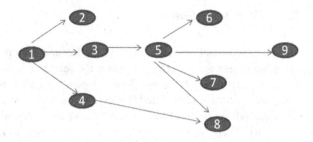

model from [5] where we keep two attributes (i.e., the Nodes and Link) after visiting each node. The node in this case can be a document or another database which contains the set t1, .., tn of term T. These attributes are represented as tuples in an array such that:

Nodes = [url, title, format, size, date, topic or term (text)]
and,
Link = [source-url, target-url, label, link-type].

8.1 The Linear Search

This is the commonest algorithm on which most existing data mining tools are built; probably because it is straightforward to implement and it has a complexity cost of $O(n)$. Our linear search methodology explores an entire vector (search) space starting from the current node (root) and going through the child nodes one after the other. So in Fig. 5, the linear search from the root will consider child nodes 2, 3, and 4. Then it will go to node 2 and will reach a dead-end. After which it will go to node 3, and will also determine that node 5 is a child of node 3. It will then visit node 5 and determine child nodes 6, 7, 8, and 9. It will further search through these individual child nodes and reach a dead-end in each case. After that, it will come back to node 4 and determine that node 8 is a child of node 4. But, in this case, it will not visit node 8 because it has already visited node 8 when it traversed node 3 and node 5 links. This measure of not visiting an already visited link makes the search not to enter into an infinite search loop. Similarly, the algorithm can be described as a recursive search algorithm because of how it searches through the links and determines which node to visit next from the current node.

Further, we refer to the model as random because the system determines which child node to visit without user intervention. For instance, the choice of traversing node 2, 3, or 4 as the first choice follows no particular order. The only criterion is every child node must be visited.

8.2   Parallelization

Our proposed parallel search employs the linear search in two concurrent functions but randomness is not permitted. Since the search is in a directed graph, the search for terms starts from the root node and depending on the number of child nodes, two concurrent functions are called that divides the search space by numbering nodes as even and odd. Assuming the entire vector space is N with layers such that $N = \{1, 2, 3 \ldots n\}$. Then, for each layer two linear functions, X and Y are called such that, $X = \{$search through odd numbered nodes of N$\}$ and $Y = \{$search through even numbered nodes of N$\}$. So, for every node that has more than one child node, the linear functions X and Y will be activated in order to halve the search space vector in the previous linear search algorithm. After all the layers in N are visited and the terms are extracted, the *Serializer* component is activated which combines all the search terms into a single extracted document structure just as the linear search. In the framework, the serializer works only with the parallel search in order to integrate the results from the segregated functions. That is, combining the array values of the various search results into a single array with duplicates eliminated.

In order to explain the concept of the parallel search further to the reader using Fig. 5, we can say that $N = 4$ layers counting from the root node (i.e. node 1). The first layer which has the child nodes of the root are three nodes (i.e., nodes 2, 3, 4). So the two parallel linear functions will be activated and the function X will search node 3 and function Y will search node 2 and 4. Node 2 is a dead-end and node 4 has a child node 8 so the Y function will be called to search through node 8 (since its only one node and we treat one node as odd) and then we reach a dead-end. Node 3 however will be searched by X and then node 5 will be found as a child. The search space in node 5 will be divided among X and Y again since the child nodes are more than one. X will search node 6 and node 8, and Y will search node 7 and node 9. Now there are two cases to explain here. There is the repetition of searching through node 8 because the initial search was done by Y and in the second case, the search is being carried out by X. So, during the serialization of the results (i.e., JSON Clustering in the main architecture), the duplicate nodes will be eliminated. However, assuming the use case is different and Y initially searches through node 8 and then based on the search space division between X and Y at node 5 it happens that Y is assigned to node 8, the search will not be carried out all because Y already knows that it has visited 8. It works just as the linear search algorithm and this further saves cost (time).

8.3   Pessimistic and Optimistic Search Algorithms

Pessimistic and optimistic constants have been employed extensively in software engineering to accomplish tasks such as detection of the existence of software artifacts in source code, traceability link detection, bug triaging and fixing, and so on [38]. The pessimistic search assumes that the search term may not be found based on some probability while the optimistic search is the reverse. The reason we found the pessimistic and optimistic search relevant to our work is because we employ it to search for the existence of topics, terms, and documents in the unstructured data source but not necessarily the links and the dependencies of the keywords. In essence, the pessimistic and optimistic search is a linear search but with restrictions as to which sources to search or not. For example, looking for the term "Bleeding Disorder" from a pile of digital files, the pessimistic search will ignore all nodes that the user thinks the term may not be present. Hence, from the directed graph illustration, the pessimistic search can be set to ignore say nodes 3 and 4. In that case, the search is not going to go through all the nodes for example in Fig. 5 if the algorithm assumes that the topic cannot be found in node 3 or 4 or some other node. The search is user specified hence, the user has to provide the search term and also provide the document names or files or directories that should not be searched. The optimistic search on the other hand is when the user provides a search term; and then specifies files or directories in which the user thinks those search terms can be found.

The next section focuses on the evaluations of the various algorithms.

9   Evaluating the Algorithms

Several tests have been conducted based on the aforementioned algorithms. The main focus is to highlight the pros and cons of each of the adopted methodologies. To do this, we seek to prove the accuracy of the extracted terms based on each of the adopted methodologies. Thus, the following parameters are explored: True Positive (TP)—refers to the extraction of expected results, False Positive (FP)—refers to the extraction of perceived to be desired results from the data source but in reality the terms are not needed, True Negative (TN)—is when the term is not found because it does not exist, and False Negative (FN)—the term could not be found but it exists in the data source.

9.1   The Bernoulli Model and the HMM

The Bernoulli algorithm is analysed in this section and the results are reported in Tables 1 and 2. The experiments focus on one-word and two-words extraction. For each category of specified terms, we analyzed the result for the single term Bernoulli, two-terms Bernoulli, and the Hidden Markov Model. In Table 3, we observed that the "Two-Term" Bernoulli model has a better accuracy index due to the fact that the true positive value is higher and the false negative values are less. As expected, the one-word terms are better represented than the two-word terms.

Table 2 The analysis of the extracted term for psychiatry

| | Bernoulli model | | | | Hidden Markov Model | |
| | Single-term | | Two-term | | | |
	One-word (%)	Two-words (%)	One-word (%)	Two-words (%)	One-word (%)	Two-words (%)
True positive	96.20	80.02	100.00	99.90	97.22	83.22
False positive	9.91	10.23	0.00	0.00	2.30	7.71
True negative	96.80	94.23	100.00	99.93	98.33	93.75
False negative	17.27	19.09	5.45	8.83	12.34	19.23
Precision	90.66	88.66	100.00	100.00	97.69	91.52
Recall (sensitivity)	84.78	80.74	94.83	91.88	88.74	81.23
Specificity	90.71	90.21	100.00	100.00	97.71	92.40
Accuracy	87.65	85.60	97.35	95.77	93.03	86.79
F1 score	87.62	84.52	97.35	95.77	93.00	86.07

The improvement in the two-term Bernoulli model is as a result of the fact that the search contains both negative and positive terms.

In case a term is specified, the negative list aids the analytics tool to eliminate undesired terms which leads to significantly low false negative values.

An interesting observation however is that, the Hidden Markov Model (HMM) has higher accuracy value than the single-term Bernoulli model but lower accuracy in comparison to the two-term Bernoulli model. A possible reason for this phenomenon is due to the fact that the HMM relies on the frequency of term occurrence. The limitation however arises when two-words appear in the same data source when individual terms are also existing terms. For example, "heart" and "disease" are individual and completely separate terms while "heart disease" is another term. The HMM therefore has higher FN results with two-word terms because it counts the single frequency of the individual terms.

In order to validate the results and the arguments, we conducted the experiment using different data sets for Psychiatry. The result is recorded in Table 2. The outcome follows exactly as recorded in the previous case. The TP, TN, FP, and FN values all follow the same trend. Our aim here is not to get the same result but, similar pattern in determining which of the module works better.

9.2   The Apriori and HMM

In Tables 3 and 4, we reproduced the results of the experiments on the Apriori algorithm and the HMM in [36]. For every dataset, the extracted terms (artifacts)

Table 3 Terabyte JSON text on Hemophilia related records in CouchD

	500K artefacts		1 million artefacts		1.5 million artefacts		2 million artefacts	
	Hidden Markov Model (%)	Apriori (%)	Hidden Markov Model (%)	Apriori (%)	Hidden Markov Model (%)	Apriori (%)	Hidden Markov Model (%)	Apriori (%)
True positive	92.20	93.14	92.81	93.00	92.09	92.67	93.11	93.43
False positive	14.34	7.86	17.33	9.43	24.34	9.85	31.50	10.21
True negative	99.40	99.21	99.45	99.23	98.72	99.12	99.54	99.32
False negative	4.21	4.34	4.36	4.43	4.63	4.98	5.11	5.06
Precision	86.54	92.22	84.27	90.79	79.09	90.39	74.72	90.15
Recall (sensitivity)	95.63	95.55	95.51	95.45	95.21	94.90	94.80	94.86
Specificity	87.39	92.66	85.16	91.32	80.22	90.96	75.96	90.68
Accuracy	91.17	94.04	89.86	93.27	86.82	92.82	84.03	92.66
F1 score	90.86	93.85	89.54	93.07	86.41	92.59	83.57	92.45

Table 4 Terabyte JSON text on psychiatry related records in CouchDB

	500K artefacts		1 million artefacts		1.5 million artefacts		2 million artefacts	
	Hidden Markov Model (%)	Apriori (%)	Hidden Markov Model (%)	Apriori (%)	Hidden Markov Model (%)	Apriori (%)	Hidden Markov Model (%)	Apriori (%)
True positive	90.09	91.87	89.45	92.06	87.45	90.33	87.02	90.33
False positive	19.32	7.52	23.09	8.46	29.76	9.08	36.98	9.20
True negative	99.61	99.66	99.13	99.01	98.10	98.89	98.36	98.99
False negative	8.22	4.50	11.21	5.02	13.00	5.90	17.23	7.49
Precision	82.34	92.43	79.48	91.58	74.61	90.87	70.18	90.76
Recall (sensitivity)	91.64	95.33	88.86	94.83	87.06	93.87	83.47	92.34
Specificity	83.76	92.98	81.11	92.13	76.72	91.59	72.68	91.50
Accuracy	87.32	94.09	84.61	93.41	81.27	92.66	77.37	91.90
F1 score	86.74	93.86	83.91	93.18	80.35	92.34	76.25	91.54

are analyzed in groups of 500 thousand, 1 Million, 1.5 Million, and 2 Million. The extraction is grouped so that we can further observe the behavior of the model with increasing data set and diversity.

The overall accuracy of the proposed Apriori model is 93.11 % while the Hidden Markov Model (HMM) is 85.31 %. In order to understand this result, the various factors are observed critically. We realized that the factors return identical results across the dataset except for the False Positive data. The Hidden Markov Model returns a lot of FP data because the model identifies the expected terms plus other keywords that the system dim correct.

In most cases, the keywords that are dimed correct are not so, they contribute to unwanted result (pollution). Further, as the number of extracted artefacts increases, the FP value increases. This phenomenon reduces the accuracy of the search result across the two datasets.

The Apriori model on the other hand returns low FP value since the result is filtered based on previously acceptable terms. Practically, the Apriori model identifies the same terms as the HMM but, the former filters the result and eliminates unwanted artefacts. This situation causes the FP value to be almost the same regardless of the data size and dataset. Moreover, the FP does not vary across the datasets as was in the case of the HMM. The only issue is that, when there is no historical data for a particular search term, then the result will contain more FP values.

To further explain the various phenomenon exhibited by both methodologies, we shall explain the output of the graphs in Fig. 6 which focuses on the True Positive (TP) plot, Fig. 7 which focuses on the Accuracy plot, and Fig. 8 which illustrates the level of falsehood in the dataset.

In Fig. 6a, we plot the True Positive (TP) indices for the Hemophilia dataset and Fig. 6b is the plot for the Psychiatry dataset. In both plots, we can see that the true positive results for both the HMM and the Apriori algorithms are almost identical. Especially in Fig. 6a, considering the cumulative average for the entire terms from 500K to 2 Million, the average TP value for the HMM is 0.9255 and the TP value of the Apriori is 0.9306. In Fig. 6b, which represents the Psychiatry dataset, the TP averages are 0.8850 and 0.9115 for the HMM and Apriori respectively. This goes to

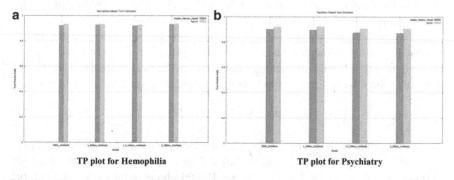

TP plot for Hemophilia   **TP plot for Psychiatry**

Fig. 6 (a) TP plot for Hemophilia. (b) TP plot for Psychiatry

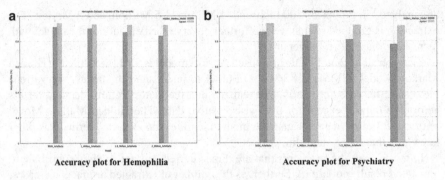

Accuracy plot for Hemophilia   **Accuracy plot for Psychiatry**

Fig. 7 (**a**) Accuracy plot for Hemophilia. (**b**) Accuracy plot for Psychiatry

show that both algorithms are able to identify the expected terms in the entire search result. However, the high competition and closeness in the TP value is different from the accuracy of the result. We can have high TP values and when the False Positive (FP) and False Negative (FN) values are also high, the accuracy will be minimal. This is a practical case where a search is conducted and what is sort for is found plus other irrelevant artefacts known as noise or pollutants. The accuracy therefore is about how much of relevance the search result meets the user's criteria. This means accuracy is enhanced in a system if the FP and FN values are minimized.

So, in Fig. 7a, b, we turn our attention to the accuracy of both methodologies. The accuracy plot in the Hemophilia dataset is shown in Fig. 7a and the Psychiatry dataset is shown in Fig. 7b. In these two cases, we can clearly see that the accuracy of the Apriori methodology outperforms that of the HMM. The cumulative average value of the accuracy of the Apriori methodology is 0.9320 and that of the HMM is 0.8797 in the Hemophilia dataset. Investigating the same phenomenon in the Psychiatry dataset, the cumulative accuracy of the Apriori methodology is 0.9302 and that of the HMM is 0.8264. Though the cumulative averages over the entire set of terms show that the proposed Apriori methodology shows better accuracy, we have also observed some traits in the results. We realized that the accuracy index of the HMM declines as the data set increases. At this point, we can assume that the decline in accuracy is due to increasing FN and/or FP values since the same result shows competitive true positive indices for both methodologies.

So, we decided to evaluate the level of falsehood in the returned result. In our estimation, falsehood includes the cases of misclassified results, wrongly perceived terms, overlooked terms, and wrongly tagged terms. We calculate the falsehood as the sum of the false positive and false negative, which can be formalized simply as:

$$Falsehood = FP + FN$$

The falsehood is shown in Fig. 8a, b for the Hemophilia and Psychiatry datasets respectively. In both graphs, our assumption is confirmed true as the level of falsehood increases as the dataset increase. The falsehood in the case of the Apriori

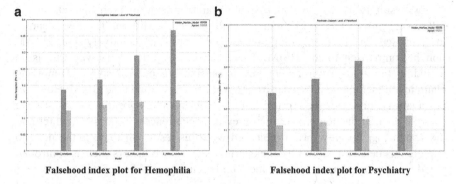

Falsehood index plot for Hemophilia   **Falsehood index plot for Psychiatry**

Fig. 8 (**a**) Falsehood index plot for Hemophilia (**b**) Falsehood index plot for Psychiatry

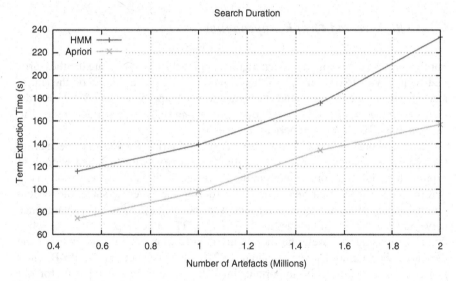

Fig. 9 The search duration

stabilizes across the high-dimensional data because of its reasoning from previous searches. In the practical case, we realized that the contributing factor to the high falsehood in the HMM is misclassification.

9.2.1 The Search Duration

Apart from testing the reliability of both methodologies in terms of the accuracy and false perceptions, we are also concerned about the search duration. In today's data economy where the data quantum is huge and can be spread across several layers, the time spent to retrieve terms is crucial. We recorded the time spent on retrieving a search result from the NoSQL. The result for both algorithms is graphed in Fig. 9.

The result is the average plot of the search time from both datasets at the following points 500K, 1 Million, 1.5 Million, and 2 Million. The result shows the proposed Apriori methodology retrieves the terms in a relatively shorter duration in comparison to the HMM. There can be several factors why this is so including the cloud environment that is outside our control so we cannot lay claim to the fact that in all scenarios, the Apriori is faster than the HMM. However our analysis show that the Apriori is faster because the algorithm does not have much to do after the determination of previous occurrences of the specified term in the search log. For now, we are pleased with this result but there is the need to explore this behavior further by considering other macro factors such as controlled cloud environment, equal search time with less noisy neighbors, and so on.

9.3   The Directed Graph Approaches

For the purpose of testing the directed graph approaches, we populate the thesaurus of RSenter with terms related to "Psychiatry"; which is a subset of the entire medical record we acquire. The thesaurus contains approximately 3200 records, their dependency keywords, possible synonyms, and all other artifacts related to "Psychiatry". The result is reported in Table 5.

There is about 0.2 % data loss in the Linear Search (i.e., 99.80 % TP) because at the end of the search, we realised that the thesaurus was not detailed enough to capture those information. Though in the Extracted Artifacts storage, we observed that the TP for the Linear Search is 100 %, during the Filtering stage, the system removed some of the words because they were not considered to be relevant since they were not defined in the thesaurus. Thus, the TP value can be improved when these relationships are well and thoroughly defined in either the dictionary or the thesaurus. Furthermore, there is about 1.02 % FP value because while RSenter perceive those words to be important, in reality they were not relevant for our

Table 5 Evaluated metrics of the proposed algorithms

	Linear search (%)	Parallel search (%)	Pessimistic search (%)	Optimistic search (%)
True positive	99.80	97.22	84.31	89.33
False positive	1.02	1.74	0.00	0.00
True negative	100.00	100.00	99.22	99.01
False negative	0.00	0.00	34.31	36.74
Precision	98.99	98.24	100.00	100.00
Recall (sensitivity)	100.00	100.00	71.08	70.86
Specificity	98.99	98.29	100.00	100.00
Accuracy	99.49	99.13	84.25	83.68
F1 Score	99.49	99.11	83.09	82.94

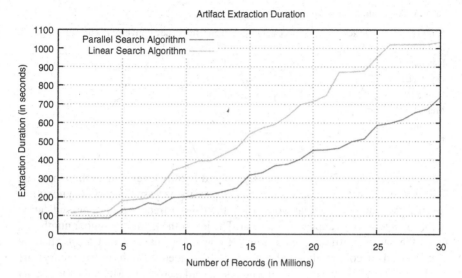

Fig. 10 The term extraction duration

search. Since the Parallel Search is an extension on the linear search (i.e., multiple linear searches that run concurrently), the observations from the linear search are replicated in the parallel search.

In the case of the Pessimistic Search, there is huge data loss (i.e., 84.31 % TP) because the search is based on the user preferences.

In most cases, the CouchDB databases that we specify should not be queried contain some relevant terms. Also, there are some errors in the Optimistic Search which has eventually affected the accuracy because the user specified CouchDB nodes are not the only sources for the important terms. However, it is important to state that the results from the Pessimistic and Optimistic searches will vary based on the user of the system. This is because the criteria that user A will set for the query can/will be different from the criteria of user B.

The next evaluation is to determine the speed of the framework with respect to the amount of data we have. The result is represented in Fig. 10.

The Linear Search took significantly larger amount of time especially as the number of distributed NoSQL databases increase. The Parallel search however reduces the term mining duration and completes the process faster. The parallel search result we show in this work employs ten concurrent linear searches, so it reduces the waiting queue by almost 300 %. Since the underlying programming environment of the framework is Erlang [40], the framework supports high concurrency through multi inter-process communications, thus, several parallel linear requests can be started concurrently. The only concern will be the consideration for the hardware on which the framework is running.

Finally, we report the characteristics of the terms extracted for "Psychiatry" and how they are rated. Though there are a lot more terms (about 3200 unique artifacts),

Table 6 Associations in sample terms

Sample artifacts	Difficulty level	Success ratio (%)	Term frequency—inverse document frequency (tf-idf)
Psychiatry	1	100	0.0014
Psychiatric	2	98	0.0033
Hospital	1	100	0.0011
Mental	3	95	0.0056
Treatment	2	98	0.0021
Research	4	93	0.081

we focus on the most frequently accessed. The difficulty level from high to low (i.e., 1–4) is which sample artifacts (or, terms) are easily accessed even if a synonym is specified instead of the actual word. Also, the tf-idf as reported gives an indication of the most terms that appeared the most. The lesser the tf-idf, the higher number of times the sample artifact occurs. From Table 6, we realized that terms that are standardized or commonly used among the documents (such as Psychiatry) are easily accessed. However, dependency keyword such as "Mental" has higher difficulty level. Also, "Hospital" has a low difficulty index but other frequently appeared word such as "Research" has very high difficulty indices. This is because though psychiatry research has appeared a lot of times in the NoSQL sources, the relationship between the two keywords is not well-defined in the thesaurus. From these outcomes, we can conclude that the more frequently occurred terms are easily extracted with high success ratio.

10 Conclusion

Analytics-as-a-Service (AaaS) is becoming an important area for the purposes of making sense of the immense data at our disposal. Today's data economy ("a.k.a., Big Data") boasts of huge amount of data which comes in different representations and formats. The heterogeneity in the data structure calls for new ways of analyzing the data.

Currently, NoSQL databases are being proposed to store the highly unstructured data. This means, previously designed data mining approaches for schema-oriented storages have to be modified to meet the modern standards. Our work focuses on how terms extraction can be achieved in NoSQL environment. Specifically, we focus on document-style NoSQL databases which are gaining prominence.

In this chapter, several algorithmic models are presented and the performance of each is evaluated. The proposed algorithms are the: Bernoulli model, Hidden Markov Model (HMM), Apriori, Linear Search, Parallel Search, Pessimistic Search, and Optimistic Search. Comparing the search durations, the Parallel Search shows minimal window in comparison to the Linear Search. Similarly, the Apriori has minimal window in comparison to the Hidden Markov Model. While the

Hidden Markov model aligns with graph technology and can be a very important algorithm for data in distributed nodes, the accuracy must be considered. The Bernoulli model shows higher accuracy when it comes to dual-word artifact extraction in comparison to the HMM. Further, the Optimistic and Pessimistic Searches can be adopted to extract terms without going through the entire data source. In this case, it is important to say that the algorithms are only encouraged when the user is not particularly interested in the accuracy of the result. Where, accuracy can be affected by the presence of high false positive results.

Beyond this chapter, there are a lot to do in the area of unstructured data, NoSQL, and terms analytics. Further questions can be asked on how the analytics platform can be trained for sentence extraction especially in mining medical diagnostics reports? Further questions that arise are centred on language adaptability and generalization of the platform for cross-enterprise adoption. There are other rising issues such as "big security" which focuses on the privacy, protection, and security of data for secondary usage and against violations.

Acknowledgement
- Special thanks to grad students in the MADMUC Lab, University of Saskatchewan.
- Thanks to Prof. Patrick Hung of the IT Security Unit, University of Ontario Institute of Technology.
- Final thanks to the Editors and Reviewers of this chapter for their feedback.

References

1. M.R. Wigan, R. Clarke, Big data's big unintended consequences. Computer **46**(6), 46–53 (2013). doi:10.1109/MC.2013.195
2. R. Akerkar, C. Badica, C. B. Burdescu, Desiderata for research in web intelligence, mining and semantics, in *Proceedings of the 2nd International Conference on Web Intelligence, Mining and Semantics (WIMS '12)*. ACM, New York, NY, USA, Article 0, 5 pages. DOI= 10.1145/2254129.2254131 http://doi.acm.org/10.1145/2254129.2254131
3. P. C. Zikopoulos, C. Eaton, D. de Roos, T. Deutsch, G. Lapis, Understanding Big Data: Analytics for Enterprise Class Hadoop and Streaming Data, Published by McGraw-Hill Companies, 2012. https://www.ibm.com/developerworks/community/wikis/home?lang=en#!/wiki/Big%20Data%20University/page/FREE%20ebook%20-%20Understanding%20Big%20Data
4. K. Rupanagunta, D. Zakkam, H. Rao, How to Mine Unstructured Data, Article in Information Management, June 29 2012, http://www.information-management.com/newsletters/data-mining-unstructured-big-data-youtube--10022781-1.html
5. IBM Research, Analytics-as-a-Service Platform, Available: http://researcher.ibm.com/researcher/view_project.php?id=3992
6. J. Sequeda, D. P. Miranker, "Linked Data," Linked Data tutorial at Semtech 2012, Jun 07, 2012. Available: http://www.slideshare.net/juansequeda/linked-data-tutorial-at-semtech-2012
7. Google Knowledge Graph, Available: http://www.google.ca/insidesearch/features/search/knowledge.html
8. NoSQL, http://nosql-database.org/

9. EMC, EMC Accelerates Journey to Big Data with Business Analytics-as-a-Service, http://www.emc.com/collateral/white-papers/h11259-emc-accelerates-journey-big-data-ba-wp.pdf
10. SAS, Analytics as a Service: Customer Experiences, http://www.sas.com/offices/europe/uk/resources/brochure/aaas_research_brief.pdf
11. X. Sun, B. Gao, L. Fan, W. An, A Cost-Effective Approach to Delivering Analytics as a Service, IEEE 19th International Conference on Web Services (ICWS 2012), vol., no., pp.512,519, 24–29 June 2012, doi: 10.1109/ICWS.2012.79
12. P. Deepak, P. M. Deshpande, K. Murthy, Configurable and Extensible Multi-flows for Providing Analytics as a Service on the Cloud, 2012 Annual SRII Global Conference (SRII), vol., no., pp.1,10, 24–27 July 2012, doi: 10.1109/SRII.2012.11
13. D. Keim, J. Kohlhammer, G. Ellis, F. Mansmann, Mastering the Information Age Solving Problems with Visual Analytics, Printed in Germany, Druckhaus "Thomas Müntzer" GmbH, Bad Langensalza ISBN 978-3-905673-77-7
14. F. S. Gharehchopogh, Z. A. Khalifelu, Analysis and evaluation of unstructured data: text mining versus natural language processing, Application of Information and Communication Technologies (AICT), 2011 5th International Conference on, vol., no., pp.1–4, 12–14 Oct. 2011, doi: 10.1109/ICAICT.2011.6111017
15. V. Tunali, T. T. Bilgin, PRETO: A High-performance Text Mining Tool for Preprocessing Turkish Texts, 2012 International Conference on Computer Systems and Technologies
16. S.V. Vinchurkar, S.M. Nirkhi, Feature extraction of product from customer feedback through blog. Int. J. Emerg. Technol. Adv. Eng. **2**(1), 314–323 (2012). ISSN 2250-2459
17. D. Kuonen, Challenges in bioinformatics for statistical data miners. Bull. Swiss Stat. Soc. **46**, 10–17 (2003)
18. J. Y. Hsu, W. Yih, Template-Based Information Mining from HTML Documents, American Association for Artificial Intelligence, July 1997
19. M. Delgado, M. Martín-Bautista, D. Sánchez, M. Vila, Mining Text Data: Special Features and Patterns, Pattern Detection and Discovery, Lecture Notes in Computer Science, 2002, Volume 2447/2002, 175-186, DOI: 10.1007/3-540-45728-3_11
20. Q. Zhao, S. S. Bhowmick, Association Rule Mining: A Survey, Technical Report, CAIS, Nanyang Technological University, Singapore, No. 2003116, 2003
21. W. Abramowicz, T. Kaczmarek, M. Kowalkiewicz, Supporting topic map creation using data mining techniques. Aust. J. Inf. Syst. **11**(1), 63–78 (2003)
22. B. Janet, A. V. Reddy, Cube index for unstructured text analysis and mining, in *Proceedings of the 2011 International Conference on Communication, Computing & Security (ICCCS '11)*. ACM, New York, NY, USA, 397–402
23. L. Han, T.O. Suzek, Y. Wang, S.H. Bryant, The text-mining based PubChem Bioassay neighboring analysis. BMC Bioinformatics **11**, 549 (2010). doi:10.1186/1471-2105-11-549
24. L. Dey, S. K. M. Haque, Studying the effects of noisy text on text mining applications, in *Proceedings of the Third Workshop on Analytics for Noisy Unstructured Text Data (AND '09)*. ACM, New York, NY, USA, 107–114
25. S. Godbole, I. Bhattacharya, A. Gupta, A. Vea, Building re-usable dictionary repositories for real-world text mining, in *Proceedings of the 19th ACM international conference on Information and knowledge management (CIKM '10)*. ACM, New York, NY, USA, 1189–1198
26. R. Feldman, M. Fresko, H. Hirsh, Y. Aumann, O. Liphstat, Y. Schler, M. Rajman, Knowledge Management: A Text Mining Approach, *Proc. of the 2nd Int. Conf. on Practical Aspects of Knowledge Management (PAKM98)*, (Basel, Switzerland, 29–30 Oct 1998)
27. R. Feldman, M. Fresko, Y. Kinar, Y. Lindell, O. Liphstat, M. Rajman, Y. Schler, O. Zamir, Text mining at the term level, *Proc. of the 2nd European Symposium on Principles of Data Mining and Knowledge Discovery (PKDD'98)*
28. J. C. Scholtes, Text-Mining: The next step in search technology, DESI-III Workshop Barcelona, June 8, 2009

29. J. Lee, D. Grossman, O. Frieder, M. C. Mccabe, Integrating structured data and text: a multi-dimensional approach, *Proc. of Information Technology: Coding and Computing, 2000. International Conference on*, vol., no., pp. 264–269, 2000

30. V. Gupta, G.S. Lehal, A survey of text mining techniques and applications. J. Emerg. Technol. Web Intell. **1**(1), 60–76 (2009)

31. R.K. Lomotey, R. Deters, Analytics-as-a-Service framework for terms association mining in unstructured data. Int. J. Bus. Process Integrat. Manag. **7**(1), 49–61 (2014)

32. Y. Gu, C. Kallas, J. Zhang, J. Marx, J. Tjoe, Automatic Patient Search Using Bernoulli Model. in *Proc. of 2013 I.E. International Conference on Healthcare Informatics (ICHI 2013)*, pp. 517–522, Sept 9–11 2013, (Philadelphia, PA, USA, 2013)

33. R. K. Lomotey, R. Deters, Terms extraction from unstructured data silos, 8th International Conference on System of Systems Engineering (SoSE 13), (2013) pp. 19–24, 2–6 June 2013, doi: 10.1109/SYSoSE.2013.6575236

34. T. Scheffer, C. Decomain, S. Wrobel, Mining the Web with active hidden Markov models, ICDM 2001, *Proceedings IEEE International Conference on Data Mining*, vol., no., pp. 645–646, 2001, doi: 10.1109/ICDM.2001.989591

35. S. Mukherjee, S.J. Mitra, Hidden Markov Models, grammars, and biology: a tutorial. J. Bioinform. Comput. Biol. **3**(2), 491–526 (2005)

36. R. K. Lomotey, R. Deters, Data Mining from NoSQL Document-Append Style Storages. *Proc. of the 2014 I.E. International Conference on Web Services (ICWS 2014)*, pp. 385–392, June 27–July 02, 2014, (Anchorage, Alaska, USA, 2014)

37. R. K. Lomotey, R. Deters, RSenter: tool for topics and terms extraction from unstructured data debris. *Proc. of the 2013 I.E. International Congress on Big Data*, pp. 395–402, Santa Clara, California, 27 June–2 July 2013

38. S. Haiduc, G. Bavota, R. Oliveto, A. de Lucia, A. Marcus, Automatic Query Performance Assessment during the Retrieval of Software Artifacts, *Automated Software Engineering 2012 (ASE '12)*, September 3–7, 2012, Essen, Germany

39. A. Balinsky, H. Balinsky, S. Simske, On the Helmholtz Principle for Data Mining, Published by Hewlett-Packard Development Company, L.P. (2010). Available: http://www.hpl.hp.com/techreports/2010/HPL-2010-133.pdf

40. Erlang Programing Language, http://www.erlang.org/

VLAB-C: Collaborative Virtual Laboratory in Cloud Computing and Its Applications

Jianjun Yu, Kejun Dong, and Yihua Zheng

Abstract Scientific Virtual Laboratory (SVL) provides an online research environment for inter-disciplinary e-science applications, where researchers can do remote experimentation, create online chat rooms, share costly equipments and resources that otherwise are available to limited number of users due to constraints on time and geographical distances. Whereas traditional SVL may meet issues like access performance, adaptable, extensible and scalable framework adoption when provided to large number of researchers with "Big Data" processing in CAS (Chinese Academy of Science). "Big Data" system usually includes datasets with sizes beyond the ability of commonly-used software tools to capture, manage, and process the data within a tolerable elapsed time. Cloud computing enables "Big Data" processing of all sizes by delivering massive distributed computing and storage capacity as a transparent and centralized service to different communities of inter-disciplinary scientists, which inspires us to develop a SaaS (Software as a Service) cloud for scientific virtual laboratory named VLAB-C. VLAB-C provides three key features: (1) the ability of high performance on massive data processing and large number of communities' collaboration; (2) elastic computing for collaborative services; (3) extensible open framework for customized service integration through developing the micro-kernel container, the cloud infrastructure, and the open service. We introduce VLAB-C system, its SVL applications, and several experiments on performance, which shows that VLAB-C achieves considerable efficiency with cloud computing technique.

Keywords Cloud computing • Software as a service (SaaS) • Big data • Virtual laboratory

J. Yu • K. Dong (✉) • Y. Zheng
Computer Network Information Center, Chinese Academy of Sciences, Beijing 100190, China
e-mail: yujj@cnic.ac.cn; kevin@cnic.ac.cn; zyhua@cnic.ac.cn

© Springer International Publishing Switzerland 2016   145
P.C.K. Hung (ed.), *Big Data Applications and Use Cases*, International Series
on Computer Entertainment and Media Technology, DOI 10.1007/978-3-319-30146-4_7

1 Introduction

With the development of Internet, and the exceptional increase in computing power, storage capacity and network bandwidth, online collaboration is widely taken place, especially for researchers. At the meantime, the changing scale and scope of experimental science requires a new research paradigm, where researchers can collaborate to each other globally via Scientific Virtual Laboratory (SVL). SVL, in our opinion, offers an online collaborative environment that focuses on a specialized scientific discovery problem comparing to the traditional concept, which essentially helps to utilize the infrastructures (such as scientific equipments and instruments), share scientific datasets, discover correlated resources to assist researchers' scientific discoveries.

Broadly speaking, a SVL should provide features like: (1) independent virtual laboratories while with common collaborative services. For example, astronomers may build their owner pulsar discovery virtual laboratory, and physicists can build a neutron star analysis one sharing the same telescope and storage server; (2) transparent usage of ever-increasing resources, such as computers, storage, equipments; (3) customized discipline-related collaborative services. Traditional work introduces simple yet incomplete one or two features to construct SVL, which is insufficient for researchers to unitize collaborative services or develop customized ones upon the ever-increasing distributed scientific datasets and computing resources transparently. Cloud computing based virtual laboratory [1, 2] is prevailing nowadays since it provides computation, software applications, data management and storage without requiring users to know the location and other details of the underlying infrastructure [3]. Whereas performance issues such as big data processing and large number of communities' collaboration are not further discussed.

In our opinion, SVL is a typical "Big Data" application since the capability of scientific datasets exceeds 2 PB, and the storage capability is over 22 PB. Consequently, it brings the problems of scalable storage and high performance processing when applied for hundreds of SVLs on such large scale of datasets. "Big Data" is high-volume, high-velocity, and/or high-variety information assets that requires new forms of processing to enable enhanced decision making, insight discovery and process optimization [4]. In our opinion, the rise of cloud computing and cloud data stores have been a precursor and facilitator to the emergence of "Big Data", i.e., cloud computing gives the implementations for "Big Data". Whereas "Big Data" would be focus more on the applications issues, such as how to process tremendous datasets on cloud computing techniques. Thus, when we construct "Big Data" applications (scientific virtual laboratories), we would implement them under the cloud computing framework.

In this paper, to support the complete features of SVL while solving "Big Data" issues, such as high performance concurrency, data-intensive processing and extensibility for collaborative resources under the cloud computing framework, we scheme a solution of "Software as a Service" (SaaS) based SVL named VLAB-C.

VLAB-C aims to fill the gap between the requirements of online collaborative services with big data processing and providing different cloud based collaborative services through capsulating distributed, heterogeneous and ever-increasing scientific resources. The main contributions of VLAB-C can be summarized as: (1) We scheme a micro-kernel model for runtime collaborative services of diverse virtual laboratories, which supports elastic computing and promotes resource utilization; (2) We develop a cloud infrastructure for scientific resources integration, and support big data processing and computing, which provides the basic functions for diverse data-intensive processing applications; (3) We release an open service that integrates the common services and develops composed collaborative services to form customized virtual laboratories. VLAB-C intends to achieve high performance on big data processing and large number of communities' collaboration, elastic computing, and scalable open service.

The rest of the paper is organized as follows: In Sect. 2, we discuss related work. Section 3 gives several supported collaboration patterns in scientific virtual laboratory. Section 4 introduces our previous scientific virtual laboratory solution VLAB. Section 5 provides the cloud computing based VLAB-C, and introduces its core components. Section 6 presents the VLAB-C system and its applications. Section 7 shows our experiment results. Finally, we conclude and discuss some future work.

2   Related Work

We hope to construct a cloud based SVL for scientific collaboration since most of big data applications are developed with cloud computing technique. Cloud based SVL in nature helps to realize information interaction and knowledge sharing among researchers with the ability of big data processing and large number of communities' collaboration through integrating computing, storage and equipment resources, and therefore facilitate online scientific activities. In this paper, we would separate these work into two parts: virtual laboratory and cloud computing/big data. Researchers have done much work in these fields.

2.1   Virtual Laboratory

From the point of view of researchers, virtual laboratory is composed of a series of collaborative services, which utilizes the cyber-infrastructure to support world wide range collaboration through supplying resource integration and knowledge sharing, applying new Internet technologies like collaborative editing, remote control, computing simulation, instant message, to form cross-disciplines, cross-organizations online scientific communities. Projects, like NSF Cyberinfrastructure [5], UK e-Science [6], and CAS informatization plan [7], all aim to provide such cyber-infrastructure supporting online collaborative research. These projects present big picture of the cyber-infrastructure, and the sub-systems of them give in-depth analysis and discussion on specific technical issues, such as collaborative virtual laboratory, cloud computing, and so on. TeraGrid Science Gateway [8] is a Web or application portal which provided access to tools customized to meet the needs of a specific community of researchers and is connected to TeraGrid resources. VRE (Virtual Research Environment) [9] aimed to comprise digital infrastructure and services for scientists with huge amounts of data. ViroLab [10] provided a common space for planning, building, improving and performing experiments by different groups of users, which enables access to distributed, heterogeneous data resources, computational resources in Grid systems, clusters and standalone computers. Josep et al. [11] presented an integrated structure for a virtual laboratory consisting on nine resources divided into pedagogical, human, and technological factors. Jara et al. [12] provided a new tool which integrated virtual laboratories inside a synchronous collaborative e-learning framework. Disciplinary efforts are also presented, such as chemistry concept learning [13], medical image analysis [14] planetary materials [15] and so on. At the meantime, virtual laboratory systems are widely used in computer supported collaborative work and learning areas, such as GIMOLOUS [16], ISIlab [17], DARE [18], for examples.

In our opinion, these efforts emphasize more on the software design of the middleware for teamwork and community collaboration. Whereas our work focuses more on Internet collaboration and aims to offer big data processing and large number of scientific communities' collaboration based on the cyber-infrastructure.

2.2 Cloud Computing/Big Data

Cloud computing is a model for enabling convenient, on-demand network access to a shared pool of configurable computing resources that can be rapidly provisioned and released with minimal management effort or service provider interaction [19].

Dittrich and Quian-Ruiz [20] gave a tutorial for big data processing on Hadoop Map-Reduce that focused on different data management techniques, going from job optimization to physical data organization like data layouts and indexes. Zhang and Zhou [21] presented seven architectural principles and derived ten interconnected architectural modules to form a reusable and customizable cloud computing open architecture. De Assuno et al. [22] investigated six scheduling strategies that considered the use of resources from the cloud, to understand how these strategies achieved a balance between performance and usage cost, and how much they improved the requests' response times. Matthews et al. [23] proposed Virtual Machine Contracts (VMCs), a platform independent way of automating the communication and management of such requirements. Also the cloud computing techniques are applied into many scientific area, like biomedical information sharing [24], 3D GIS data processing [25], and cyber-physical systems [26]. Most of work focus on cloud computing technique, and they should be optimized and customized for scientific virtual laboratory.

Nowadays, converting traditional software packages to cloud based services is quite prevailing. There are many papers addressing various issues related to converting legacy systems to cloud based services from the perspective of applications [27], data [28, 29], service [30], and network [31]. In our opinion, these work support the same pictures of our scenarios, whereas we focus on migrating scientific virtual laboratory to cloud services, and concentrate on big data processing applications.

As cloud computing has become a research hotspot among modern technologies, researchers pay more attentions to its applications for virtual laboratory. EduCloud [2] gave a systematic evaluation of different types of cloud technologies in an advanced course on network overlays. Zhang et al. [32] provided virtual basic laboratory and experiment teaching resources platform based on cloud computing to promote college information teaching. Also cloud computing based virtual laboratories are presented in [33–35]. Until now the research applying cloud computing to SVL is not significantly reported. On the one hand, most of solutions are based on the virtual machine, and provide Paas (Platform as a Service) or IaaS (Infrastructure as a Service) architecture.

In this paper, we aim to provide a SaaS based SVL to integrate heterogeneous and distributed scientific dataset while keeping the best performance. Simmhan et al. [36] and Erickson et al. [37] proposed a similar idea to our model. Simmhan et al. [36] compared and contrasted science application and data valet workflows through exemplar e-Science projects to drive shared and unique requirements for scientific workflows across diverse users in a Science Cloud. Erickson et al. [36] provided a cloud-based platform that inverted the traditional application-content relationship enabling users to rapidly build customized solutions around their content items. Different from these solutions, VLAB-C focuses more on how to integrate distributed and heterogeneous resources, transform our previous collaborative software VLAB to SaaS services, and get the best performance of big data processing and large number of scientific communities' collaboration based on cloud computing technique.

3 Supported Collaboration Patterns

The cloud based scientific virtual laboratory aims to support big data processing along with traditional collaborative services, such as collaborative editing, instant message service, video conference, and so on. In addition to the common services, the cloud based scientific virtual laboratory should provide open service to support customized collaborative services, i.e., disciplinary related services, such as astronomy, geography, biology big data processing. We then give several typical supported collaboration patterns for the scientific virtual laboratory.

3.1 Collaborative Editing

Collaborative editing is the practice of groups producing works together through individual contributions which would be written by more than one person. People may discuss what they are going to write before they start, and discuss what they have written after they finish each draft they write. Effective choices in group awareness, participation, and coordination are critical to successful collaborative writing outcomes.

Comparing to the traditional collaborative editing, the cloud based collaborative editing supports transparent resource utilization, and elastic computing when more people involve in the current group.

3.2 Video Conference

Video conference brings researchers together in meetings, discussions, conferences, live events, consultations, coaching and of course casual community chat. Web based video conference provides researchers together instantly and without travel costs and time loss. These benefits open a wide range of new specifical opportunities for researchers in different cities or institutes.

Comparing to the traditional video conference, the cloud based video conference develops a universal portal to create an online conference immediately. Also researchers can select those online people easily for current conference group.

3.3 Cloud-Based File Storage

It's important to reserve all research achievements, including the critical data, documents, and wilderness photographs for scientists. Now, they can be securely backed up to the cloud, with the highest level of encryption.

Cloud-based file storage offers the feature for researchers that all files can only be read, opened or retrieved, by connecting to the secure cloud backup space through their own private login. Also they are encouraged to back up as many files as they want. Cloud-based file storage doesn't limit the amount of storage space since our upgrades are always available to expand the cloud file storage space as needed. Cloud-based file storage should be designed to be easy to use, regardless of how basic or advanced researchers' computer skills are. Finally the cloud-based file storage should allow accessing the backed up files from any computer with an Internet connection, at any time, from anywhere in the world.

This is a new feature for scientific virtual laboratory, which can be realized with the cloud infrastructure.

3.4   Virtual Collaborative Environment

Virtual collaborative environment provides a universal platform for collaborative services. We exploit virtual collaborative environment for scientific research aiming at providing the users with a much enjoyable experience while doing research online. In all cases the users can join a virtual world and then manipulate and interact with the scientific apparatus as in the real world.

In our opinion, cloud based virtual collaborative environment needs privacy, high performance on concurrency while reducing resource waste. We need to design a new architecture to accommodate these features.

3.5   Big Data Processing

Big data processing provides opportunities to discover deeper, more complete scientific achievements insights through the analysis and visualization of significant volumes of rapidly changing structured and unstructured scientific data. Traditional data-intensive processing systems struggle to analyze big data because they were designed for the analysis of relatively small amounts of structured data and simply cannot easily analyze unstructured data, large data sets or data sources that change quickly.

Big data processing originates with disciplinary researchers who had the need to index and analyze large volumes of scientific datasets, for example, the astronomical fit files. In our opinion, big data processing would mainly use the cloud infrastructure for scalable storage, distributed computing.

3.6   Customized Service

It's difficult to build a scientific virtual laboratory for all disciplinary researchers. Different researchers have their owner processing approaches along with the common collaborative services. Both the granularity and the convenience of the interfaces for customized service should be designed carefully when we provide an open service for all disciplinary researchers.

4   Scientific Virtual Laboratory

As described above, SVL is an online research environment for inter-disciplinary e-science applications where researchers can collaborate to each other and share resources.

Our previous version of SVL is basically a set of collaborative services to support online research for disciplinary scientific communities named VLAB, which neglects the differences of diverse scientific research tasks and requirements, and deploys almost the same software packages for different communities for their collaborative activities and scientific research purposes.

4.1 VLAB Architecture for Virtual Laboratory

VLAB develops an integrated collaboration environment to support virtual laboratory applications. The resources are generated or from other disciplinary e-Science applications, which is an information island and cannot be shared to each other conveniently. Accordingly, these resources are integrated by the Resource&Service component of VLAB separately. This component also includes several plugins that provide pipelines encapsulating different resources, like computing resources plugin, AV plugin, device plugin, database plugin, digital library plugin and others. It also provides a scientific workflow upon these resources that can easily draft complex business logic and consume resources to generate innovative scientific knowledge. To integrate, share and manage massive and distributed resources, VLAB also builds three core toolkits for online collaboration including activity collaboration toolkit, instant message toolkit, and document collaboration toolkit. For front-end researchers, VLAB offers a virtual laboratory console to help them to access, organize and manage resources easily and quickly (Fig. 1).

We developed VLAB software since 2007, and the latest version is 3.0. Until to now, we have deployed more than 100 VLAB packages in different institutes or collaborative teams in CAS. There are more than 12,000 active users in these systems.

4.2 The Obstacles of Current VLAB

Software package based VLAB achieves great success for knowledge sharing in a relatively small community since it can be customized with puglin framework, whereas when this architecture is applied to more communities with big data processing, especially for all researchers in CAS, it would meet obstacles if we continue to use current architecture. These obstacles include:

1) How to support ever-increasing resource integration. CAS has built a scientific database with the capability of 22 PB storage that is distributed in nine cities in China, such as Beijing, Shanghai, Guangzhou. Moreover, the capability of storage is ever-increasing, and more cities would involve in. VLAB architecture doesn't consider the issues of the scalability and extendibility for "Big Data"

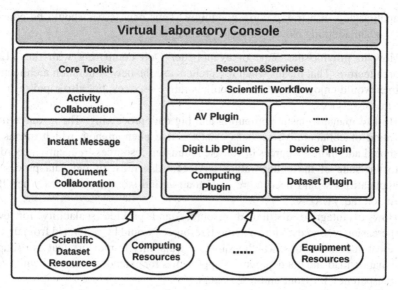

Fig. 1 VLAB architecture for virtual laboratory. We need to deploy VLAB software for each newly-created virtual laboratory since it's a software package

integration, which results in the difficulty supporting transparent utilization of back-end massive and distributed resources.

2) How to support online collaboration. When developing VLAB system for 100+ institutes, 100,000+ researchers, and even more communities in CAS, we need to deploy thousands of software suites theoretically. That would waste effort of duplication and involve painstaking maintenance. We need a universal cyber-infrastructure for collaborative services despite of disciplinary differences.

3) How to develop customized services. As for specialized applications, VLAB meets obstacles to support third-party applications, which prevents disciplinary researchers to develop their own customized applications and promote the quality of collaborative services.

To solve the issues of current architecture and offer new features, we adopt Software-as-a-Service (SaaS) and cloud computing technique to develop the new generation collaborative cloud services for virtual laboratory.

5 Cloud Based VLAB-C

Ideally, cloud computing technique should easily solve the issues of VLAB architecture through its inherent nature. Whereas, considering that all researchers would utilize the centralized virtual laboratory portal to collaborate with each other, it would bring new issues like one point of failure, poor performance with parallel computing and web traffic correspondingly. Thus new issues should be concentrated when adopting cloud computing technique:

1) How to provide the same or even better QoS comparing with the VLAB architecture. That means when researchers use the new-generation architecture, they would enjoy not only more collaborative services, but also rapid response time of services.
2) How to manage elastic computing and big data processing. The resource utilization of collaborative services exist the tide phenomenon, which means we should add more resources or release redundant resources frequently according to the state of the collaborative services. Also most of bid data processing applications would need more computation and storage resources when they run on the VLAB-C.
3) How to integrate distributed resources and provide scalability for ever-increasing resources. More and more resources would be generated from diverse research communities, which requires a scalability framework that can support dynamic load and hot deployment approaches for extended resources while keep transparency for front-end researchers.

5.1   Overview of VLAB-C Architecture

In this section, we introduce cloud based VLAB-C that tries to solve the issues described above, and present its core components.

We develop the VLAB-C architecture based on cloud computing and Web services techniques. Different from the VLAB architecture, the new architecture would integrate services from the lower component and provide restful Web services interfaces to the upper component, which helps to promote scalability and deliver a loose-coupled architecture.

We integrate and encapsulate all kinds of resources into a universal resource pool, including scientific datasets, virtual machines, distributed storage, equipments, and online applications. These resources would be shared to all researchers from diverse virtual laboratories with agreed permissions. The cloud infrastructure supports distributed resources integration based on the concept of cloud computing, helps to promote the performance of big data processing and parallel computing, and provides elastic computing for collaborative services. We realize a resource pool to integrate distributed resources and provide scalability for ever-increasing resources. The metadata of all resources are stored in a heap list and classified with different types, e.g. computing resources, storage resources. The resource pool would check the metadata in the heap list, release available resources to the collaborative services, and label them as "unavailable" for the monopolized resources or add the consumption count for the shared resources at runtime. The micro-kernel runtime container delivers essential elements for collaborative services based on the light-weighted micro-kernel model, which is composed of

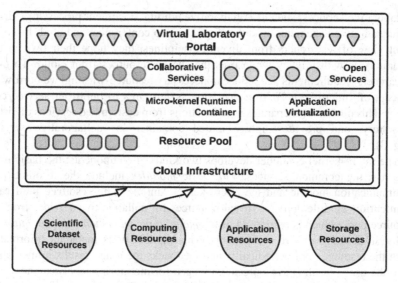

Fig. 2 Cloud computing based architecture of VLAB-C with restful Web services interfaces

several kernel services and communication protocols. The application virtualization offers disciplinary-oriented processing tools for upper level collaborative services. We also develop diverse disciplinary collaborative services, such as the protein visualization service, the astronomy FITS (Flexible Image Transport System) file processing service, and the atmospheric monitoring service. The open service provides SDK to access the cloud infrastructure and the scientific resources through a series of encapsulated interfaces. Finally we present different collaborative services and provide customized portal for diverse disciplinary communities (Fig. 2).

The cloud based architecture of VLAB-C would solve issues that exist in the current architecture and support new features for massive disciplinary communities while improve significant efficiency. These features includes: (1) distributed and massive resource integration and processing through the cloud infrastructure and the resource pool; (2) virtual resource utilization and collaborative service composition through the micro-kernel container; (3) scalability and loose-coupled architecture through the open service. We then introduce these core components in the new architecture.

5.2   Micro-kernel Container for Collaborative Service

The vision of micro-kernel container is to provide the independence of each front-end virtual laboratory for different communities while keep considerable performance. In the meantime, most of virtual laboratories have almost the same collaborative services, such as collaborative editing, document processing, virtual organization management, instant message, video conference, and et al. From the point view of researchers from diverse disciplines, they hope their own virtual laboratory is with privacy while uses the shared resources from cloud. To meet researchers' requirements and reduce unnecessary resource-wasting, we borrow the concept of "micro-kernel" from operation system area to build our service container. This new model separates core functions from customized services of virtual laboratory, and provides light-weighted container for collaborative services (Fig. 3).

The micro-kernel container develops two kinds of components: the basic modules and the common services. *The basic modules* include the resource pool communication module and the micro-kernel runtime. **The resource pool communication module** delivers virtual resources for collaborative services from the resource pool, which is composed of the *metadata management*, *state monitoring*, and *resource dispatching* components. This module pulls metadata information from the resource pool periodically, and feedbacks the usage results immediately. Also the usage results of resources are logged for monitoring, analysis and scheduling. It provides several scheduling policies, such as FIFO (First In First Out), SJF (Shortest Job First), priority based scheduling, to minimize resource starvation and ensure fairness amongst the collaborative services when competing resources.

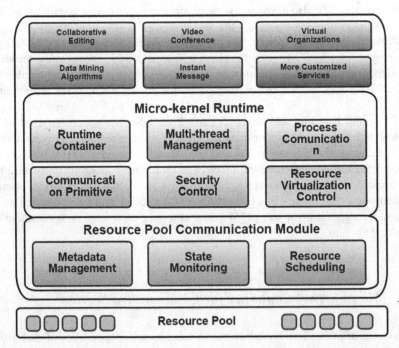

Fig. 3 The micro-kernel container for collaborative services, which includes basic modules and core collaborative services to assure light-weight and extendibility

The micro-kernel runtime plays a key role of coordinator between virtual resources and collaborative services. **The multi-thread management** provides concurrency control for a collaborative service. Considering that most of resources cannot be consumed in a parallel mode, such as updating and querying a record in a distributed database simultaneously, we design a concurrency lock for those shared resources to assure the maximum concurrency on a single resource for more collaborative services. **The process communication** interchanges processing results of different collaborative services through a message queue. **The container management** delivers the basic functions to start, stop, or restart a specialized collaborative service. **The communication primitive** supports the asynchronous mechanism allowing different processes to communicate with each other, by sending messages. It also interacts the resource pool, and provides the API to collaborative services or other components. **The security control** keeps information safety for different processes and collaborative services, assuring that users can only operate permitted resources with individual privilege. **The resource virtualization control** allows administrators to build proper copies of virtual resources, such as running 20 collaborative services in one virtual machine.

The micro-kernel container also provides several common collaborative services, including collaborative editing, map-reduce supported data mining algorithms (such as Support Vector Machine, Naive Bayes, K-Nearest Neighbors, Collaborative Filtering, and et al.), instant message, video conference and virtual organization. These common services are pre-installed and can be utilized by all virtual laboratories. Other customized collaborative services can be deployed with standardized API provided by the micro-kernel container.

5.3   The Cloud Infrastructure

The cloud infrastructure enables distributed resources' management and supports elastic computing while promotes the performance of the virtual laboratories with big data processing and large scale of collaboration.

The cloud infrastructure builds a cloud computing platform including distributed storage, parallel computing, big memory, which helps programmers to develop and deploy their owner collaborative services on the cloud platform without the complexity of managing the underlying hardware and software resources. Moreover, the cloud infrastructure offers the elastic computing through dispatching underlying computer and storage resources automatically to meet application demands such that researchers from diverse disciplines do not have to schedule resources manually.

As shown in Fig. 4, The cloud infrastructure delivers several components based on Hadoop[1]:

---

[1] http://hadoop.apache.org

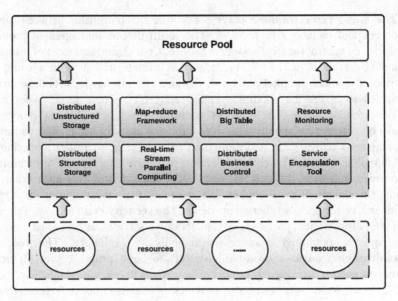

Fig. 4 The cloud infrastructure for scientific virtual laboratory

- *The distributed structured storage*, which constructs a structured storage service for massive scientific datasets expressed as key/value pairs. We build a mongodb[2] cluster for these kinds of datasets that supports PB scale storage and scalability. The cluster supports master/salve mode with asynchronous replication. A master can have multiple slaves. Slaves are able to accept other slaves connections in a graph-like structure.
- *The distributed unstructured storage*, which constructs an unstructured storage service for files that cannot be expressed as key/value pairs such as images, documents and videos. We build a Hadoop HDFS (Hadoop Distributed File System) based storage system, where massive files are cached and partitioned into HDFS according to different policies and usage purposes. For example, if we store a file with size 128 GB into HDFS. This file would be compressed firstly, and then inserted as a "SequenceFile" (a storage format of HDFS) into HDFS, which would be split into 2000 blocks (64 MB a block in default) and inserted into data nodes in HDFS cluster.
- *The map-reduce framework*, which supports parallel scientific data processing upon distributed computing resources, and is developed with the MapReduce component.
- *The real-time stream parallel computing framework*. There exist applications that are time sensitive, and the processing results need to be published

---

[2] http://www.mongodb.org

immediately. We develop the real-time stream parallel computing component to support data steam processing with Twitter Storm.[3]

- *The distributed big table*, which combines distributed computers to form a federated memory with memcached.[4] It would support memory based massive storage for high performance applications.
- *The distributed business control*, which locks the related resources for the separated applications and keeps the atomicity and safety for parallel access.
- *The service encapsulation tool*, which encapsulates initial resources, assembles atomic services to provide specified services.
- *The resource monitoring*, which monitors the status of each resources and components. If the resources for a collaborative service exhausts and results in poor performance, it will provide more resources, such as computing resources to assure the enhanced performance for the current service.

5.4 Open Service

When a group of researchers decide to make their virtual laboratory more specialized for their research purpose, i.e. develop customized collaborative services for their research tasks, they would use restful Web services interfaces provided by the open service module to test and deploy customized collaborative services, which can access required resources and reuse the cloud infrastructure provided by VLAB-C.

Before delivering open interfaces to researchers, VLAB-C provides a universal user authentication mechanism to manage different users' and roles' privileges, which includes a SSO (Single Sign On) passport center and identify federation to attract scientific applications that would facilitate end users to log in once and gain access to all VLAB-C services via their emails.

5.4.1 Universal User Authentication

The universal user authentication framework aims to provide researchers to access and share resources among SVLs, whereas different SVLs has owner user management systems currently since most of them has run for a long time. We should make more efforts to support SSO and identify federation with only one account.

The CSTNET passport[5] is a universal passport for all applications developed by VLAB-C. CSTNET Passport is realized with OAuth 2.0 protocol.[6] OAuth is an

---

[3] http://storm-project.net
[4] http://memcached.org
[5] http://passport.escience.cn
[6] http://oauth.net

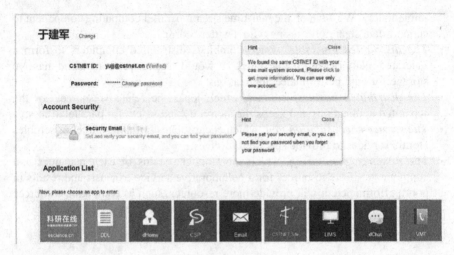

Fig. 5 CSTNET Passport UI from passport.escience.cn

open protocol to allow secure authorization in a simple and standard method from web, mobile and desktop applications, which enables a third-party application to obtain limited access to an HTTP service, either on behalf of a resource owner by orchestrating an approval interaction between the resource owner and the HTTP service, or by allowing the third-party application to obtain access on its own behalf. With CSTNET passport, all applications can not only reduce miscellaneous and toilsome effort on developing user management systems, but also share user resources from CSTNET passport, which has 20,000 users and integrate other OAuth passport services (e.g. Sina Weibo[7]) nowadays. As shown in Fig. 5, when a researcher uses his/her unique email account to access VLAB-C, he/she can enjoy all services without relogin again.

If a new SVL (e.g. SVL4) has not built its user management system, it can use standard OAuth protocol or interfaces provided by CSTNET Passport to make this passport as its user management system. If a SVL has built its own user management system, or share user information with other SVLs, such as SVL5–SVL7. They need to deploy SP component of Shibboleth[8] implements, develop a new IDP (IDP B in Fig. 6), and built themselves as SPs. In this scenario, We also should develop CSTNET passport as another IDP (IDP A). Thus a standard identify federation would be formed to complete user authentication connecting users to applications between IDPs, including SP, IDP, and DS (Discovery Service). For example, when users from a IDP want to access resources protected by other IDPs (e.g. user in SVL7 wants to access resources in SVL1), it will take ten steps to finish authentication and acquire restricted resources as described in Fig. 7: (1) The user starts by attempting to access the protected resource in SVL1. (2) If the user has an

---

[7] http://weibo.com
[8] http://shibboleth.net

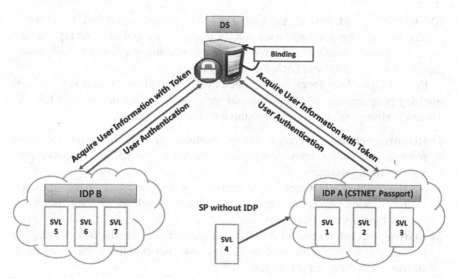

Fig. 6 A universal user authentication framework

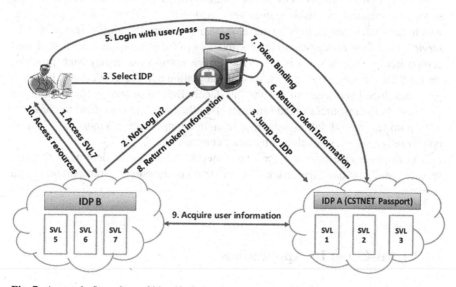

Fig. 7 A sample flow chart of identify federation

active session, then directs to the resources; if not, directs he/she to the DS. (3) The user selects which IDP he/she would log in. (4) Directs the user to the IDP A. (5) When the user arrives at IDP A, it checks to see if the user has an existing session. (6) IDP A authenticates and returns auth token. (7) Binding user token to

IDP B. (8) After identifying the user, DS sends auth token to SVL7. (9) SVL7 validates the response, creates a session for the user, and makes some information retrieved from the response. (10) With user's information, the resource will service the user's request and send back the requested data.

Restful Open Interfaces. Restful open interfaces deliver an open service SDK inspiring programmers to enjoy common services and core function of VLAB-C. These interfaces are categorized into three types:

1) **Resource-related interfaces**. These interfaces provide functions to access resources, including physical resources, virtual resources, and resource pool with allowed privileges.
2) **Service-related interfaces**. These interfaces presents methods to manage common collaborative services or customized ones, such as binding, invoking, composition operations on services.
3) **System-level interfaces**. VLAB-C offers Web services interfaces for third-party to utilize inner functions, such as the micro-kernel container, the cloud infrastructure with allowed privileges.

Also the open service provides several tools to help better building discipline-oriented virtual laboratory. *The service management* provides the functions like service description, publishing, discovery, matching, versioning and monitoring, which facilitates researchers to develop their own collaborative services. *The service workflow management* offers the functions to manage workflow based composited collaborative services. *The service integration framework* provides restful Web services interfaces for service integration and encapsulation. The third-party developed services can use the interface&SDK to interact with the runtime container or the resources in the lower levels. When researchers intend to construct a customized virtual laboratory, they can integrate diverse kinds of scientific collaborative services developed by other comminutes.

The open service provides the open interfaces helping to deploy third party services and invoke the back-end distributed resources transparently and automatically.

6   VLAB-C and Its Applications

We develop VLAB-C with the new architecture and deploy it at www.escience.cn, which is an open environment for researchers in CAS to select standard collaborative services or develop customized ones to form their own virtual laboratories. With VLAB-C, researchers could build virtual communities for online collaboration based on discipline-oriented virtual laboratories.

6.1   VLAB-C Overview

We integrate over 2 PB scientific datasets distributed in the institutes at CAS, 1024 computers, 22 PB data storage, thousands of devices, and about 30 collaborative services into the cloud infrastructure. We offer a cluster for each virtual laboratory, which is allocated with 8 or 16 virtual machines, 1 TB storage, and moreover, it can apply for more shared resources if standard ones are not enough. VLAB-C develops a universal portal for all virtual laboratories to access back-end resources through the resource pool.

To better use the front-end collaborative services, we also deliver several applications through integrating the basic collaborative services, such as "cloud storage", "cloud conference", "scientist homepage", and "laboratory management" (Fig. 8).

"*cloud storage*" provides limitless storage for scientific datasets and files like Dropbox. "*cloud conference*" helps to organize academic conference and paper review like EasyChair. "*scientist homepage*" is a social network system facilitating researchers to discover persons with the same research interests like Microsoft Renlifang.[9] "*laboratory management*" is a laboratory information system delivering collaborative communication between devices and researchers.

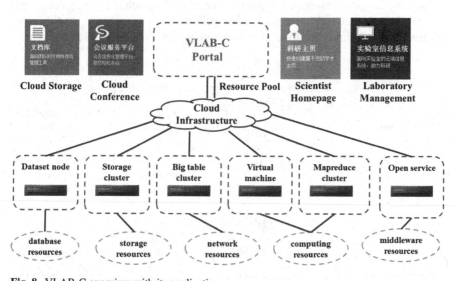

Fig. 8 VLAB-C overview with its applications

---

[9] http://renlifang.msra.cn

6.2 Discipline-Oriented Virtual Laboratories

The collaborative services based virtual laboratory at VLAB-C has been applied into many disciplines, such as astronomy, geography, biology, HEP (High Energy Physics), and etc. We take several typical virtual laboratories for examples.

6.2.1 Research Interest Learning Virtual Laboratory

In CAS, there are more than 100,000 researchers from different disciplines, moreover, they have different user interests. How to capture user interest, thus find those researchers with common interests, and recommend related papers or other scientific research productions to them is a primary mission of "scientist homepage".

Actually, the original research productions are so tremendous to run the user interest learning model in one machine. Moreover, researchers would update their scientific research productions frequently and thus bring the change of user interest. In this paper, we decide to use the Hadoop Map-Reduce framework to run the learning model to acquire the final user interest.

As shown in Fig. 9, to capture the user interest, we take three steps to get the final results.

1) We first crawl researchers' original scientific research productions, such as papers, projects, patent, monographs, and et al. For each crawler, we dispatch 10~50 sub-crawlers to acquire more original data since most portals have limitation of crawlers. Up to now, we have gotten over 3,145,280 researchers,

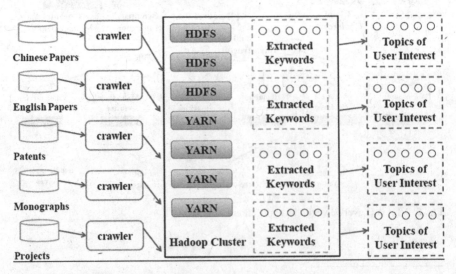

Fig. 9 Research interest learning model on Map-Reduce framework

Table 1 The performance of learning model with Map-Reduce and without Map-Reduce framework

Approaches	100 Iterations (h)	200 Iterations (h)	500 Iterations (h)	1000 Iterations (h)
LDA with Map-Reduce	409	492	579	928
LDA without Map-Reduce	2037	3856	4423	8875

3,867,348 Chinese papers, 15,437,225 English papers, 10,256 projects, 322,789 patents, 8967 monographs.

2) When the datasets are crawled, the original information would be generated as HDFS blocks, and the keywords would be splitted to represent current user's scientific research productions.

3) We use Mahout LDA tools to learn latent topics from the keywords. It's time-consuming activity to learn latent topics. As we observed, most of researchers may concern few fields, which inspires us set the number of topics as 1–5. Also the number of iterations in LDA model would also affect the computation efficiency. More iteration would bring more accuracy, and also result in more computation time as shown in Table 1. In our scenario, 200 iterations would give the best balance between the accuracy and the computation time, so we decide to set the number of LDA iterations as 200.

We run this learning model in a Hadoop cluster with ten PC servers. We give a preliminary comparison of the efficiency for the learning model with Map-Reduce and without Map-Reduce framework.

With current dataset, we need about 20 days to get the final learning results, which would help to capture the user interest more accurately.

6.2.2   Transportation Virtual Laboratory

Learning transportation patterns of city, especially big city like Beijing, is important for traffic planning, cutting down traffic jams and pollution. Usually the transportation patterns are learned through GPS (Global Positioning System) data from various independent sources, especially from floating car, mobile phone, bus, metro in and around the city (Fig. 10).

The transportation virtual laboratory provides distributed dataset storage, parallel computing through the cloud infrastructure. The original traffic data with different formats would firstly be pre-processed to a universal structural type. Then these datasets are cached and compressed into HDFS block files or HBase key-value pairs. In this virtual laboratory, there exist 100,000 taxis in Beijing, and each taxi would generate one records (about 160 Bytes) for 10 s, whereas we would store all data from all taxis as one file for each day to the distributed massive storage, so we cache a 128 GB file for each day and then store into HDFS, or

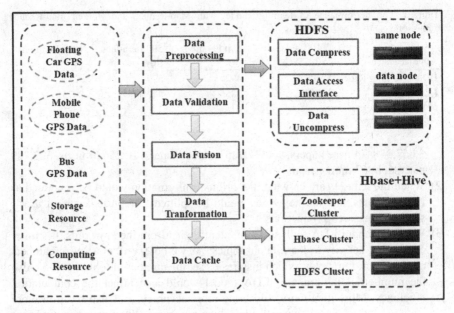

Fig. 10 The architecture of transportation virtual laboratory

864,000,000 records to Hbase. In HDFS storage, the file would be compressed firstly, and then inserted as a "SequenceFile" (a storage format of HDFS) into HDFS, which would be split into 2060 blocks (64 MB a block) and inserted into data nodes in HDFS cluster. In Hbase storage, each record would be indexed with "datatype_taxiid_time" for complete query because many mining applications require to acquire all traffic data of a specialized taxi, whereas it's difficult to meet this kind of need when we store them as a file in HDFS. Certainly we index more columns in Hive table for extended mining applications, such as current position, current velocity, current direction of the taxi.

We should emphasize that the mining algorithms are data-insensitive, which means map function can read each record randomly and doesn't change the final result. The transportation virtual laboratory presents several mining algorithms for transportation patterns discovery based on map-reduce framework, such as traffic jams detection, traffic accident detection, outlier detection, route planning, transportation investment decision.

6.2.3 Economy Virtual Laboratory

The impact on economic development is enormous in economic cycle, therefore how to set up a monitoring system of economic developments effectively becomes an important goal for macro economy. They hope to be provided a visualized interface without considering the technical details, such as how to store massive datasets, how to build up the correlation between datasets and figures, and data visualization.

Economy virtual laboratory offers a cloud based monitoring service, which allow scientists upload owner economical datasets into "cloud storage", select economic indicators in advance, analyze the statistical materials by statistics, draw economic climates figures or GIS based ones without involvement of pro-grammers. With the help of economy virtual laboratory, economists can obtain economical status and tendency in the future fully, accurately and promptly, carry on macro economic situation analysis, measure prosperous circulation, which enables them not only to be aware of the pulse of economical operation in time accurately, but also make judgments on the developing trend in the future.

6.3 Experience Learned from VLAB-C

When developing diverse kinds of virtual laboratories on VLAB-C, we conclude several principles as follows:

1) The open service with Web services interfaces is necessary since most of virtual laboratories need common services, such as user passport service, data access service, virtual machine service, and so on. Different developers select and integrate needed services to compose their own virtual laboratories.
2) Micro-kernel model would help to reduce resource consumption and promote service performance. Most of researchers would collaborate together in a short time, then these virtual laboratories are in idle state for a long time; Most of big data processing applications adopt intensive computation models. These requirements inspire us to develop the micro-kernel container that includes only those needed functions. When the applications need more resources, such as computation, storage resources, we just dispatch more micro-kernel con-tainers for them. Consequently, when they are in idle state, redundant micro-kernel containers would be released.
3) Different big data applications should adopt different storage models for flexible access. Most of applications would choose HDFS blocks to store their original datasets. If they want to index more keys and promote query efficiency with more fields on Hive, they should store the original datasets in HBase.
4) The efficiency of Hadoop for Map-Reduce computation needs to be promoted since Hadoop jobs run on disk. We plan to run existing jobs on Spark platform.[10] Spark can run programs up to 100+ faster than Hadoop MapReduce in memory, or 10+ faster on disk.
5) It's a challenge for researchers to develop their owner virtual laboratories. Most of virtual laboratories customized by users can only integrate those common and

---

[10] http://spark.apache.org

simple services, such as user passport service. They need more time and technical support for complex service integration. On the one hand, we should make the interfaces of the service easy to use, on the other hand, we need to give more training for users.

7 Experimental Evaluation

Generally speaking, it's complicated to evaluate the performance of VLAB-C since it's a portal for all virtual laboratories. Whereas we would measure the performance of the cloud infrastructure, and the efficiency of the virtual laboratory for scientific collaboration, since these metrics would reflect the overall performance of VLAB-C.

The experimental environment is constructed with an infrastructure that has 512 virtual machines (each machine has 1-core processor, 16 GB memory, 1 TB disk), 400 TB distributed storage, 200 TB scientific dataset (covering over 100 disciplines, such as HEP, astronomical, traffic, economical datasets), 30 collaborative services. We develop a cloud infrastructure to integrate these resources and provide universal interfaces for access. We construct 1000 virtual laboratories based on the micro-kernel container selecting ten collaborative services randomly. We repeat each experiment with 100 times to calculate the average results.

7.1 Performance of Cloud Infrastructure

The cloud infrastructure may meet I/O bottlenecks since most of applications are data-intensive and it's a resource universal interface for collaborative services. i.e. the throughput performance of the cloud infrastructure is the most important metrics when massive data processing tasks arrive. As we know, different storage format would influence the final throughput efficiency; therefore we make the evaluation with structured datasets and unstructured ones separately considering the factor of virtual machine and the number of data copies.

As for structured datasets, we present the experiment on the writing performance of the cloud infrastructure with data servers ranging from 1 to 25 with increment of 5 (data copies are 3). We collect 100,000 records (each record is with the size of 136 Bytes) each time, and then make batch insert into the structured storage. The writing performance is shown in the left side of Fig. 11. We can find that the writing speed is about 12,000 records per second for a sole server and maximum value 35,000 for the cluster. The limitation of writing is caused by two reasons: (1) the I/O throughput limitation of mongodb which needs build more indexes when massive structured records are inserted; (2) the resource pool which is a bottleneck since it's a universal interface for lower-level resources and upper-level services. Therefore,

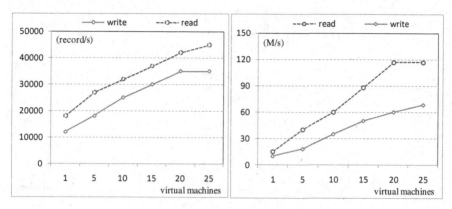

Fig. 11 I/O throughput for the massive storage with three data copies

we build the structural storage with 21 virtual machines (one for query, and others for storage).

In the meantime, the writing speed of the unstructured storage would continuously increase when we add more virtual machines. This is because we utilize standard HDFS components to store unstructured dataset, which would promote I/O throughput efficiency when more data nodes are involved in. Considering that the unstructured storage with the writing speed 60 MB/s is enough for our applications, we also deploy the HDFS cluster with 21 virtual machines (one for name node, and others for data nodes).

When evaluating the reading performance of the cloud infrastructure, as we observed, the reading speed of both storage would increase until they meet the limitation. We should mention that the reading limitation of unstructured storage is caused by the network bandwidth which is 1000 Mb/s in our experimental environment.

As we all know, cloud based storage would reserve multiple backup copies to ensure redundancy, which also affects the performance. We construct unstructured and structured storage separately with 21 virtual machines and with the data copies ranging from 1 to 5 with increment of 1. The I/O throughput performance of the structured storage is shown in the left side of Fig. 12. We can find that the reading speed of structured storage is about 11,000 records per second for one copy of data. The more the number of copy is, the faster the reading speed is. The reading speed of the unstructured storage is about 11 MB/s for one copy of data, and also the reading speed would increase when we set more copies. As we observed, when more copies are set, the lower writing speed would achieve. This is because both of two kinds of storage are distributed services, which needs more time to communicate with the data servers when more copies are stored. Considering both the factors of the cost and the performance, we set the number of data copies as 3.

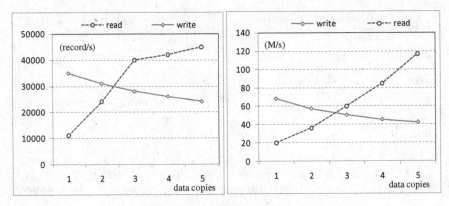

Fig. 12 I/O throughput for the massive storage with fixed count of virtual machines

7.2   The Efficiency of Virtual Laboratory

When analyzing the efficiency of virtual laboratory, we evaluate the count of the micro-kernel container supported in a virtual machine, the concurrency access of virtual laboratory portal, and the count of needed virtual machines for collaborative services. The concurrency access of virtual laboratory portal means how many affordable threads of current web portal simultaneously.

The first problem is how many micro-kernel containers should run in a virtual machine to achieve the best performance. We present this evaluation with a micro-kernel container including only the common collaborative services.

As shown in Fig. 13, we can find that when we add more micro-kernel containers on a virtual machine, we get more concurrency access to the maximum value 100. When we run 11 micro-kernel containers or more on one virtual machine, the value of concurrency access would decrease, this is because the micro-kernel container itself would consume resources though it's light-weighted. To achieve the best performance, we set ten micro-kernel containers on each virtual machine in our new VLAB-C architecture. In the meantime, we provide the experiment with the sole deployment of the VLAB software suite. We can find that the value of concurrency access keeps almost the same or worse when we add more sole containers.

The virtual laboratory portal provides access of all communities that aims to provide the best performance of the concurrency access, which acts as the most important metrics for VLAB-C applications. We give the experiment results on the concurrency access with the virtual machines ranging from 1 to 100 with increment of 10 comparing with the performance of the previous VLAB architecture (Fig. 14).

VLAB-C would get about 100 concurrency access for a single instance. For the previous VLAB system, we would run a VLAB instance on each virtual machine, which gets about 30 concurrency access for each VLAB system. When we add more virtual machines for the virtual laboratories, the concurrency access of VLAB-C would increase more slowly than the linear rate, this is because that

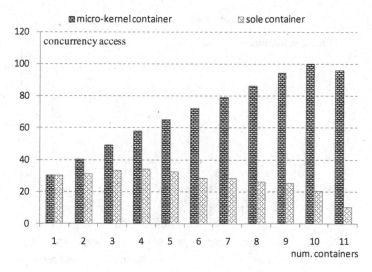

Fig. 13 The performance of the micro-kernel container that includes the common collaborative services

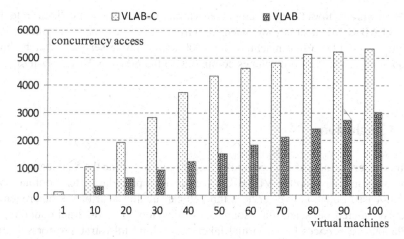

Fig. 14 The concurrency access of VLAB-C and VLAB

when more users collaborate via virtual laboratories, the micro-kernel container and the resources would reach their best affordable performance for services.

To evaluate the number of needed virtual machines supporting collaborative services, we set the same execute time for each service, and evaluate the needed virtual machines for different collaborative services. For simplicity, we select the collaborative editing (100 users edit ten different web pages) as the testing collaborative service.

As shown in Fig. 15, we need about 33 virtual machines for 100 collaborative services, and 330 virtual machines for 1000 collaborative services for the VLAB

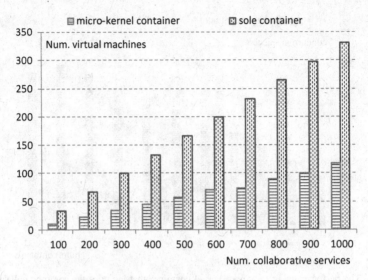

Fig. 15 The virtual machines needed for collaborative services

system, which shows the requirements of virtual machines with the linear rate. For the VLAB-C architecture, we need 10 virtual machines for 100 collaborative services, and 117 virtual machines for 1000 collaborative services, which shows that we need less virtual machines comparing to the previous VLAB system.

8 Conclusions

In this paper, we adopt cloud computing technique to scheme the SaaS based virtual laboratory and develop the VLAB-C system, which provides different cloud computing based collaborative services through capsulating distributed, heterogenous and ever-increasing scientific resources. We develop a micro-kernel container for collaborative services based virtual laboratory, cloud infrastructure for scientific resources integration supporting elastic computing, and open service model for customized collaborative service. VLAB-C supports high performance of big data processing and large amount of communities' collaboration, elastic computing and scalable open service.

We did experiments on the performance of the cloud infrastructure, and the efficiency of the virtual laboratory for scientific collaboration. The experimental results indicate that our system is suitable for most cases of cloud based collaborative service applications.

Still there are several issues should be solved. The first one is that we should develop more open interfaces for researchers to develop their own collaborative services more easily. The second problem is that we should evaluate the performance of mapreduce parallel algorithms and provide data query interfaces with different granularity. In our future work, we would analyze these issues further and deliver the new version of VLAB-C.

Acknowledgment This research is supported by NSFC Grant No. 61202408, CNIC Grant CNIC-PY-1407, and CAS 125 Informatization Project XXH12503.

References

1. M.L. Bote-Lorenzo, L.M. Vaquero-Gonzlez, G. Vega-Gorgojo, J.I. Asensioprez, E. Gmez-Snchez, Y.A. Dimitriadis, GRIDCOLE: A Grid Collaborative Learning Environment, in *Proceedings of IEEE International Symposium on Cluster Computing and the Grid (CCGrid'04)*
2. L.M. Vaquero, EduCloud: PaaS versus IaaS cloud usage for an advanced computer science course. IEEE Trans. Educ. **54**(4), 590–598 (2011)
3. B. Hayes, Cloud computing. Commun. ACM **51**(7), 9–11 (2008)
4. M.A. Beyer, D. Laney, *The Importance of 'Big Data': A Definition* (Gartner, Stamford, CT, 2012)
5. NSF-Cyberinfrastructure-Council, NSF's Cyberinfrastructure Vision for 21st Century Discovery, http://www.nsf.gov/od/oci/ci v5.pdf
6. H. Tony, E. Trefethen Anne, Cyberinfrastructure for e-science. Science **308**(5723), 817–821 (2005)
7. G. Wenzhuang, What is e-science. eScience Technol. Appl. **1**(1), 1–7 (2008)
8. N. Wilkins-Diehr, D. Gannon, G. Klimeck, S. Oster, S. Pamidighantam, TeraGrid science gateways and their impact on science. Computer **41**(11), 32–41 (2008)
9. D.D. Roure, C. Goble, R. Stevens, The design and realisation of the virtual research environment for social sharing of workflows. Future Gener. Comput. Syst. **25**(5), 561–567 (2009)
10. W. Funika, D. Harlak, D. Krl, M. Bubak, Environment for Collaborative Development and Execution of Virtual Laboratory Applications, in *Proceedings of 8th International Conference on Computational Science (ICCS'08)*
11. P.-B. Josep, A.-M. Joan, H.-J. Jordi, An integrated structure for a virtual networking laboratory. IEEE Trans. Ind. Electron. **55**(6), 2334–2342 (2008)
12. C.A. Jara, F.A. Candelas, F. Torres, S. Dormido, F. Esquembre, O. Reinoso, Real-time collaboration of virtual laboratories through the internet. Comput. Educ. **52**(1), 126–140 (2009)
13. D. Tsovaltzi, N. Rummel, B.M. McLaren, N. Pinkwart, O. Scheuer, A. Harrer, I. Braun, Extending a virtual chemistry laboratory with a collaboration script to promote conceptual learning. Int. J. Technol. Enhanc. Learn. **2**(1), 91–110 (2010)
14. S.D. Olabarriaga, T. Glatard, P.T. De Boer, A virtual laboratory for medical image analysis. IEEE Trans. Inform. Technol. Biomed. **14**(4), 979–985 (2010)
15. P.R.C. Da Silveira, M.N. Valdez, R.M. Wenzcovitch et al., Virtual Laboratory for Planetary Materials (vlab): An Updated Overview of System Service Architecture, in *Proceedings of 2011 TeraGrid Conference: Extreme Digital Discovery (TG'11)*
16. S. Wesner, K. Wulf, M. Muller, How Grid Could Improve E-learning in the Environmental Science Domain, in *Proceedings of 1st LEGE-WG International Conference on Educational Models for GRID Based Services (LeGE-WG'02)*
17. A. Bagnasco, A.M. Scapolla, A Grid of Remote Laboratory for Teaching Electronics, in *Proceedings of the 2005 Conference on Towards the Learning Grid: Advances in Human Learning Services*
18. G. Bourguin, A. Derycke, Integrating the CSCL Activities into Virtual Campuses: Foundations of a New Infrastructure for Distributed Collective Activities, in *Proceedings of Euro-CSCL'01*

19. P. Mell, T. Grance, The NIST definition of cloud computing. Comput. Inform. Sci. **5**(6), 50 (2009)
20. J. Dittrich, J.-A. Quian-Ruiz, Efficient big data processing in Hadoop MapReduce. Proc. VLDB Endowment **5**(12), 2014–2015 (2012)
21. L.-J. Zhang, Q. Zhou, CCOA: Cloud Computing Open Architecture, in *Proceedings of IEEE International Conference on Web Services (ICWS '09)*
22. M.D. De Assuno, A. Di Costanzo, R. Buyya, Evaluating the Cost-Benefit of Using Cloud Computing to Extend the Capacity of Clusters, in *Proceedings of 18th ACM International Symposium on High Performance Distributed Computing (HPDC '09)*
23. J. Matthews, T. Garfinkel, C. Hoff, J. Wheeler, Virtual Machine Contracts for Datacenter and Cloud Computing Environments, in *Proceedings of 1st workshop on Automated control for datacenters and clouds (ACDC '09)*
24. A. Rosenthal, P. Mork, M.H. Li, J. Stanford, D. Koester, S.P. Reynold, Cloud computing: a new business paradigm for biomedical information sharing. J. Biomed. Inform. **43**(2), 342–353 (2010)
25. J.W. Park, Y.W. Lee, C.H. Yun, H.K. Park, S.I. Chang, I.P. Lee, H.S. Jung, Cloud Computing for Online Visualization of GIS Applications in Ubiquitous City, in *Proceedings of IEEE International Conference on Cloud Computing (CLOUD '10)*
26. M. Olson, K.M. Chandy, Performance Issues in Cloud Computing for Cyberphysical Applications, in *Proceedings of IEEE International Conference on Cloud Computing (CLOUD '11)*
27. M. Hajjat, X. Sun, Y.-W.E. Sung et al., Cloudward Bound: Planning for Beneficial Migration of Enterprise Applications to the Cloud, in *Proceedings of the ACM SIGCOMM 2010 Conference*
28. S. Strauch, V. Andrikopoulos, T. Bachmann, Migrating Application Data to the Cloud using Cloud Data, in *Proceedings of 3rd International Conference on Cloud Computing and Service Science (CLOSER '13)*
29. A. Thakar, A. Szalay, Migrating a (Large) Science Database to the Cloud, in *Proceedings of 19th ACM International Symposium on High Performance Distributed Computing (HPDC '10)*
30. Y. Kwon, E. Tilevich, Cloud refactoring: automated transitioning to cloud-based services. Autom. Softw. Eng. **21**(3), 345–372 (2014)
31. H. Jamjoom, VirtualWire: System Support for Live Migrating Virtual Networks Across Clouds, in *Proceedings of 7th International Workshop on Virtualization Technologies in Distributed Computing (VTDC '13)*
32. L. Zhang, M. Liu, Z. Shi, X. Ma, Research on Virtual Basic Laboratory and Experimental Teaching Resources Platform based on Cloud Computing, in *Proceedings of 9th International Symposium on Linear Drives for Industry Applications (LDIA '14)*
33. S. Chen, The view of scientific inquiry conveyed by simulation-based virtual laboratories. Comput. Educ. **55**(3), 1123–1130 (2010)
34. R.C. Correia, J.M. Fonseca, A. Donellan, Euronet Lab a Cloud based Laboratory Environment, in *Proceedings of 2012 I.E. Global Engineering Education Conference (EDUCON '12)*
35. R. Dinita, G. Wilson, A. Winckles, M. Cirstea, A Cloud-Based Virtual Computing Laboratory for Teaching Computer Networks, in *Proceedings of 13th International Conference on Optimization of Electrical and Electronic Equipment (OPTIM '12)*
36. Y. Simmhan, R. Barga, C. Van Ingen, E. Lazowska, A. Szalay, On Building Scientific Workflow Systems for Data Management in the Cloud, in *Proceedings of Fourth IEEE International Conference on eScience (e-Science '08)*
37. J. Erickson, S. Spence, M. Rhodes, D. Banks, J. Rutherford, E. Simpson, G. Belrose, R. Perry, Content-centered collaboration spaces in the cloud. IEEE Internet Comput. **13**(5), 34–42 (2009)

Self-Adaptive Parameters Optimization for Incremental Classification in Big Data Using Neural Network

Simon Fong, Charlie Fang, Neal Tian, Raymond Wong, and Bee Wah Yap

Abstract Big Data is being touted as the next big thing arousing technical challenges that confront both academic research communities and commercial IT deployment. The root sources of Big Data are founded on infinite data streams and the curse of dimensionality. It is generally known that data which are sourced from data streams accumulate continuously making traditional batch-based model induction algorithms infeasible for real-time data mining. In the past many methods have been proposed for incrementally data mining by modifying classical machine learning algorithms, such as artificial neural network. In this paper we propose an incremental learning process for supervised learning with parameters optimization by neural network over data stream. The process is coupled with a parameters optimization module which searches for the best combination of input parameters values based on a given segment of data stream. The drawback of the optimization is the heavy consumption of time. To relieve this limitation, a loss function is proposed to look ahead for the occurrence of concept-drift which is one of the main causes of performance deterioration in data mining model. Optimization is skipped intermittently along the way so to save computation costs. Computer simulation is conducted to confirm the merits by this incremental optimization process for neural network.

Keywords Neural network • Incremental machine learning • Classification • Big data • Parameter optimization

S. Fong (✉) • C. Fang • N. Tian
Department of Computer and Information Science, University of Macau, Macau, SAR, China
e-mail: ccfong@umac.mo; flyhero@live.com

R. Wong
School of Computer Science and Engineering, University of New South Wales, Sydney, NSW, Australia
e-mail: wong@cse.unsw.edu.au

B.W. Yap
Faculty of Computer and Mathematical Sciences, Universiti Teknologi MARA, Selangor, Malaysia
e-mail: beewah@tmsk.uitm.edu.my

© Springer International Publishing Switzerland 2016   175
P.C.K. Hung (ed.), *Big Data Applications and Use Cases*, International Series
on Computer Entertainment and Media Technology, DOI 10.1007/978-3-319-30146-4_8

1   Introduction

Recently a lot of news in the media advocate the hype of Big Data that are manifested in three problematic issues. They are the 3V challenges known as: Velocity problem that gives rise to a huge amount of data to be handled at an escalating high speed; Variety problem that makes data processing and integration difficult because the data come from various sources and they are formatted differently; and Volume problem that makes storing, processing, and analysis over them both computational and archiving challenging.

In views of these 3V challenges, the traditional data mining approaches which are based on the full batch-mode learning may run short in meeting the demand of analytic efficiency. That is simply because the traditional data mining model construction techniques require loading in the full set of data, and then the data are used to infer the weights in the hidden layer(s) of a neural network in order to represent the nonlinear relations between the input values and the expected output; two classical algorithms are activation functions in neural networks [1] and Rough-set discrimination [2]. Each time when fresh data arrive, which is typical in the data collection process that makes the big data inflate to bigger data, the traditional induction method needs to re-run and the model that was built needs to be built again with the inclusion of the fresh data.

In contrast, the new breed of algorithms known as data stream mining methods [3] are able to subside these 3V problems of big data, since these 3V challenges are mainly the characteristics of data streams. Data stream algorithm is not stemmed by the huge volume or high speed data collection. The algorithm is capable of inducing a classification or prediction model from bottom-up approach; each pass of data from the data streams triggers the model to incrementally update itself without the need of reloading any previously seen data. This type of algorithms can potentially handle data streams that amount to infinity, and they can run in memory analyzing and mining data streams on the fly. It is regarded as a computationally cost-effective method for solving big data analytics problems. Lately researchers concur data stream mining algorithms are meant to be solutions to tackle big data for now and for the future years to come [4, 5].

In both families of data mining algorithms, stream-based and batch-based, classification has been widely adopted for supporting inferring decisions from big data. In supervised learning, a classification model or classifier is trained by inducing the relationships between the attributes of the historical records and the class labels which are usually the predictor features of all the data and their predicted classes respectively. Subsequently, the classifier is used to predict appropriate classes given unseen samples.

Among classification applications, artificial neural network (ANN) has been a popular choice of learning method throughout the years. ANN is inspired from biology where individual neurons are layered and they respond to input values by producing a predicted value which is computed from the weights of the internal states of the neurons. An ANN can be trained by adjusting the internal states and weights of the neurons, given some labeled training samples. An ANN can be trained and retrained in this fashion depending on the application scenarios. In case of Big Data analytics a so-called "Deep" neural network can be built by constructing many hidden layers that incorporate with learning a huge amount of information from the big data. How deep should a neural network be, in terms of the complexity of the structures and number of neurons? What is the optimal complexity of the neural network that is just sufficient to offer the maximum predictive power?

On the other hand, another type of learning called Online Learning or Incremental Learning, is a train-and-forget strategy where only a segment of the data is learnt one at a time and it is unnecessary to recall the historical data for the current testing. This is likewise equivalent to data stream mining where the machine learning algorithm is trained and predicts using a continuous stream of incoming data. The algorithm needs to quickly adapt to the latest contents of the data stream as the underlying contexts of the data stream may vary in time—a phenomenon known as concept drift. For example in marketing applications fashion and food items that sell well in summer may not do so in winter. Concept drift is crucial in incremental learning that decides how frequent a machine learning model needs to be refreshed when processing online data streams.

In the literature a lot of research efforts were dedicated in innovating new ANN learning model where its network architecture expands according to the varying concepts from data streams. They range from polynomial neural networks to self-organizing map where the neurons and layers are prone to increase in complexity in order to deal with the ever-changing contents in the data streams. In this paper an alternative method is proposed in optimizing the parameters of a neural network in data stream mining while keeping the network topology and structure constant. The implication of reusing the same structure of the neural network is simplicity that may be suitable for memory-constrained applications, such as sensor-network monitoring and micro-controller embedded modules.

It is assumed that in normal supervised learning scenarios, there is always a compact neural network architecture that would work well for a given input dataset [6]. However, it was pointed out in [7] that it is difficult to find the right parameters for that network structure for achieving maximum performance because online learning is unique that continuous data are passing through the neural network from time to time. Given such motivation, our proposed method tunes only the parameters in real-time with respect to the variations in the data streams, in terms of concept drifts. It is anticipated that the complexity of the neural network remains stable as the structure does not change; and the selected parameter values enable the neural network to attain an acceptable level of performance with the ongoing analytics tasks in Big Data. Instead of exhaustively rebuilding the neural network every time as the incoming data arrive, a self-adaptive optimization mechanism is devised using a loss function which activates the parameter selection process when the trained model becomes obsolete.

The remaining of the paper is organized as follow. Section 2 reviews the current research on incremental learning using neural networks, in particular of several school of algorithms and neural network designs. Our proposed self-adaptive parameter tuning method for neural network incremental learning is described in Sect. 3. An empirical temporal data set of electricity consumption is tested in experimentation with the aim of verifying the efficacy of the proposed method. The results are then discussed. Lastly Sect. 5 concludes the paper.

2   Related Work

It is well known that incremental learning can often be difficult for traditional neural network systems, due to newly learned information interfering with previously learned information. Throughout the history of related works on solving the problems of incremental neural network learning, mainly there are three schools of thoughts on achieving the same purpose—(a) incremental construction algorithms on expanding the topology of the neural network; (b) evolving neural networks; and (c) hyperparameters optimization.

The algorithms that control and decide how the neural network structure expands vary. They commonly keep a flexible structure allowing the hidden layers expandable or modifiable depending on the given situations. Aran and Alpaydın [8] proposed a constructive algorithm called Multiple Operators using Statistical Test for controlling the architecture. The networks are allowed to have multiple hidden layers with multiple hidden units in each layer. The algorithm uses node removal, addition and layer addition and determines the complexity of nodes in layers by heuristics. Statistical tests are applied to compare different architectures. Similar approach was pioneered by Soviet scientist Prof. Alexey G. Ivakhnenko [9] called Group method of data handling (GMDH) which a breed of polynomial algorithms for modeling multi-parametric problems by growing the structure and complexity of neurons automatically. Lately adaptive neural network architecture [10] was devised that grows or trims its structure with respect to variations in the incoming data by using a simple incremental auto-encoder model to reward or compensate a validation error. Similarly a reinforcement learning algorithm is devised where long-term memory is stored at a resource allocating network [11]. In their approach, the reinforcement learning algorithm has a corrective ability in recalling the right memory from the long-term cache in such a way that the newly learned knowledge would not cause 'interference' to the long-term memory. This concept extended to the recent hype so-called Deep Learning; the authors in [12] show how to use "complementary priors" to suppress the explaining away effects that cause inference in densely-connected belief neural networks that are constructed with many hidden layers. A greedy algorithm using complementary priors is developed for deep learning while leaving the top double layers for storing undirected associative memory.

This type of incrementally growing neural network is gaining momentum in research community. Instead of using reinforcement algorithm, the authors in [13] used SoftMax function to estimate the approximation error in an incremental manner. This measure is applied to tune the neural network growth rate. As early as 1993 [14], an incremental neural network model was proposed for sequence learning by progressively increasing higher-order connections and new units. It adds higher orders to the network when required by introducing new units that dynamically change connection weights. In this way, information from the distant past can be retained on each prediction. Along with the same concept the authors [15] refined the approach by a new algorithm expectation–maximization, which starts with a single component and incrementally adds more components at appropriate positions in the data space. The addition of a new component is not random but heuristically depends on the detection of a region in the data space that is advantageous to goal of the classification task. When all the components are added, the algorithm divides the network into subcomponents, one for a corresponding classification class. In 2012, Tscherpanow [16] further enhanced the approach by using Adaptive Resonance Theory by tapping on the ability of noise-insensitive, incremental clustering and topology adapting at hierarchical levels of a neural network from hyperspherical categories. For parsing language processing, a recursive neural network is developed [17]. Recursive neural network architecture is extended for producing predictions after a training phase on samples drawn from a corpus of parsed sentences, the Penn Treebank. The design is to fit the incremental parsing algorithm in syntactic analysis where the structure is continually prolonged as more texts are to be processed.

The other type of related work is evolutionary neural network. Similar to incremental structure for neural network, a neural network is evolved so the overall structure is optimized and the vitality of the prediction is enhanced. The evolution is beyond merely the network structure or neuron weights. A survey report [18] has summarized a number of growth strategies that include evolution in the following: number of neurons, connectivity, asymmetry, sideways connection, skipping layers, feedbacks and bias, etc. In the paper [19] the authors demonstrated how evolutionary computation techniques are able to produce incremental neural network models that improve their performance over the non-incremental ones. In addition it was claimed that a favorable feature of evolving neural networks embraces optimization of any parameter of the neural network through evolutionary process. The parameters may get simultaneously interacted in complex manners during evolution. This implies users are relinquished from the hassles of configuring a neural network of which the most optimal structure and parameters values are unknown in advance; the extremely difficult but crucial task of setting the parameter values for a neural network is left to the evolutionary process. Learn++ system is one of the most widely cited for its implementation of evolutionary neural network by this concept.

In addition to optimizing topology and connectivity of neural network, recently a contemporary type of adaptive neural network model is on hyperparameters optimization. Hyperparameters are parameters which are crucial to the performance of a neural network, and their values have been optimized through some optimization techniques such as swarm optimization. Hyperparameters in the context of machine learning by neural network include but not limit to the architecture (structure) of the

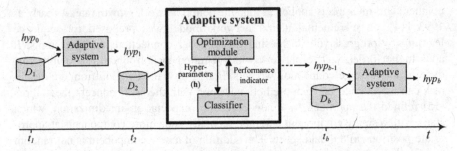

Fig. 1 A generalized view of adaptive system learning various hypotheses over a data stream

network, number of hidden nodes, the number of layers and type of activation functions. In incremental learning, a neural network that is setup initially may either have to be totally retrained from the start to the latest cumulative bulk nor evolved into a more complex structure. But its parameters values may have to be fine-tuned just to refresh or update the existing weights on the neuron pairs in each layer. In Fig. 1, a generalized view of how an adaptive system refreshes itself by the hyperparameters for incrementally learning different concepts or hypotheses along a data stream. (Image courtesy from [20]).

An incremental learning scenario is shown in the above diagram where new segment of data continuously arrive and they are used to retrain a classifier over time. Starting with the initial data D_1, the system is trained to recognize hyp_1; and so on for D_2, hyp_2 ... D_b and hyp_b. Hyperparamter optimization happens whenever a new segment of D arrives and the classifier needs to be refreshed as signaled possibly by the indication performance drop. Adaptation is reflected by the iterative training process where the optimization module finds an optimal set of hyperparameters values h. With an optimal set of h, the classifier is supposed to be properly tuned in order to attain the highest possible performance in the events of recognizing different hypotheses along the way. The authors [20] tested the vitality of this adaptive system by using fuzzy ARTMAP neural network and PSO in video-based face recognition. The model that was initially trained to recognize few samples of faces are subjected to further enrollments of face data. The neural network is optimized in parameters and incrementally learning new concepts through new data. Superior results are obtained by using hyperparameters compared to standard model without using hyperparameters.

This profound and adaptive concept of hyperparameter optimization along with the incremental construction of neural network gives rise to the impetus of this research project. Some drawbacks of incrementally growing neural networks including those with and without using evolutionary algorithms are the ever-increasing complexity of the neural network structure and the overhead in managing the balance of the memories of short and long terms. In review of the literature, there is no simple and effective method available that a neural network can learn incrementally with respect to the changing contents of the data stream, yet keeping the network structure constant. Our proposed model is designed to overcome the challenge of incremental classification learning using a lightweight parameter optimization mechanism on a simple neural network.

3 Proposed Method

3.1 Data Stream Classification Operation

A generalized algorithm is proposed here for adaptively controlling the hyperparameter optimization process for incremental learning using only a simple configuration of neural network. It is directly applicable to classifying multi-attributed data in continuous data stream. The data is represented by values of multiple attributes, one of which is a target class. The neural network learns by recognizing the relations between the attribute values and the output target class by supervised learning. That is when old data samples are used to induce a memory model making it ready to classify new unseen samples into one of the output classes. A learn-and-forget approach is taken as new samples arrive some of the learnt knowledge would be replaced by the new knowledge from the new samples, though this happens gradually in the form of progressively updating weights at the neurons. By this approach the neural network with its simple architecture carries both long-term memory and short-term memory. We do not however calibrate their proportions for we want a simple and fast classifier which aims at achieving high classification accuracy by adapting to new samples. Rather, at each cycle of model update, there is an opportunity for a hyperparameter optimization to occur for the sake of finding the best parameter values upon the arrival of new training samples. The optimization is carried out under some control. The control mechanism is implemented by a loss function which is triggered by the detection of a concept drift arisen from the data stream. Hence three types of data stream mining operations are possible, and they are illustrated in Fig. 2.

In Fig. 2(a), it shows a typical segment-based training/testing process where a classifier is trained by one segment of data and then being tested on the subsequent data segment. For example, by the time t_2, the classifier is already trained with data samples that arrived between t_0 and t_1. It is then ready for making prediction during the testing phase between t_1 and t_2. While a copy of the trained classifier is used for testing during the period between t_1 and t_2, the classifier model is subject to retraining simultaneously by using the newly arrived data samples in the same time period. The dual phases of training-and-testing repeat from window to window as time progresses. Intermediate performance of the classifier can be collected at the end of each time window in the testing phases.

In our proposed methods, as shown in Fig. 2(b), hyperparameter optimization can be conducted upon each training phase, one round per window cycle. The purpose of the hyperparameter optimization is to find a suitable combination of parameter values for the refreshed classifier to achieve the best performance. The

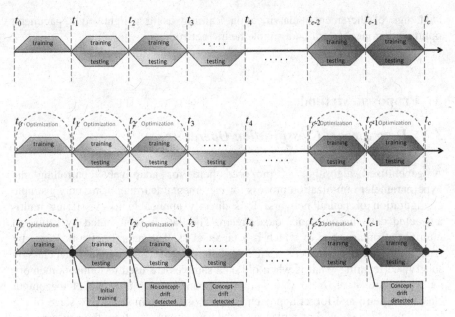

Fig. 2 Three possible types of training/testing operations of incremental learning over data streams: (a) *Top*: training/testing without any optimization; (b) *Middle*: training/testing with optimization at all times; (c) *Bottom*: training/testing with smart optimization

hyperparameter optimization function implemented in our experimentation is called *CVParameterSelection* [21] in *Weka* which is a Java-based open source machine learning platform. It automatically searches for the best parameters values by trying out all the combinations via-brute force using cross-validation on the training data. Readers who are interested in the detailed implementation are referred to the online documentation of URL http://weka.wikispaces.com/Optimiz ing+parameters. The search is however by brute-force which may be justifiable for its use because of simplicity in program code and the fact that only two parameters are used—Learning rate and Momentum. Learning rate [0, 1] dictates the amount of weights to be updated in each training epoch, with 1 means all the weights are to be updates in full learning, 0 means none in not learning. Momentum is an intensity control parameter [0, 1] that is applied to the weights during updating. By default their values are 0.2 and 0.3 respectively in Weka. These values nevertheless do not guarantee best results in training a neural network. Hence the motivation for optimizing the parameter values in the hope of building an accurate classifier along the process of incremental classification over the data stream. For more sophisticated neural network or other classification algorithms which carry more parameters than two, the program designer can replace the optimization function *CVParameterSelection* by any of the other swarm searches, such as those listed in [22] for shortening the search time.

It is argued that doing optimization by whichever search algorithm incurs significant overheads in the training phases, and such over-doing may not be necessary especially when the data samples across consecutive time windows are about the same in contents. In other words, repeating the same optimization while the underlying hypotheses reflected by the data stream are about the same does not yield any major performance improvement but to waste computing resources. Therefore a streamlined approach which we call smart-optimization is proposed in this paper that activates the optimization process only when necessary. That is, a new set of parameters values are needed to be generated only when the underlying concept changes which are anticipated to affect the model performance. Otherwise when the model is still effective at times of no concept change, the same set of parameters values inherited from the previous training cycles are used again for model refreshing. Graphically the operation of smart-optimization is illustrated in Fig. 2(c). Hyperparameter optimization runs only when concept-drift is detected to occur at the incidences represented by red-spots at t_3 and t_{c-1}. By default, hyperparameter optimization runs for the first time at t_1 initially. At other times the retraining proceeds without running the optimization function for saving computing resources. This resource-saving mode of optimization should offer improved performance almost near to full optimization as long as concept-drift is detected properly along the way.

3.2   Detecting Concept-Drift by Loss Function

How then concept-drift is detected in data stream? As a lightweight method, an auxiliary classifier (AC) in the simple form of decision table is implemented as an early-warning alarm alerting the event of a possible concept drift in the data stream. Each time when fresh data arrives, the prediction by the auxiliary classifier is tested against the prediction by the neural network. If the discrepancy between the predictions is at large, it implies the neural network which is the main classifier needs to be reset by a newly optimized set of hyperparameters in order to accommodate the significant changes in the contents of the data stream.

In this paper, an alternative solution that detects the presence of concept drifts and skips certain time-consuming optimizations when it is unnecessary is proposed. The alternative solution which is simpler than reviewed in Sect. 2 uses a lightweight auxiliary classifier in a sliding window and a loss function. The AC serves as a watchdog to observe the prediction performance of the neural network. The proposed solution is suitable for on-going incremental classification learning from unbounded data stream distorted with problems of concept-drifts. AC works with a loss function which determines whether or not the neural network needs to be totally retrained by a newly optimized set of hyperparameters whenever new data arrive.

The AC is lodged within a sliding cache window that renews the data instances whenever fresh data arrives. The AC is updated accordingly as a decision-table classifier [23] using the local data lately cached in the window. The window size, although it is chosen arbitrarily, it is related to the data transmission rate. W is defined as the maximum amount of instances that a window can hold, hence the window size. The window is refreshed periodically by intervals, of length W for each round. Let the amount of instances that have been cached temporarily in a window at time t be $|D_t|$. The data caching process thereby takes the following steps and repeats itself in the sliding-window:

1. Accumulate incoming data samples into the window until it full when $|D_t| \rightarrow W$;
2. Refresh AC with the currently cached bulk of data samples D_t;
3. Make a prediction from AC, and flush the cached bulk of data sample, $D_t = \text{NULL}$. Return to Step 1.

The decision table in the AC should have its prediction performance similar to that of the main neural network except when concept drift occurs. The decision table is more susceptible or sensitive to the concept drift problems hence the discrepancy between the predictions of the two classifiers would emerge. Moreover a decision table can be rebuilt at a low computation cost, and a total model reconstruction is much faster than that of a neural network. So with a slight computational overhead the AC is rebuilt at each interval of length W, while fully rebuilding the main neural network (MN^2) is delayed only when concept-drift is detected to occur at a large extent.*

Suppose the MN^2 gets its weights updated (retraining) by learning through all of the streaming instances. As a result, it would have a global perspective over all of the cumulative data since the beginning or the last concept-drift. On the other hand, the AC computes the relations between the attributes and the classes on a decision table by learning the instances that are currently cached within the sliding window. The AC adopts a local and close-up view of the data stream as it is rebuilt in every interval. When a new instance (X, y_k) arrives, where $X = \{x_1, x_2, .. x_m\}$ is a set of m-dimensional attribute values and y_k is the expected output of class k, the MN^2 and the AC are to make a prediction separately. The counts of true or false predictions are retained for both classifiers as in Eqs. (1) and (2), where T_k and F_k are variables that record the correct and incorrect predictions respectively for a corresponding class k.

$$MN^2(X) \rightarrow \hat{y_k} \begin{cases} = y_k \Rightarrow T_k^{MN^2} = T_k^{MN^2} + 1 \\ \neq y_k \Rightarrow F_k^{MN^2} = F_k^{MN^2} + 1 \end{cases} \tag{1}$$

$$AC(X) \rightarrow \hat{y_k} \begin{cases} = y_k \Rightarrow T_k^{AC} = T_k^{AC} + 1 \\ \neq y_k \Rightarrow F_k^{AC} = F_k^{AC} + 1 \end{cases} \tag{2}$$

After T_k and F_k are being updated from the prediction results of MN^2 and AC, the following loss variables are calculated that represent the loss in prediction accuracies between the local and global classifiers.

$$Loss_k^{MN^2} = T_k^{MN^2} - F_k^{MN^2} \tag{3}$$

$$Loss_k^{AC} = T_k^{AC} - F_k^{AC} \tag{4}$$

To unify the loss variables to a single variable that measures the prediction performance of the AC and the overall MN^2 for a certain class y_k, a coefficient P_k is used with respect to class k.

$$\frac{\sum_{m=1}^{M}\sum_{j=1}^{J} n_{mjk}}{N} = P_k \times \frac{Loss_k^{AC}}{Loss_k^{MN^2}}, \tag{5}$$

where M is the total number of attributes, J is the total number of different values for a nominal attribute (otherwise binning would be required for numeric attributes), N is the total number of instances with which the MN^2 so far has been trained, and the worth of the adequate statistic that counts the amount of arrived instances belonging to class y_k within W is n_{mjk}. After the AC has been updated and made a prediction, the values in the decision table are reset to zero for the next window, $Loss_k^{AC}$ is initialized to null. So the coefficient P_k is simplified from Eq. (5) to the following:

$$P_k = \frac{Loss_k^{MN^2} \times \sum_{m=1}^{M}\sum_{j=1}^{J} n_{mjk}}{(N+1)\left(Loss_k^{AC}\right)}. \tag{6}$$

When $P_k \to 0$, the MN^2 is yielding perfect overall accuracy. Small value of P_k indicates a good prediction performance. Two performance indicators are being tracked whenever a new window of data instance arrives, one for the current window cycle and the other one for the previous window cycle, which are P_k^t and P_k^{t-1} respectively. Keeping two (or more) successive performance indicators allows us to detect if the performance is declining that suggests a concept-drift problem emerged.

If ever the coefficient value of the current window cycle is greater than that of the previous window cycle, i.e., $P_k^t > P_k^{t-1}$, the prediction accuracy of the MN^2 in relation to the AC is on decline. A variable known as the bound ϵ_k for predicting class k is used as a sensitivity control. A bound can be interpreted as a threshold after seeing so many times of accuracy declines in exponential trend, one can decide whether there is anticipating a concept drift with a preset confidence level control δ. The bound ϵ_k is derived from the performance coefficients that are computed from the statistics of the loss variable, $Loss_k^{AC}$ and m_k which is the harmonic mean of the P_k^t and P_k^{t-1} as defined in the following Eq. (7).

$$\epsilon_k = \sqrt{\frac{1}{2m_k} \times \ln\left(\frac{4}{\delta'}\right)}, \quad \text{where } m_k = \frac{1}{\frac{1}{P_k^t} + \frac{1}{P_k^{t-1}}}, \quad \text{and } \delta' = \frac{\delta}{P_k^t + P_k^{t-1}} \quad (7)$$

In order to decide whether the whole neural network needs a total reconstruction with a new set of hyperparameters, the bound is used to compare with the difference between the best version of the model and the second best version of the model. Some heuristic criterion such as information gain or mutual information is used to gauge the goodness of the model, where $H(.)$ is computed by information gain. For the case of taking n independent observations of $H(.)$, that has a limiting range of $\log_2 n_k$ and a confidence level of $1 - \delta$. The true mean of $H_{true}(.)$ is at least $H_{observed}(.) - \epsilon_k$, where $H_{observed}(.)$ is the observed mean of the heuristic values. Therefore when the event, $H(best) - H(second\_best) > \epsilon_k$ happens it is time to rebuild the neural network by doing optimization over the parameters. The process of fully rebuilding the neural network with optimized parameters is expressed in pseudo code as in Table 1. The retraining of the neural network is referred to Sect. 3 of [24] whose details are not repeated here.

4 Experiments

4.1 Setup

For validating the applicability of the adaptive optimization method in data stream mining scenario, a back-propagation neural network that is implemented as *MultilayerPerceptron*[1] in Weka and a dataset of electricity power consumptions[2] are used in a performance experimentation. This dataset used in the experiment was originally collected from the electricity market of New South Wales, Australia. The electricity prices in the Australian electricity market are elastic. They are determined by the dynamics of the demand and supply of the consumer market. The data are recorded in every 5 min that include information about date/time, day of the week, current demand and current supply in both states of NSW and Victoria. The target class for prediction or classification is the movement of change in price with respective to a moving average of prices from the last 24 h. There are a total of 45,312 instances in the dataset sorted in temporal order. 19,237 records belong to the UP trend class, and the remaining 26,075 belong to the DOWN trend class. No missing value is reported. The data of the electricity consumption are visualized in Fig. 3 where the x-axis is the time domain. It can be noticed that some attribute values drastically change their ranges over time thereby possibly leading to

---

[1] http://weka.sourceforge.net/doc.dev/weka/classifiers/functions/MultilayerPerceptron.html
[2] http://sourceforge.net/projects/moa-datastream/files/Datasets/Classification/elecNormNew.arff.zip/download

Table 1 Pseudo code of smart optimization

1. Initialize all variables.
2. A sample instance of data arrives to W from the data stream $D_t = (X, y)$.
3. If MC^2 is not constructed, build MC^2.
4. When the volume of the current cache is less than $|W|$, continue to add D_t to the cache. Or else, rebuild AC from the currently cached data, make a prediction and flush the cache.
5. Take D_t as testing samples, make prediction by the neural network with respect to k, such that $MC^2(X) \rightarrow \widehat{y_k}$; update the counts $T_k^{MC^2}$ and $F_k^{MC^2}$.
6. Use AC to classify the same testing sample with respect to k, $AC(X) \rightarrow \widehat{y_k}$, then update T_k^{AC} and F_k^{AC}.
7. Update n_k as the number of instances being classified so far by MC^2 with respect to y_k.
8. If all instances classified so far with respect to k do not belong to k, reset $(n_k \bmod n_{min} = 0)$.
9. Compute $H(x_{best})$ and $H(x_{2ndBest})$ as the highest and second-highest $H(.)$.
10. Computer ϵ_k, from the loss function where k is the class index belonging to $x_{2ndBest}$.
11. If $(H(x_{Best}) - H(x_{2ndBest}) > \epsilon_k)$, then activate hyperparameter optimization and fully rebuild MC^2.
12. Goto 2

concept-drifts. For examples, the values of the two attributes Vicdeman and Transfer remain rather in a narrow range between 0.4 and 0.42 from time zero to time 17.5×10^3. And the values of the same two attribute fluctuate greatly in the range of 0–1 there afterwards. So a neural network that was trained with instances earlier on, is expected to fail to cope with the changes from time $= 17.5 \times 10^3$ onwards. Model retraining is then required to maintain a good level of prediction accuracy.

To simulate the sliding window mechanism, the whole dataset is sequentially divided into 20 portions of equal length. Thus each portion contains approximately 2265 instances amounting to 5 % of the whole data. A back-propagation neural network (MC^2) is trained and retrained by adjusting its neuron weights by loading 2265 instances in each of the window cycle. When necessary, the neural network is reset and retrained from scratch by using a new set of parameter values during smart optimization. The sliding window runs from the first instance with timestamp $= 0$ incrementally to last instance towards the end of the dataset; the AC and MC^2 are trained and tested along the way with windows W instances at each round.

The experiment was conducted on the computing platform of a Dell Precision T7610 PC workstation with Intel Xeon Processor E5-2670 v2 (Ten Core HT, 2.5GHz Turbo, 25 MB) and 128GB RAM. The programming environment is Java Development Kit 1.5. For the algorithms, they are implemented on Weka platform. Default parameter values are set for all experimentation runs except the learning

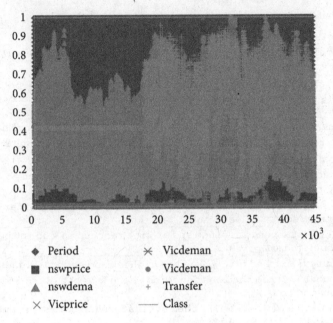

◆	Period	✳	Vicdeman
◼	nswprice	•	Vicdeman
▲	nswdema	+	Transfer
✕	Vicprice	——	Class

Fig. 3 Visualization of the electricity dataset on the time domain

rate and momentum of the neural network that are optimized each time with the contents of the given data. For a fair evaluation over the efficacy of the data mining approaches, a tenfold cross-validation is used for obtaining the optimized parameter values. The data in the current window that are used for testing are subsequently used for model retraining. So both training data portion and the testing (or validation) data portion are assumed to be of equal length. The performance is measured in terms of accuracy which is defined as how well the neural network is able to predict whether there is an up or down in change of price given an instance of attributes values; accuracy is computed as $\frac{TP+TN}{TP+FP+FN+TN}$, where T/F is true/false of the actual results, and P/N is positive/negative of a prediction. The epoch or the maximum training time is set at 500 cycles for capping a upper limit in runtime in both batch training mode and incremental training mode.

4.2 Results

The experiment is designed to test three phenomena pertaining to (1) optimization approaches, (2) the effect of window sizes on the other performance aspects such as Kappa statistics and time-taken, and (3) the complexity of neural network. In the first experiment, three incremental classification approaches with no optimization, always optimization and smart optimization are run over the electricity dataset that

Table 2 Accuracy of neural network under various incremental classification approaches

Data	Original	Optimized	Smart-optimized
ALL	78.3347	99.3363	99.3363
data4	51.5487	99.3284	94.469
data9	54.646	98.0088	93.5841
data14	49.115	99.5575	99.5575
data19	56.6372	99.7788	99.7788
data24	63.0531	98.4513	98.4513
data29	67.0354	100	99.5575
data34	63.9381	99.7788	99.115
data39	52.4336	99.3923	98.8938
data44	64.1593	97.7876	97.1239
data49	47.5664	100	99.7788
data54	47.5664	98.6726	97.7876
data59	50.6637	99.7788	99.3363
data64	65.0442	97.7453	95.8621
data69	53.7611	96.8966	96.1962
data74	56.1947	97.9518	97.7586
data79	50.6637	99.3103	98.0207
data84	45.354	99.3103	97.4355
data89	41.8142	98.7931	95.852
data94	44.6903	97.931	96.747
data99	44.469	98.2759	96.4888
Average	55.7647	98.8589	97.6729
Min	41.8142	96.8966	93.5841
Max	67.0354	100	99.7788

is divided in 20 segments of equal length. The results are tabulated in Table 2 and they are also graphed in Fig. 4.

It is apparent that the neural network that has not been optimized in any way, suffer in poor accuracy in both full batch training model and incremental training model, in comparison to the neural network that has been optimized. As shaded in grey in the first row of Table 2 one can easily see that over 99.3 % of accuracy can be attained by either optimization mode, where the neural network without any optimization remains at 78.3 %. Batch training model means all the dataset are loaded into training the neural network as inputs at once. Incremental training model trains a neural network by updating its weights with the locally cached data in a window one at a time. When the neural network is subject to these two training models with and without parameter optimization, something interesting is observed in Fig. 4—the original neural network without any optimization has its accuracy curve fluctuate along the data stream. There are several abrupt declines in accuracy line probably due to the concept drift which is in tally with the changes of attributes values depicted in Fig. 3. Overall when the accuracies which are resulted from incremental classification by the neural network without optimization, are added with a linear trend line, a decline is obvious with a negative gradient -0.633

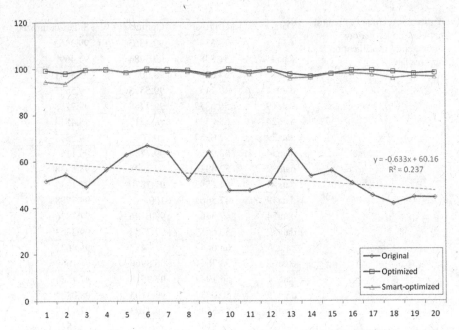

Fig. 4 Line graph of accuracy of neural network under various incremental classification approaches

and R^2 value 0.237. In contrast, it is evident that the parameter optimization help lift up the accuracy to very high levels at the average values of 98.9 % and 97.7 % for always optimization and smart optimization modes respectively, where a neural network without optimization gets stuck at average of 55.8 %. On the other hand, there is not much difference in accuracy performance between the two modes of optimization—always and smart. Running the optimization in always on mode outperforms the smart mode by only 1.2 % improvement. As seen in Fig. 4, the always-on optimization has a slightly higher accuracy curve than smart optimization near the initial period and ending period of time.

Nonetheless when it comes to computational time consumption, the major overhead is the parameter optimization process over the given training data of size W which is a variable to be set by users. In order to have a fair comparison between mainly the always-on optimization and smart-optimization, a total of four datasets from the Dataset section of Massive Online Analysis website[3] are tested as sample data streams for the experiments. The performances of concerns are Accuracy, Kappa and Time-taken in seconds. Kappa statistics is roughly interpreted as how generalized the classification model is when it works for another dataset besides the one that was used for inducing the model. The Time-taken is the measure of time in unit of seconds starting from the beginning of the

---

[3] http://moa.cms.waikato.ac.nz/datasets/

Table 3 Averaged performances of neural network under various incremental classification approaches over four Datsets

Window size	2 %		5 %		10 %	
	Av.	Std. Dev	Av.	Std. Dec	Av.	Std. Dev
Original						
Accuracy %	75.91182	±1.93913	78.14965	±2.19745	78.88019	±4.54572
Kappa	0.76378	±0.19824	0.792412	±0.1035	0.87123	±0.06022
Optimized						
Accuracy %	98.47708	±0.17899	99.2547	±0.69097	99.36283	±1.788863
Kappa	0.969082	±0.00359	0.975445	±0.00219	0.98549	±0.00018
Time taken (s)	179.1645	±3.01481	785.64	±86.43784	1790.75	±168.13602
Smart-optimized						
Accuracy %	96.36029	±3.01657	97.17539	±5.75412	98.40707	±9.46679
Kappa	0.931636	±0.05279	0.9429	±0.04558	0.96676	±0.0307
Time taken (s)	75.15363	±24.31232	177.1955	±59.44298	347.204	±123.01134

CVParameterSelection function till its end. Training time of neural network is considered negligible here as there is a fixed number of epoch learning of 500 rounds, which is constant in all situation given the same format of the datasets in terms of rows and columns. Three window sizes are tested as well, varying from 2, 5 to 10 % of the total dataset length. The averaged results and the standard deviations over the four Big Data datasets are tabulated in Table 3. The corresponding performance results are also plotted on radial and bar charts in Figs. 5, 6 and 7 respectively.

The timing results in Fig. 5 show that the ratio of time consumption for always-on optimization and smart-optimization is as much as 70/30. When the window size is small the savings of time are less than large window size. Small window size implies that optimization overhead can be perhaps more frequently saved; on the other hand large window size incurs relatively long time in optimization as the search has to go over a long data cache and repeated so for multiple folds of cross-validation. Nevertheless the results point to a fact that smart-optimization can significantly save a lot of computation time at the slight cost of 1.2 % of accuracy loss. For the results in Figs. 6 and 7, they show that the window size should be moderately large—as W is too small, (e.g. $W = 2$) it is hardly possible to gain a high level of accuracy and Kappa despite optimization is applied. When W is 10, the results are best relatively to $W = 2$ and $W = 5$. Having a large W, may lead to long computation time for optimization and it may not be able to predict well as the data stream may contain unforeseen changes in the testing data ahead while the model lacks of prior knowledge from the training samples. After all, the results in both Accuracy and Kappa indicate that smart-optimization is a feasible approach which yields relatively good performance (almost on par with always-on optimization) and it can save significant amount of computation time.

The last part of the experiment is to test the complexity of the neural network in respective to training time required (given a fixed number of epochs). So far for the

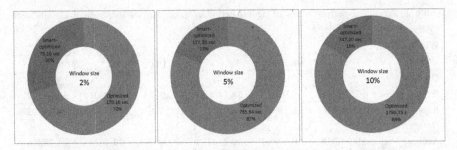

Fig. 5 Radial graphs of time consumption of neural network under various incremental classification approaches and W's

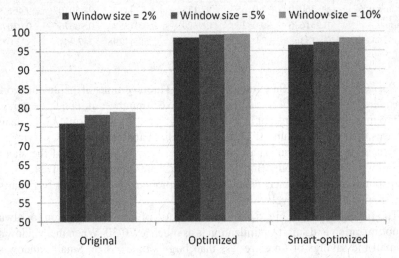

Fig. 6 Bar chart of averaged accuracy of neural network under various incremental classification approaches and W's

experimentation, an auto-build option is selected; hence the neural network structure always follows the default formulae: the number of points in the topology equals to (#attributes + #classes)/2. So for the electricity data there are 14 attributes, 2 classes, the number of points is $(14 + 2)/2 = 8$. Figure 8 shows a visualization of a simple neural network built for classifying electricity data. There are exactly eight nodes in the hidden layer.

Our proposed optimization approach however is for generic structures of neural network, which may not follow the standard rule of to (#attributes + #classes)/2; but users should have the liberty of scaling up or down the neural architecture as they wish. Therefore it is mandatory to test the time taken with respective to different configurations of neural network structures (as a matter of complexity) by repeating the same electricity classification experiment which was conducted earlier on. This time, only smart optimization is tested since it is by far the best data stream mining

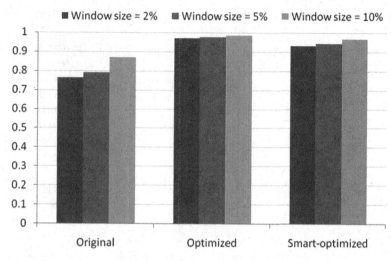

Fig. 7 Bar chart of averaged Kappa of neural network under various incremental classification approaches and W's

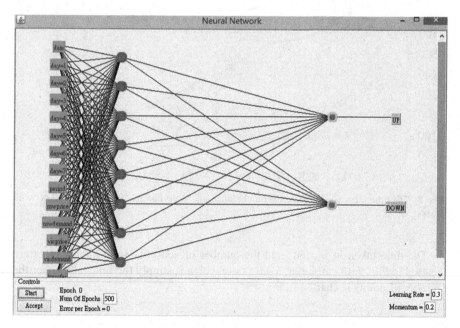

Fig. 8 Neural network structure for classifying electricity dataset

strategy, $W = 2$. The time performance results of electricity classification by smart optimization using different configurations of neural networks are tabulated in Table 4.

Table 4 Time taken for different configurations of neural network in classiflying electricity dataset

Size	Number of points	Time taken (s)	Time/number of points
11*11	121	861.12	7.116694215
9*11	99	706.9066667	7.14047138
9*9	81	577.58	7.130617284
7*11	77	549.82	7.140519481
7*9	63	429.9133333	6.824021164
7*7	49	336.68	6.871020408
5*7	35	240.64	6.875428571
5*5	25	172.05	6.882
5*3	15	103.4566667	6.897111111
3*3	9	61.8	6.866666667

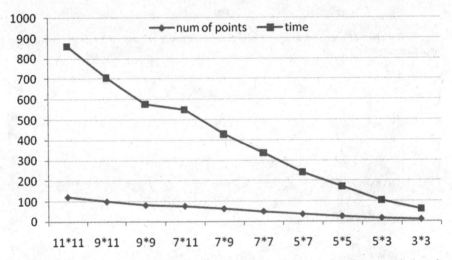

Fig. 9 The time taken for the incremental classification as the complexity of the neural network varies

The time taken in seconds and the number of neurons in the hidden layer are charted in Fig. 9. In particular, a gain ratio which is simply the time taken over the number of points is charted in Fig. 10.

5 Conclusion

In Big Data analytics, the streaming nature of the incoming data aggravates great computational challenges in data mining. Big Data grows continually with fresh data are being generated at all times; hence it requires an incremental computation approach which is able to monitor large scale of data dynamically. Lightweight

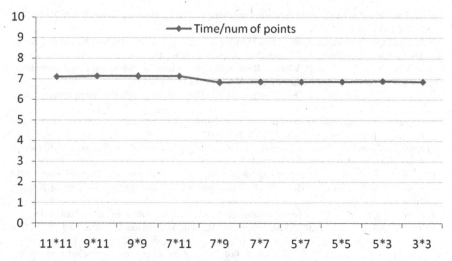

Fig. 10 The gain ratio as the complexity of the neural network varies

incremental algorithms should be considered that are capable of achieving robustness, high accuracy and minimum pre-processing latency. In this paper, we investigated the possibility of using a simple neural network coupled with an adaptive hyperparameter optimization process for fast-classification data streams, accurately and efficiently. In particular a smart-optimization approach is proposed and studied, which makes use of a simple loss function for detecting concept-drift problems in data stream so to activate the time-consuming optimization process only when it is necessary. As a case study empirical data streams taken from an Australian Electricity Market were used in the experimentation for verifying the efficacy of our proposed incremental classification approaches using neural network. The results show that smart-optimization approach is able to significantly enhance the accuracy of incremental classification by neural network. The complexity of the neural network is also verified to have little impact on the time-requirement which is stringent in fast data stream mining environment.

Acknowledgement The authors are thankful for the financial support from the research grant "Rare Event Forecasting and Monitoring in Spatial Wireless Sensor Network Data," Grant no. MYRG2014-00065-FST, offered by the University of Macau, FST, and RDAO.

References

1. P. McCullagh, J.A. Nelder, *Generalized Linear Models*, 2nd edn. (Chapman & Hall, London, 1989)
2. P.-F. Pai, T.-C. Chen, Rough set theory with discriminant analysis in analyzing electricity loads. Expert Syst. Appl. **36**, 8799–8806 (2009)
3. M.M. Gaber, A. Zaslavsky, S. Krishnaswamy, Mining data streams: a review. ACM SIGMOD Rec. **34**(2), 18–26 (2005)

4. W. Fan, A. Bifet, Mining big data: current status, and forecast to the future. SIGKDD Explor. **14**(2), 1–5 (2012)
5. A. Murdopo, Distributed decision tree learning for mining big data streams. Master of Science Thesis, European Master in Distributed Computing, July 2013
6. B. Yoshua, A. Courville, P. Vincent, Representation learning: a review and new perspectives. IEEE Trans. Pattern Anal. Mach. Intell. **35**(8), 1798–1828 (2013)
7. G. Zhou, K. Sohn, H. Lee, Online incremental feature learning with denoising autoencoders. *AISTATS*, 2012
8. O. Aran, E. Alpaydın, An incremental neural network construction algorithm for training multilayer perceptrons. ICANN/ICONIP'03, 2003
9. A.G. Ivakhnenko, Heuristic self-organization in problems of engineering cybernetics. Automatica **6**, 207–219 (1970)
10. A. Fang, F. Ramos, Tuning online neural networks with reinforcement learning. 2014 Research Conversazione, The School of Information Technologies, University of Sydney, 2014
11. N. Shiraga, S. Ozawa, S. Abe, A reinforcement learning algorithm for neural networks with incremental learning ability. Proceedings of the 9th International Conference on Neural Information Processing, 2002. ICONIP '02, vol. 5, November 2002, pp. 2566–2570
12. G.E. Hinton, S. Osindero, Y.-W. Teh, A fast learning algorithm for deep belief nets. Neural Comput. **18**(7), 1527–1554 (2006)
13. A. Carlevarino, R. Martinotti, G. Metta, G. Sandini, An incremental growing neural network and its application to robot control. Proceedings of the IEEE-INNS-ENNS International Joint Conference on Neural Networks, 2000. IJCNN 2000, vol. 5, pp. 323–328
14. M. Ring, Sequence learning with incremental higher-order neural networks. Technical Report, University of Texas at Austin, Austin, TX, USA, 1993
15. C. Constantinopoulos, A. Likas, An incremental training method for the probabilistic RBF network. IEEE Trans. Neural Netw. **17**(4), 966–974 (2006)
16. M. Tscherepanow, Incremental on-line clustering with a topology-learning hierarchical ART neural network using hyperspherical categories, Advances in data mining, poster and industry. Proceedings of the 12th Industrial Conference on Data Mining (ICDM2012) (ibai-publishing, Fockendorf 2012), p. 22
17. F. Costa, P. Frasconi, V. Lombardo, G. Soda, Learning incremental syntactic structures with recursive neural networks. Proceedings of the Fourth International Conference on Knowledge-Based Intelligent Engineering Systems and Allied Technologies, 2000, pp. 458–461
18. C. MacLeod, G.M. Maxwell, Incremental evolution in ANNs: neural nets which grow. Artif. Intell. Rev. **16**(3), 201–224 (2001)
19. T. Seipone, J.A. Bullinaria, Evolving improved incremental learning schemes for neural network systems. The 2005 I.E. Congress on Evolutionary Computation, vol. 3, pp. 2002–2009
20. J.-F. Connolly, E. Granger, R. Sabourin, Incremental adaptation of fuzzy ARTMAP neural networks for video-based face classification. Proceedings of the 2009 I.E. Symposium on Computational Intelligence in Security and Defense Applications (CISDA 2009), July 2009, pp. 1–8
21. R. Kohavi, *Wrappers for Performance Enhancement and Oblivious Decision Graphs* (Department of Computer Science, Stanford University, Stanford, 1995)
22. S. Fong, S. Deb, X.-S. Yang, J. Li, Feature selection in life science classification: metaheuristic swarm search. IT Prof. **16**(4), 24–29 (2014)
23. R. Kohavi, The power of decision tables. 8th European Conference on Machine Learning, pp. 174–189, 1995b
24. S. Ioannou, L. Kessous, G. Caridakis, K. Karpouzis, V. Aharonson, S. Kollias, Adaptive on-line neural network retraining for real life multimodal emotion recognition. Artificial Neural Networks—ICANN 2006. Lecture notes in computer science, vol. 4131, 2006, pp. 81–92

Case Studies of Government Use of Big Data in Latin America: Brazil and Mexico

Roberto da Mota Ueti, Daniela Fernandez Espinosa, Laura Rafferty, and Patrick C. K. Hung

Abstract Big Data is changing our world with masses of information stored in huge servers spread across the planet. This new technology is changing not only companies but governments as well. Mexico and Brazil, two of the most influential countries in Latin America, are entering a new era and as a result, facing challenges in all aspects of public policy. Using Big Data, the Brazilian Government is trying to decrease spending and use public money better by grouping public information with stored information on citizens in public services. With new reforms in education, finances and telecommunications, the Mexican Government is taking on a bigger role in efforts to channel the country's economic policy into an improvement of the quality of life of their habitants. It is known that technology is an important part for sub-developed countries, who are trying to make a difference in certain contexts such as reducing inequality or regulating the good usage of economic resources. The good use of Big Data, a new technology that is in charge of managing a big quantity of information, can be crucial for the Mexican Government to reach the goals that have been set in the past under Peña Nieto's administration. This article focuses on how the Brazilian and Mexican Governments are managing the emerging technologies of Big Data and how it includes them in social and industrial projects to enhance the growth of their economies. The article also discusses the benefits of these uses of Big Data and the possible problems that occur related to security and privacy of information.

Keywords Big Data • Brazil • Mexico • Government

R.M. Ueti • D.F. Espinosa • L. Rafferty
Faculty of Business and IT, University of Ontario Institute of Technology,
Oshawa, ON, Canada
e-mail: rmueti@gmail.com; dany_patata@hotmail.com; Laura.Rafferty@uoit.net

P.C.K. Hung (✉)
Faculty of Business and IT, University of Ontario Institute of Technology,
Oshawa, ON, Canada

Department of Electronic Engineering, National Taipei University of Technology, Taiwan
e-mail: Patrick.Hung@uoit.ca

© Springer International Publishing Switzerland 2016   197
P.C.K. Hung (ed.), *Big Data Applications and Use Cases*, International Series
on Computer Entertainment and Media Technology, DOI 10.1007/978-3-319-30146-4_9

1   Introduction

In almost 60 years, the concept of computing has passed from limited information in many computers allocated in one place, to a massive quantity of information in many devices and servers spread around the world. This astronomical quantity of information, called Big Data, has an amazing variety and is transacted by servers and devices in a huge velocity, and could be used to help enterprises and governments solve complex problems. Brazil and Mexico, two of the most influential countries in Latin America, have been identified as the fastest growing markets for sales of Big Data Solutions in Latin America. IDC projects that revenue from Big Data software, hardware and services in Latin America will grow 64 % from 551 million USD in 2013 to $6.59 billion USD in 2018 [1].

Beyond the private sector, the governments Brazil and Mexico have also recently begun to embrace opportunities related to Big Data in order to improve their current regimes. With the ability to collect a huge quantity of information on citizens in their respective countries, these governments are faced with a range of unique opportunities for Big Data.

In Brazil, Big Data has just recently gained popularity within the past few years, in conjunction with an explosive influx of oil and gas resources, introducing international oil and gas companies into the market with a great interest and funding for Big Data initiatives [2]. The government is the fifth largest sector for investments in Big Data [3]. From a government perspective, there are also many opportunities for Big Data. While the Brazilian Government traditionally has a bad reputation regarding the administration of public money, the government has tried to use all the public information they have to help spend this money wisely. Efforts for transparency of government data, such as through the Strategic Priorities Office of Minas Gerais, aim to allow the public to access public management data and help to participate in developing new public policies [4].

Mexico is facing a new era where political reforms will play a crucial role in the economic growth of the country. The Mexican President promised big changes to the way the country was run. The legislative phase of this reform process is now complete; next comes implementation [5]. In the last 2 years, the President of Mexico in conjunction with his Parliamentary group has approved 11 reforms, which include Energetic Reform, Finances reform, Fiscal reform, Education reform, etc.

The reform in Telecommunications and Broadcasting stands out of the other reforms for its impact in the use of the Information Technology. This reform establishes that a new regulatory Institute will moderate the economic competitiveness and plural content between different social actors. The Regulatory Institute will have the power to sanction monopolistic practices that are being conducted by the companies such as TELMEX (Teléfonos de Mexico), the monopoly of Carlos Slim, the richest man of the world [6].

This reform looks really interesting and ambitious because one of the biggest problems that Mexican Government is facing is the distrust of the people regarding the usage of their private data.

According to the most recent estimates provided by the CIA, the population of Mexico is roughly 120 million people. There are 53.9 million people who have internet access [7]. So, it's really important that the Government establishes certain regulations regarding the management of data of the telecommunications companies, but, it is also important to focus on the good management of this data to provide the population with better programs and services that involve them socially.

Alessandro Maffioli mentions in his book, "Evaluating the impact of the Technology Development Funds in Emerging Economies: Evidence from Latin-America" [8], that to reach a real growth it is necessary to take a risk on new technologies. It is known that Latin America in all its history has faced problems regarding innovation, development and usage of new technologies. As Correa mentioned in his book, "Transfer of technology in Latin America: A decade of Control", "Latin America industrialization has been characterized by the predominant role played by foreign technologies as a basis for the establishment of new industries and the substitution of previously imported products" [9]. That is why the Mexican Government is committed to the use of emerging technologies as Big Data. Big Data is a key element for the development of the reforms. A clear example is the reform in Telecommunications and Broadcasting, where the Mexican government will have access to user data through IFETEL (Instituto Federal de Telecomunicaciones) to protect the consumers and prevent those private companies from making misusage of sensitive information.

This article aims to investigate the uses of Big Data by the governments of Brazil and Mexico. It has the objective to disclose the different projects which are being developed by the Mexican Government and how these projects affect directly the development of the new reforms. We try to clarify the challenges that the government has to face to ensure the confidence of the users in public institutions and how these institutions manage their personal information. Further, this article presents some uses of Big Data by the Brazilian Government to better spend the public money and to try to improve their reputation. The article will present some cases made by the Brazilian government and after that, will discuss more about some issues that Big Data use could cause in security of information.

The chapter is organized as follows: Sect. 2 will present some background information on Brazilian and Mexican context, as well as some background information on big data concepts. Section 3 will discuss about how the Brazilian government uses Big Data and all the problems about security and privacy of the data that use could cause. Section 4 will discuss some Big Data projects in Mexico. Lastly, Sect. 5 will provide a brief discussion to conclude this research work.

2 Background

Information comes from everywhere, from sensors, used to gather climate information, to posts to social media sites, digital pictures and videos, purchase transactions records, and cell phone GPS signals to name a few. For IBM, all these data are Big Data.

For Javier Puyol, Big Data is not a technology, but, it is a new way of working, where the user can get benefits from the treatment of big volumes of data. Only 0.05 % of the data extracted is object of analysis for the decision making. The information is growing up faster than the investment that the Government is putting in information and technology. For that reason, Puyol remarks that, in this moment, it is important for the governments of different countries to catch, manage and save the data and its derivatives with the objective for having benefits in the future [10].

We can list a lot of benefits that the use of Big Data offers to its users, but the focus of this work is in the benefits for public policy. Big data offers a better description of the actual situation of the resources of a country. It allows to make real simulations in different scales of possible situations and to know the impact that can cause in almost real time. It helps to know and improve the supply of the demand of making a better segmentation of the offer in every good, product or service. Finally it helps to accelerate the development of social benefits and innovator products.

A clear example of how big data helps cities to improve their public policy is the famous term "Smart Cities", where the good use of big data can help to make better decisions. Cities like Madrid, San Sebastian in Spain or Columbus in USA, show us the importance of the treatment of public data.

When the government of a city has the capability of extracting and analyzing urban elements data, it can save between 15 and 7 % of consumption of water for irrigation and drinking water. It can reduce almost 25 % in garbage recollection, 17 % in use of energy and 30 % of the emissions of CO_2 [10]. It is important to remark that the data has to be valid in a statistical sense; this means that it has to be a clear evidence of the reality.

The New Mexican era is happening now; with the new reforms, Mexico has the opportunity of becoming one of the most important emerging economies like India and Brazil. One of the problems that Mexico is facing is that the cost of an investment in the use of big data in public policy looks higher than the real benefits that its use can bring. This means that to make a correct treatment of the data with the basic characteristics of quality, veracity and immediacy can cost more than the use that can have in the future.

Puyol proposes that for the developing countries, it is best to have an Open Government. An Open Government uses technology to promote transparency, participation and collaboration between the different social actors. Obama in 2009 used this term (Open Government) to refer his new way to create public policy [11].

In this way, the only role of the Mexican government would be to publish data in a general format using techniques of Open Data and external agents would have the possibility of using this data to supply their necessities.

The Open Governments guarantee transparency to their citizens because they can have access to data that proceeds from the official source. Also it promotes efficiency and opportunities for equality, because all citizens and companies would have access to data in the same condition of equality, promoting a fair competition between all the social actors in conjunction with the government.

Sharing responsibilities in the use of data can be the key for the Mexican government in the application and success of its new reforms. The technology and the participation of the society in making decisions will make Mexico a paragon of public policy in all Latin America.

2.1 Big Data

According to the IBM Website, we can define Big Data as huge quantity of information that is created by any device, such as sensors to gather climate information to posts, videos and digital pictures that are posted in social media sites [12]. For Lohr, the definition of Big Data is, a "shorthand for advancing trends in technology that open the door to a new approach to understanding the world and making decisions" [13]. That definition is more subjective and abroad, even more different than what we learn and read. However, the majority of people define big data as one group of data from digital or other kinds of sources that could represent a source of ongoing discovery and analysis [14]. These three definitions show that Big Data is one new rich area which could be the answer for the new difficulties that big companies are having nowadays.

Oracle has released one paper that has a deeper definition and some important characteristics about Big Data. Oracle defines big data as a large amount of information coming from three sources: traditional enterprise data, machine-generated like sensors and social data. Oracle points out that the volume of data is just one of four important aspects about Big Data, which includes also the high velocity of transitioned data, huge variety of information and the value of all this data [15]. The definition from Oracle is more technical and more tangible than the definitions given above.

Nowadays, Big Data shows one important resource for big companies, since it could extract relevant information in years of compiled stored data. Another point that needs to be discussed is, the world has never produced this quantity of information like at present, where the information continues to increase exponentially. Is expected an increase of 40 % for 2015. The volume of global data today is just 1.8 zettabytes, however some forecasts say this volume could reach 7.9 zettabytes in a few years [16]. This quantity of information become to be a problem for the enterprises since with more information, more time needs to be spent for mining relevant data.

2.2 Information Security

According to Anderson, one definition for information security is, "a well-founded sense of assurance that the controls and risk information are well balanced" [17]. To the Brazilian Government the meaning of Information Security is:

> Protection of information systems against denial of service to authorized users, as well as against the intrusion, and the unauthorized modification of data or information stored in processing or in transit, covering even the safety of human resources, documentation and of material, areas and facilities of communications and computing, as well as to prevent, detect, deter and document any threats to its development [18].

To Maia, information security has three basic principles: confidentiality (meaning the information needs to be granted only for whom that have the right), integrity (the information needs to be stored without any change) and availability (the information needs to be available for the users when they need) [19]. Information security is very important in any company since they have as a main objective, "to protect the confidentiality, integrity and availability of information assets, whether in storage, processing, or transmission. It is achieved via the application of policy, education, training and awareness, and technology" [20].

2.3 Information Privacy

Clarke defines information privacy as "the interest an individual has in controlling, or at least significantly influencing, the handling of data about themselves" [21]. In other words, information privacy is when you have the partial or complete control about the data that you made about anything or somebody made about yourself.

For Junior, the concept of privacy is closely connected with liberty. The concept of liberty is, any person can do what he wants to do without any kind of discomfort. One person who has liberty has the right to refuse their personal information to be released to people they do not want or do not know. In terms of privacy of information, we talk about information or data available on internet [22]. Fernandes and Filho agree with this concept since for them, for a person to have privacy, they need to have two important things: the control of all information existent from himself, and practice the consistent control with their interests and personal values [23]. Fernandes and Filho continue discussing about the privacy threats which could be numerous, and in particular these threats that are present on internet and are very important, which are the transaction data, cookies, invasions and company's interests.

3 The Uses of Big Data by Brazilian Government

3.1   The Uses of Big Data by State of Goiás in Public Education

The Brazilian Government has started to use Big Data to help cities, and even entire states to help administrators to make important decisions. The State of Goiás has begun to use Big Data in order to help decisions on public education [24].

The stored data has more than 200,000 users and the traffic of data could reach one thousand and half of requests per second. This new information collected by the Big Data analysis helped the Learning Unities to improve the quality education in all the State with new tools like the *Portal do Diretor*—Principal Website—and the *Diário Eletrônico*—Electronic Diary—which helps teachers and principals in their daily tasks [24].

According to Ricardo Pereira Borges, the head of Educational Technology Center of Goiás Department of Education, this huge database that is used, has all the information of all students who study in any public school in the Goiás State, which means one user could know the frequency of any student, information about the meals that is used to feed the students and other privacy information. To Borges, these Big Data Analysis Tools could help all employees with dynamic information in the right moment. Moreover, not only the public employees have access of all this information, but also the parents of all the children could access the school year and the registration via the website [24]. The software utilized by the Government has the capability to cross information about the administrative and educational registers for having more efficiency on the decision taking. The core of the software is the Microsoft SQL Server, a platform made by Microsoft, which have the power to analyses a huge quantity of information [25]. The software utilized by the Government has the capability to cross information about the administrative and educational registers for having more efficiency on the decision taking. At the core of the software is Microsoft SQL Server, a platform made by Microsoft, which has the power to analyze a huge quantity of information [25].

3.2   DataViva: The Project of State of Minas Gerais Using Big Data

On November 27th, 2013 the State of Minas Gerais with Professors of Massachusetts Institute of Technology (MIT) and the Harvard University released one portal that could be used by anyone to see the occupation of any Brazilian citizen and all the products that is exported of Brazil to any other country [26]. The website has eight applications where all users have access to more than 100 million interactive visualizations. The entire platform is open source and has open access for any person [27].

The analysis used information from 2002 until the last completed year. Emilia Paiva, the vice president of Strategic Priorities of the Government of Minas Gerais, said in the beginning the objective was mapping all the State, however after the information gathered from many departments around all the Brazil, they stated to think not only in the State of Minas Gerais, but the whole country [26].

3.3   Big Data and Security for City of Sao Paulo

Another city that wants to use Big Data is Sao Paulo, but focused in the security of population. The *Detecta* system is software made by the partnership between the Public Security Bureau of Sao Paulo and Microsoft, and the main idea of the project is connect all the security cameras and a huge database to help the Military Police of State to catch the criminals [28]. The software could merge information from security devices, like surveillance cameras, radiation detection, emergency calls, license drivers, and any other kind of information that could be necessary to find and catch the outlaws [29].

The project started thinking to connect just the security cameras of the government, more than a 100 cameras. However, the state governor, Geraldo Alckmin, started one discussion with the private enterprises to connect their cameras into this big system, like the New York system called Domain Awareness System, most commonly known as DAS, increasing the number of cameras to more than 6000 [28].

3.4   Rio de Janeiro Uses Big Data as a Strategy to Help Citizens

The Town Hall of the city Rio de Janeiro started to use Big Data to help the citizens of the city in the most variable cases. The city is beginning to use the Big Data to help in huge events like the World Cup and the Olympic Games, but the benefits are not just for these two events. The city has also used Big Data to help the cyclists of the city, creating cycle lanes in places that are already needed, without spending unnecessary money [30].

Another important benefit of this project is the analysis of this Big Data was to identify spots of Dengue Fever, one of the most problematic diseases in tropical countries. The public government made one huge movement to combat this disease since one of these spots was in a place that had many schools and could be problematic since many children should be infected, causing not just problems for themselves but for their parents and even for the entire city, because they will help the disease spread even more [30].

The project of the city also helps to solve problems of traffic jams, since they used information caught by the citizens in some cellphones applications to know where there are places that have traffic jams, car accidents or where the quantity of cars increased [30].

3.5 The Big Data and the Increase of Efficiency of the Public Money

According to *FGV Projetos* (Getulio Vargas Faculty Projects) the use of Big Data has helped the government to save more than 860 million Brazilian Reais just in the ministry of education between the years 2008 and 2010. The system started to be used in 2006 after a government request for one software that could help them to optimize the acquisition of informatics materials. According to the government, just in uniforms for students the government saves 40 %. This system uses Big Data merged with economic analysis to help the public employees to make a decision about, what, when and how quantity they need to buy of one simple material [31].

3.6 Another Face of Big Data

Big Data has helped the Brazilian Government to compile information and helped on decision making in some projects which involve public money, however since this information has become public, people have started to think about their privacy and security, not just talking about information but in large aspect.

In regards to Big Data used in the State of Goias for example, all the professors and principals have access to all information about any children who have studied in the school. If some bad intentioned professor wants to get some private information about the child or about their parents it could be done. In the case of the DataViva project, the impact is even worse, since anyone can have the capability to know about the professional information like how much income some people receive for their jobs monthly. This kind of information could be problematic for a person who receive a high salary, since if a criminal knows the person and their salary, this person become a potential target.

In regards to the use of Big Data in Rio de Janeiro, the problem is not so complicated, since in this case the focus will be on privacy for whether a person wants to share their information with the government or not, since when you use a public hospital you do not have the possibility to opt out of sharing your information.

The city of Sao Paulo and how it uses Big Data is the most problematic for the privacy and security of the citizens, even if the main objective is the security. If the security of information was not good or if someone hacks the software, the population will not have security anymore, since someone bad intentioned can use the cameras to follow a person or even know the places that could be used for crimes.

All the information could be stored and transmitted with security, since the people and enterprises behind all of the projects have good feedback of other clients, like Microsoft. However, in Brazil the problem is how people use these applications, since they unfortunately could give access to the wrong person with or without consent about what this person will do with this technology.

Since this problem is just solved by education, privacy becomes one important question. The Brazilian government must carefully consider whether to give citizens the right to protect their own privacy by opting out of publicizing their information, or to decline this right in order to fully embrace the benefits of big data for the entire population.

4 The Uses of Big Data by the Mexican Government: Actual Projects and Future Work

4.1 SECTUR (Tourism Secretary) and the Use of Twitter as a Source of Information

Lovelace et al. point out that Geographic Information in social networks has a big potential for improving the geographic model of behaviors. Location tweets represent 2 % of the total production of tweets [32]. That is why it is important to be careful in the treatment of this information. The use of models, which simplify geographic information, can predict the behavior of tourists. Lovelace et al. propose three kinds of behaviors [32]:

a) Multipurpose travel: Link the travel, for example Home-School-Job-Store-Gym-Bar-Home or a simple travel to the Home
b) Seasonal travel which depends on the frequency of travel
c) Update Information for the user, traffic information in real time from Google or from GPS on the car

The Tourism Department in Mexico considers Twitter as one of the most important social networks used in the country [33]. The use of this social network brings a lot of benefits for the scientific data: low cost for a big volume of data, fast and easy access to a big number of users and better possibilities of extracting contextual information, considering the geographic area.

The Tourism Department is trying to offer better services to tourism by extracting geographic information of Twitter. They already make an experiment in two important Touristic cities: Guanajuato and Puebla. In this experiment with twitter information they analyze which national tourists prefer to visit Guanajuato depending on their geographic location. The below image shows that people in the

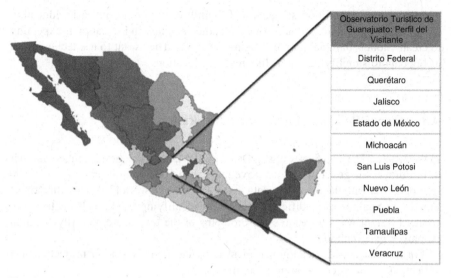

Observatorio Turístico de Guanajuato: Perfil del Visitante
Distrito Federal
Querétaro
Jalisco
Estado de México
Michoacán
San Luis Potosi
Nuevo León
Puebla
Tamaulipas
Veracruz

Fig. 1 Elaboration of SECTUR and INEGI with Twitter information [33]

surrounding states are more available to visit Guanajuato than people who live in the states that are far (Fig. 1).

After this experiment, SECTUR considers that the use of big data extracted from Twitter is a good alternative to the high costs of national surveys.

4.2   Educational Reform: Census in Schools, Teachers and Students of Basic and Special Education

One of the purposes of the Educational Reform is to concentrate all the information about school, teachers and students for making better decisions related to infrastructure, academic programs and resource allocation.

The principal objectives of this reform are [34]:

– Get the data of students, teachers and schools for creating a system of information related to the management of education.
– Have the exact geographic location of schools and educational centers.
– Identify the free spaces in every school, the equipment and the physical condition of this equipment.
– Register the information of the professors and identify their principal characteristics such as which school they are working, their salary, how many students they have, which subjects they teach, special functions that they realize, etc.
– Create a site with the academic profile of all the students, where teachers and parents can have access to the academic develop of the kids.

Mexico has 25 million students and 2 million professors in basic education [35]. With the extraction of the correct data, the Secretary in Education is expecting to create models that facilitate in making decisions. They want to use technologies as big data to simplify decisions like resource location.

4.3   Fiscal Reform: A Way to Avoid Risk

In the article "The Top 5 uses of Big Data" by IBM, tax collection is ranked number 4. In Europe, the governments can save more than 100,000 million euros (149,000 million USD) with the use of big data in the cooperative work [36]. The Ministry of Finance in Spain is using different models for identifying risk and also is trying to create different ways to resolve the problems of the users automatically, without employee intervention.

For this reason, Mexican government is trying to apply similar projects of tax collection and risk reduction in fiscal offences.

In Mexico, only six out of ten people pay taxes. This means that 40 % of the population is making illegal activities [37]. Diana Ladrón, director of PRODECON (Procudaduria a la Defensa del Contribuyente), estimates that 14 million people in Mexico are doing activities related to piracy and smuggling, which means that the Mexican government is losing 950,000 million pesos every year in tax collection [37].

The principal objectives of this reform are [38]:

– Develop models to identify risk
– Reinforce the unity of the users in the SAT
– Resolve problems without employee intervention
– Improve auditing process
– Create better methods against tax evasion and fraud

Diana Ladron believes that the use of the Information Technologies in conjunction with good bureaucracy practices will be possible to reach these objectives for 2018 [37].

4.4   Energetic Reform: PEMEX and Making Decisions

PEMEX, Mexico's state oil company, is engaged in the exploration, production, transportation, refining, storage and sale of hydrocarbons and derivatives. Its products include petrochemicals, natural gas, liquid gas, sulfur, gasoline, kerosene and diesel [39]. As a result of Mexico's energy reforms, PEMEX restructured its operations and formed new subsidiaries.

In her article, "Big Data, Big Business, and Big Government", Veronique de Rugy mentions that PEMEX is a clear example of how the good use of the information in the companies can make a complete change in the dysfunctional problems [40].

Big data solutions have been used in PEMEX operations resulting in major financial improvements. For example, the company has saved 960 h/year in maintenance by installing sensors on parts of machinery to detect vibrations and alert maintenance teams before malfunctions occur [41].

PEMEX continues working with thé use of big data in its operations. The Mexican government is expecting to have better results in the next 2 years.

4.5   National Digital Strategy: National Politics of Open Data

Mexico is facing new challenges related to free, open and neutral internet. The new reform in Telecommunications forces the government to promote new projects that benefit the users and at the same time protects their information.

The National Digital Strategy is the first step to reach this goal. The Mexican government aims to open all public databases and make tools out of them that facilitate and increase the competitiveness and promote the innovation between the citizens.

The people can find the site of open data of the government under the license "Libre Uso MX" [42]. This is only a test version, but it had a really important social impact.

In April, The Mexican government in conjunction with Coordination of the National Digital Strategy asked to the society to participate in experiment related to the edition of the politic draft. During the time the draft was kept open, more than 1000 users and 300 comments were received [43].

This experiment is the first action related to Open-Government, but also there are other projects related to Open Data, like INEGI Fácil and Ramo 23. These projects had been accepted for the society that is asking for more free and neutral information [43].

This shows that Mexico is prepared to apply the concepts of Open-Government, Open-Data, and Big Data in public policy, etc.

4.6   Big Data FILOS Example

The Autonomous National University of Mexico (UNAM), considered as one of the ten most important Universities in Latin America, has created the program FILOS. This project tries to extract the important information about the theses that UNAM's students had done throughout the history of @filosunam.

The "Samuel Ramos" Library (BSM) has the backup of the files in .pdf files of the theses since 2009. The objectives of this project include [44]:

- Producing a xml-tei library with the thesis in digital format
- Generating a platform to edit and mark the files xml-tei of the digital thesis
- Creating a plan to extract and show data and information of the xml-tei library of the digital thesis
- Producing visualizations with the data and the information collected from the xml-tei library

The faculty of philosophy and letters is expecting to get results in 2 years. This project is currently in the development phase.

4.7 CUDI: Universities Network

CUDI is a civil association that manages the national network for education and research. Its principal objective is to promote development of the country and increase synergy among its members [45]. With more than 150 Members in all of Mexico (Universities, Research Centers and different social associations) as can be seen in Fig. 2, the CUDI is looking forward to connect all the research made by different centers of innovation with the purpose of increase in knowledge.

With the project "Big Data Big Networks, Better Scientific Collaborations" CUDI is looking forward to create a center of information that allows scientists, students, professors and every person who has interest in research to get the specific information they are looking for in a faster and easier way.

In this moment, only members in Mexico are available to access to this network of collaboration but CUDI is currently looking to connecting more members in all of Latin America.

4.8 Scrutiny of Depression and Anxiety on Twitter Through a Word Analysis Program

Twitter is the second most important social network used in Mexico with approximately 10.2 million of users [46]. In Mexico almost 20 % of the habitants have been diagnosed with symptoms of depression and anxiety [46].

According to information of INEGI in the last years the rate of suicidal grew up 110 % in comparison with past years [47]. For this reason, INEGI in conjunction with The Autonomous National University of Mexico is working in a project called "Scrutiny of depression and anxiety on Twitter through a word analysis program".

The importance of this research is fundamental; because for Mexican government it is important to have a tool that helps to identify individuals with special symptoms related to depression and anxiety. In a virtual environment like social network, the analysis of data like the tweets that user posts, it will mean an easier

Backbone de la red CUDI

| Ver mapa interactivo |

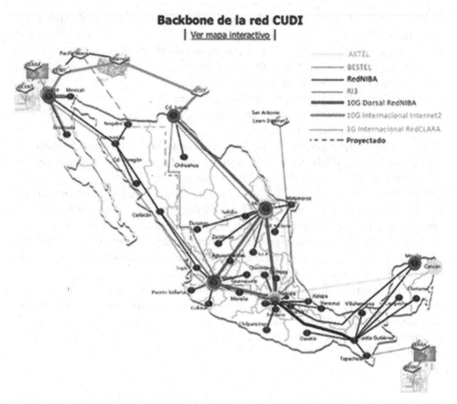

Fig. 2 Backbone of the CUDI network [45]

and faster method to prevent suicides and create specials social campaigns for individuals.

5   Conclusions

Brazil and Mexico have made significant advances in their use of Big Data in the public and private sectors. Further opportunities will continue to emerge in the coming years as these countries continue to adopt new technologies and Big Data strategies.

The Brazilian Government has made an important step in the technology path, using Big Data Analysis with Government databases to help public employees on decision making in education, security and transparency of public information. However, the government now needs to think about the privacy and security of the data of citizens, since some people who are concerned about their privacy could not want to share their information, and today. Currently there is no opt-out option for citizens.

The Brazilian Government needs to make a step towards ethics of information collection and usage, thinking about the privacy of their citizens. For security of information, the Brazilian Government needs to rethink about what is important to share to the population, and how they want to avoid the problems of bad actions, and leaking of private information.

Mexico has a long way to go, but these reforms give the citizen new opportunities to compete against big companies that in the past were the only ones with access to the government information.

Open Government combines two important concepts of this new century, big data and open data. If Mexico has the capacity of using these new technologies like a basement of its reforms, the challenges will be over in a really easy way and without the necessity of putting a lot of money in the investment of technology. Dividing responsibilities and sharing the challenges that the analysis of information brings along with it, Mexico can reach the objectives of the 11 new reforms by 2018. The Open Government guarantees transparency to their citizens and also promotes efficiency and opportunities for equality, promotes a fair competition between all the social actors and helps to reach social objectives.

Sharing responsibilities in the use of data can be the key for the Mexican government in the application and success of its new reforms. The technology and the participation of the society in making decisions will make Mexico an example of public policy in all of Latin America and the emerging economies around the world.

References

1. P. Anderson, IDC: Brazil, Mexico fastest growing big data markets through 2016 (13 de May de 2014), Obtenido de BNAmerica: Business Insight In Latin America: http://www.bnamericas.com/news/technology/idc-brazil-mexico-fastest-growing-big-data-markets-through-2016
2. R. Cohen, Brazil's Booming Business of Big Data (12 de December de 2012), Obtenido de Forbes: http://www.forbes.com/sites/reuvencohen/2012/12/12/brazils-booming-business-of-bigdata/
3. L.F. Gomes, Winter bridge: a global view of big data—snapshot of big data trends in Latin America. The Bridge. **44**(4) (Winter de 2014), Obtenido de https://www.nae.edu/File.aspx?id=128774
4. Info Online, Os cases e números do big data no Brasil em 2013 (10 de October de 2013), Obtenido de info.abril.com.br: http://info.abril.com.br/noticias/ti/2013/09/os-cases-e-numeros-do-big-data-no-brasil-em-2013.shtml
5. The Economist, Mexico's reforms: keep it up (9 de August de 2014), Obtenido de The Economist: http://www.economist.com/news/leaders/21611069-enrique-pe-nieto-has-achieved-lot-now-his-government-needs-maintain-momentum-keep-it
6. S. Luna, Carlos Slim y su Monopolio Perfecto (17 de April de 2006), Obtenido de Elcato.org: http://www.elcato.org/carlos-slim-y-su-monopolio-perfecto
7. AMIPCI, alcanza internet el 51 de penetracion entre los usuarios potenciales de mexico (19 de May de 2015), Obtenido de amipci.org.mx: https://www.amipci.org.mx/es/noticiasx/2241-alcanza-internet-el-51-de-penetracion-entre-los-usuarios-potenciales-de-mexico-amipci

8. B.H. Hall, A. Maffioli, *Evaluating the Impact of the Technology Development Funds in Emerging Economies: Evidence from Latin-America* (Inter-American Development Bank, Office of Evaluation and Oversight (OVE), Washington, DC, 2008)
9. C.M. Correa, Transfer of technology in Latin America: a decade of control. J. World Trade **15** (5), 388–409 (1981)
10. J. Puyol, Big data and public administration. Seminario Internacional: Big Data, Instituto Nacional de Estadistica Y Geografia (INEGI) (2014), Obtenido de http://www.inegi.org.mx/eventos/2014/big-data/presentacion.aspx
11. B. Obama, Open government initiative (21 de January de 2009), Obtenido de whitehouse.gov: https://www.whitehouse.gov/open
12. IBM, Big data at the speed of business (22 de 06 de 2015), (IBM) Recuperado el 06 de 04 de 2015, de http://www-01.ibm.com/software/data/bigdata/what-is-big-data.html
13. S. Lohr, The age of big data (11 de February de 2012), Recuperado el 2015 de April de 15, de http://wolfweb.unr.edu/homepage/ania/NYTFeb12.pdf
14. L. Arthur, What is big data? (15 de September de 2013), (Forbes) Recuperado el 07 de April de 2015, de http://www.forbes.com/sites/lisaarthur/2013/08/15/what-is-big-data/
15. Oracle, Oracle Website (June de 2013), Recuperado el 07 de April de 2015, de http://www.oracle.com/us/products/database/big-data-for-enterprise-519135.pdf
16. Rede Host, Rede Host Blog (18 de 02 de 2013), (Rede Host) Recuperado el 2015 de April de 2015, de http://blog.redehost.com.br/novidades/big-data.html
17. J.M. Anderson, Why we need a new definition of information security. Comput. Secur. **22**(4), 308 (2003)
18. Brazilian Government, Palácio do Planalto (13 de June de 2000), (Brazilian Government) Recuperado el 2015 de April de 07, de http://www.planalto.gov.br/ccivil_03/decreto/D3505.htm
19. M.A. Maia, Information security (19 de August de 2013), (Módulo Security Solutions) Recuperado el 2015 de April de 07, de http://segurancadainformacao.modulo.com.br/seguranca-da-informacao
20. M. Whitman, H. Mattord, *Principles of Information Security* (Cengage Learning, Boca Raton, FL, 2011)
21. R. Clarke, Roger Clarke's website (21 de October de 2013), (Roger Clarke) Recuperado el 07 de April de 2015, de http://www.rogerclarke.com/DV/Intro.html
22. R.P. Junior, Privacidade, mercado e informação. Justitia **61**, 246–248 (1999)
23. C.H. de Fernandes, F.M. Filho, Rede Linux IME-USP (08 de December de 2003), Recuperado el 07 de April de 2015, de https://linux.ime.usp.br/~carloshf/mac339/fase2/privacidade.pdf
24. M. Araujo, Microsoft News Center Brasil (08 de January de 2015), (Microsoft) Recuperado el 2015 de April de 2015, de http://news.microsoft.com/pt-br/governo-de-goias-usa-big-data-para-apoiar-decisoes-na-educacao-publica/
25. Computerworld, Aplicações: Goiás usa recursos de big data na educação publica (09 de January de 2015), Obtenido de Computerworld: http://computerworld.com.br/tecnologia/2015/01/09/goias-usa-recursos-de-big-data-na-educacao-publica
26. Oliveira, J. Hoje em Dia (27 de November de 2013), (R7 Notícias) Recuperado el 08 de April de 2015, de http://www.hojeemdia.com.br/noticias/economia-e-negocios/dataviva-governo-de-minas-entra-na-era-do-big-data-1.196329
27. T. Aquim, Big Data: Governo de Minas Gerais Lança O Dataviva (5 de December de 2013), Obtenido de Datacenter Dynamics: http://www.datacenterdynamics.com.br/focus/archive/2013/12/big-data-governo-de-minas-gerais-lan%C3%A7a-o-dataviva
28. G. Gusmão, Info Online (20 de October de 2014), (Abril) Recuperado el 08 de April de 2015, de http://info.abril.com.br/noticias/it-solutions/2014/08/executivos-da-microsoft-explicam-o-sistema-de-big-data-que-ajudara-a-policia-de-sp.shtml
29. M. Araujo, Microsoft apresenta seu portfólio de soluções para segurança e defesa na LAAD 2015 (13 de April de 2015), Obtenido de Microsoft News Center Brasil: https://news.

microsoft.com/pt-br/microsoft-apresenta-seu-portfolio-de-solucoes-para-seguranca-e-defesa-na-laad-2015/

30. P. Cerdera, Big Data becomes strategy for the Government of city of Rio de Janeiro (24 de September de 2014)
31. M. Corrêa, Uso de Big Data ajuda governo brasileiro a gastar de forma mais eficiente. O Globo **24** (2013)
32. R. Lovelace, N. Malleson, K. Harland, M. Birkin, *Geotagged Tweets to Inform a Spacial Interaction Model: A Case Study of Museums* (School of Geography, University of Leeds, Leeds, UK, 2014)
33. SECTUR, Boletín Quatrimestral de Turismo (Quarterly Tourism Newsletter) (2014), Mexican Secretary of Tourism (SECTUR), Obtenido de http://www.datatur.sectur.gob.mx/Documentos %20Publicaciones/BCT_No40fINAL.pdf
34. Secretaria de Education Publica, Census of schools, teachers and alumni from public and private education: objective (2014), Obtenido de Secretaria de Education Publica: http://www.censo.sep.gob.mx/index.php/objetivo
35. O. Alonso, Inegi: en planteles básicos, 25 millones de alumnos y dos millones de trabajadores. La Jornada Martes **33** (1 de April de 2014), Obtenido de La Jornada Martes: http://www.jornada.unam.mx/2014/04/01/sociedad/033n1soc
36. IBM, *Las Cinco Mejores Formas de Abordar Big Data* (IBM, New York, 2013). Obtenido de http://www-01.ibm.com/software/es/events/doc/pdfs/Las_cinco_mejores_formas_de_abordar_big_data.pdf
37. P.G. Robles, Seis de cata 10 personas no pagan impuestos: Prodecon (2 de April de 2013), Obtenido de El Universal Cartera: http://archivo.eluniversal.com.mx/notas/914119.html
38. G. Perez-Navarro, La Reforma Fiscal: Los Retos en Mexico (2013), Obtenido de OECD: http://www.cefp.gob.mx/foro/2013/politicatributaria/presentaciones/uno.pdf
39. BNAmericas, Petróleos Mexicanos S.A. de C.V. (2014), Obtenido de BNAmericas—Business Insight in Latin America: http://www.bnamericas.com/company-profile/en/petroleos-mexicanos-sa-de-cv-pemex
40. V. de Rugy, Big data, big business, and big government. Reason Magazine **20** (June 2015), Obtenido de http://reason.com/archives/2015/05/13/big-data-big-business-and-big
41. A. McMonagle, Take big data to new heights with corporate cultural changes (24 de February de 2015), Obtenido de Scalar: https://www.scalar.ca/en/2015/02/take-big-data-to-new-heights-with-corporate-cultural-changes-2/
42. Gobierno de México, Libre Uso MX (4 de September de 2014), Obtenido de Datos.gob.mx: http://datos.gob.mx/libreusomx/
43. I. Rosas, México: el gobierno comenzó a liberar datos abiertos (16 de July de 2014), Obtenido de Fayerwayer: https://www.fayerwayer.com/2014/07/mexico-el-gobierno-comenzo-a-liberar-datos-abiertos/
44. F. Barrón, Big data Filos (Un Ejemplo) (12 de April de 2014), Obtenido de Seminario Tecnologías Filosóficas: http://stf.filos.unam.mx/2014/04/big-data-filos-un-ejemplo/
45. CUDI, Acerca de CUDI (2015), Recuperado el 14 de August de 2015, de Corporacion Universitaria para el Desarrollo de Internet A.C.: http://www.cudi.edu.mx/acerca-de-cudi
46. T.C. Arriaga, J.A. Luna, S.H. Flores, O.F. Ayllon, A.M. Alvarez, Escrutinio de depresion y ansiedad en twitter a traves de un programa de analisis de palabras. Invest. Educ. Med. **4**(13), 16–21 (2015)
47. El Financiero, La tasa de suicidios en México aumentó 114 por ciento: Inegi (9 de September de 2014), Obtenido de El Financiero: http://www.elfinanciero.com.mx/sociedad/la-tasa-de-suicidios-en-mexico-aumento-114-por-ciento-inegi.html

Printed in the United States
By Bookmasters